THE MEMPHIS
CHILD ADVOCACY CENTER
& FOLK'S FOLLY PRESENT

Folks in the Kitchen

FAVORITE RECIPES
FROM FAMILY & FRIENDS

The Memphis Child Advocacy Center opened in September of 1992. It was the result of one of Memphis' best examples of public-private partnership, responding to the need to provide a coordinated response to the community problem of sexual abuse. The Center was founded by the Memphis/Shelby County Child Sexual Abuse Council, a grass roots organization founded in 1984 to address the problem of child sexual abuse. The Memphis Child Advocacy Center is dedicated to serving children who are victims of sexual and physical abuse. The Center provides counseling, advocacy, team investigation, education and professional training. The primary purpose of the center is to provide an atmosphere which helps victims to become children again.

Folk's First Program

At Folk's Folly, our priority is our guests. That is why we created our Folk's First program to better serve our customers. Benefits include an in-house credit card program, expedited check-out, a complimentary caramel cake for special occasions and a frequent dining program. The frequent dining program allows members to receive dining points each time they use their Folk's First card. These points are redeemable in Folk's Folly gift certificates. If you are interested in joining, please contact us at (901) 762-8200.

Acknowledgements

A special thank you to *Chuck Mitchell* for designing our cover and naming the cookbook.

Hutchison School's Odyssey of the Mind team for the design of our chapter dividers.
Catherine Folk
Katie Brindell
Jeanne Whitehead
Grace Henderson
Mary Loveless
Aubrey Sanders
Mary Beth Buchignani

Paulsen Printing for printing our letters and recipe forms.

Shields Hood for wine selections. Mr. Hood is director of wine sales at Athens Distributing Co. of Tennessee. He is currently pursuing his Master of Wine degree.

Our recipe contest judges:
Rudy Cerrito of Giovanni's Restaurant
Steven Leak of Mississippi Boulevard Christian Church
Frank Heizler and Toni Bursi of The Crescent Club
Kay Mistilis, instructor, State Technical Institute

We would like to thank all our recipe and travel contributors who made this book possible.

4

Foreword

For many years, I have considered the idea of putting together a cookbook consisting of recipes from our customers. With the arrival of Folk's Folly's 20th Anniversary, I finally decided to make this idea a reality. Folks in the Kitchen is the result of a devotion to both my customers and my community.

Having identified a project that would give Folk's First, Folk's Folly's frequent dining program, some additional visibility, we asked our members to send us their favorite family recipes. Our project took on an even more exciting purpose when The Memphis Child Advocacy Center became the target of our fundraising efforts. My wife Gloria and I have been very involved with the center and believe it offers a way out for children who are victims of abuse.

In addition to over 450 great recipes, our cookbook also includes an extensive travel section featuring the favorite restaurants of many of our well-traveled customers. I always enjoy experiencing new restaurants when I travel and thought a special section with your favorites would make the cookbook great reading.

I hope you enjoy Folks in the Kitchen and purchase additional copies for your friends, as all proceeds go to The Memphis Child Advocacy Center. Although it has been a great deal of fun for both me and my staff, I had no idea how complicated the whole process would be. We could never have done it without the efforts of so many who have given their time, ideas and sponsor dollars. To all of them, I want to give a personal thank you. A special thanks to you, as well, for supporting our cause with your purchase.

Humphrey E. Folk Jr

Sponsors

Kendall-Jackson

Turner and Nan Askew

Willard and Rita Sparks

Sara Lee Meat Group

Danny and Brenda Harris

Mike and Nancye Starnes

Jim and Carol Prentiss

Donald H. Farris

Bob Buckman and Joyce Mollerup

NewSouth Capital Management, Inc.

Charlie Rodgers

Tommy and Anne Keesee

Folk's Folly Prime Steak House

Table of Contents

October 1996

Printed on recycled paper in the United States of America by
KEEPSAKE COOKBOOKS • FUNDCO PRINTERS
407 Arendall Street - Adamsville, TN 38310
1-800-426-9827

APPETIZERS

CHIPS

SALSA

SHRIMP

ONION RINGS

SPONSORED BY

Kendall-Jackson

Appetizers

Swissy Crab Rounds

1 (7.5 ounce) can crabmeat,
   drained
1 tablespoon chopped green
   onion
1 cup grated Swiss cheese
1/2 cup mayonnaise

1 teaspoon lemon juice
1/4 teaspoon curry powder
1 package buttermilk flaky
   biscuits
Paprika

Combine crabmeat, green onion, cheese, mayonnaise, lemon juice and curry. Separate each biscuit into 3 layers. Place on ungreased cookie sheet and spoon crabmeat mixture on each biscuit layer. Bake at 400° for 10 to 12 minutes. Remove and sprinkle with paprika. Freezes well. Servings: 30. Preparation Time: 30 minutes.

Elizabeth Gillespie

Crabmeat Au Gratin in Shells

1 pound crabmeat
4 tablespoons butter
4 tablespoons flour
1/2 pint cream

4 tablespoons sherry
Grated Cheddar for topping
Salt and pepper to taste

Make cream sauce with butter, flour and cream. Add salt, pepper and sherry. Remove from heat and add crabmeat. Pour into buttered casserole or individual shells. Sprinkle with grated cheese and cook in hot oven until cheese melts. Do not overcook. Servings: 4.

Marilyn Newton

10

Best Crab Dip Ever

"With seafood a constant in our Louisiana lives, we were always proud to serve our favorite crabmeat dip."

1/2 pound butter
8 ounces cream cheese
1 pound lump crabmeat
2 onions, chopped finely
6 shallots, chopped finely
4 cloves garlic, chopped
   finely

8 ounces mushrooms, sliced
   and drained
Dash of Tabasco
Pinch of cayenne
Salt and pepper to taste

Melt butter and cream cheese over low heat. Mix in crabmeat and remaining ingredients. Serve warm in chafing dish. Preparation Time: 15 minutes. Cooking Time: 15 minutes.

Anne R. Pratt

Holiday Crab Spread

This is a holiday favorite sure to impress your guests.

8 ounces cream cheese,
   softened
11/2 teaspoons
   Worcestershire sauce
Dash Tabasco sauce
Garlic powder to taste

6 ounces chili sauce
6 ounces seafood cocktail
   sauce
1 pound lump crabmeat
1 bunch fresh parsley,
   minced

Combine first four ingredients and mix thoroughly. Refrigerate overnight. Spread onto a large glass dish and make a pie shaped rim. Top with chili sauce and seafood cocktail sauce. Spread lump crabmeat evenly over sauce. Top with parsley and serve with assorted crackers. Servings: 15 to 20. Pan Size: 14-inch round glass. Preparation Time: 30 minutes.

Sandy S. Nichols

11

Crabmeat Mold

A wonderful family recipe.

1 cup mayonnaise
8 ounces cream cheese
1 (10³/4 ounce) can tomato
   soup
2 envelopes gelatin
1/2 cup cold water

1/2 cup celery, chopped
1/2 cup bell pepper, chopped
1 (4 ounce) jar chopped
   pimentos
1 (7 ounce) can crabmeat,
   drained

Grease mold or 9x13-inch Pyrex dish with 2 teaspoons of mayonnaise. Beat together cream cheese and remaining mayonnaise. Set aside. Heat soup slowly. Dissolve gelatin in cold water and add to heated soup. Add this mixture to cream cheese and mayonnaise. Mix in vegetables and crabmeat. Pour into mold or dish. Chill one hour. Garnish and serve with crackers or rye bread.

Mrs. Ben Dlugach

Hot Crawfish Dip

1 stick butter
1 bunch chopped green
   onions

SEASONINGS:
Worcestershire
Liquid crab oil
Thyme

1/2 cup flour
1 pint half-and-half cream
1 pound crawfish tail meat

Basil
Salt and pepper

Sauté green onions in butter until tender. Add flour and cook 3 to 5 minutes. Add cream and heat on low until thick. Add crawfish tail meat (with fat) and season to taste. Servings: 15.

Margaret Monger

12

Pickled Shrimp

2½ pounds of shrimp
1 large onion, sliced into
    rings
2 bay leaves per layer (6 to
    8)
1¼ cups oil

¾ cup vinegar
1 teaspoon salt
2 teaspoons celery seed
2 tablespoons or more
    capers and juice

In covered container place 1 layer of shrimp, 1 layer of onion rings and 2 bay leaves on each layer. Combine remaining ingredients and pour over shrimp. Marinate at least 24 hours.

Mrs. J. Hal Patton

Deviled Shrimp

2 pounds medium shrimp,
    cooked, peeled and
    deveined
1 lemon, thinly sliced
1 medium red onion, thinly
    sliced
1 cup black olives, pitted
2 tablespoons pimentos,
    chopped
¼ cup oil

2 cloves garlic, minced
1 tablespoon dry mustard
1 tablespoon salt
½ cup lemon juice
1 tablespoon red wine
    vinegar
1 bay leaf, crumbled
Dash cayenne pepper
¼ cup fresh parsley

Mix first four ingredients. In separate bowl, mix remaining ingredients to make a dressing. Toss together and chill for 2 hours. Serve in a glass bowl with toothpicks.

Joyce Johnson

Appetizers

Shrimp Toast Paradise

Shrimp, boiled, peeled and
    chopped
Water chestnuts, chopped
Green onions, sliced
Shredded Parmesan cheese

Mayonnaise
Salt and pepper to taste
Garlic powder to taste
Toasted baguette

Use 3 parts shrimp to 1 part water chestnuts, green onions and
Parmesan cheese. Add enough mayonnaise to make moist. Season to
taste. Spread mixture over baguette and broil until golden. Serve
immediately.

Marilyn Newton

Cold Shrimp Pizza

1 (8 ounce) cream cheese,
    softened
1 bottle Heinz chili sauce
1/2 green pepper, chopped
3 green onions, chopped
1 small can sliced black
    olives

1 cup chopped boiled shrimp
1 cup grated Monterey Jack
    cheese
Tortilla chips

Spread cream cheese on a 13-inch round platter or pizza pan. Cover
with chili sauce and remaining ingredients in order. Refrigerate or freeze.
Serve cold with tortilla chips. Pan Size: 13-inches. Preparation Time: 20
minutes.

Anita Harris

Marinated Catfish

1/2 cup soy sauce
1/2 cup lemon juice
1 cup water

12 (2 to 3 ounce) catfish
   fillets

Mix soy sauce, lemon juice and water. Marinate fillets in mixture for 24 hours. Remove fillets from marinade and grill or broil until done, about 1 to 2 minutes. Place on serving dish and garnish with lemon wedge, parsley and lemon twist.

Folk's Folly Prime Steak House

Smoked Oyster Dip

1 can cream of shrimp soup
8 ounces sour cream
8 ounces cream cheese
1 can smoked oysters,
   rinsed and drained,
   mashed or chopped

Garlic powder to taste

Combine ingredients in a medium saucepan and cook over medium heat stirring until heated through. Serve in a chafing dish with corn chips.

Marilyn Newton

Appetizers

Savory Salmon Spread
Popular, easy and delicious.

1 large can red salmon
1 (8 ounce) package cream
    cheese
Juice of one lemon
4 green onions, chopped
    (including tops)

¼ teaspoon pepper
Sour cream
Dill weed

Blend salmon, cream cheese, lemon juice, green onions and pepper by hand. Transfer to serving bowl. Ice with sour cream. Top with dill weed. Serve with party rye or water crackers. Preparation Time: 10 minutes.

Susan Sanford

Seafood Mold

1 large can salmon, drained
2 (6 ounce) cans tuna,
    drained
16 ounces cream cheese

Lemon pepper to taste
Garlic salt to taste
Parsley flakes for topping
Cracker crumbs for topping

Blend salmon, tuna and cream cheese together. Add lemon pepper and garlic salt to taste. Mold into desired shape and cover with parsley flakes. Sprinkle cracker crumbs on top. Servings: 5 to 10. Preparation Time: 45 minutes.

Deborah Northcross

Warm Lobster Taco with Yellow Tomato Salsa and Jicama Salad

I created this dish in early 1986 and it quickly became my signature appetizer on The Mansion on Turtle Creek menu.

4 (1 pound) lobsters
6 (7-inch) fresh flour tortillas
3 tablespoons corn oil
1 cup grated Jalapeño Jack
   cheese

1 cup shredded spinach
   leaves
Yellow Tomato Salsa
Jicama Salad

Preheat oven to 300°. Fill a large stock pot with lightly salted water and bring to a boil over high heat. Add lobsters and cook for about 8 minutes or until just done. Drain and let lobsters cool slightly. Wrap tortillas tightly in foil and place in preheated 300° oven for about 15 minutes or until heated through. Keep warm until ready to use. Remove meat from lobster tails being careful not to tear it apart. Cut meat into thin medallions (or medium-sized dice, if meat breaks apart). Heat oil in a medium sauté pan over medium heat and sauté lobster medallions until just heated through. Spoon equal portions of warm lobster medallions into the center of each warm tortilla. Sprinkle with equal portions of grated cheese and shredded spinach. Roll tortillas into a cylinder shape and place each one on a warm serving plate with the edge facing the bottom. Surround the taco with Yellow Tomato Salsa and garnish each side with a small mound of Jicama Salad.

FLOUR TORTILLAS:

2 cups sifted all-purpose
   flour
1 teaspoon baking powder
1/2 teaspoon salt
1/2 teaspoon sugar

1 tablespoon vegetable
   shortening
1/2 cup warm water,
   approximately

(continued on next page)

17

Appetizers

Sift together flour, baking powder, salt, and sugar. Cut in shortening until flour looks as though it has small peas in it. Add enough warm water to make a soft dough. Mix well and knead on a well-floured board for 3 to 5 minutes or until shiny and elastic. Cover dough and let rest for 30 minutes, out of draft. Form dough into balls about 2 to 2½ inches in diameter. On a lightly floured board, roll into circles about 7 inches in diameter and ¼ inch thick. Cook on a hot, ungreased griddle for about 2 minutes or until lightly browned on the edges. Turn and cook on the other side for about 1 minute or until edges are brown. Keep warm, tightly wrapped in foil if serving right away, or reheat, tightly wrapped in foil, at 300° for about 10 to 15 minutes or until heated through. Makes 10 to 12 tortillas.

YELLOW TOMATO SALSA:

2 pints yellow cherry
    tomatoes or 1 pound
    yellow tomatoes
1 large shallot, very finely
    minced
1 large clove garlic, very
    finely minced
2 tablespoons finely minced
    fresh cilantro
1 tablespoon champagne
    vinegar or white wine vinegar

2 serrano chilies, seeded
    and minced
2 teaspoons lime juice
Salt to taste
1 tablespoon maple syrup
    (use only if tomatoes are
    not sweet enough)

In a food processor, using the steel blade, process tomatoes until well chopped. Do not purée. Combine tomatoes and their juices with shallot, garlic, cilantro, vinegar, chilies, lime juice, and salt, mixing well. Add maple syrup, if needed, to balance flavor and sweeten slightly. Cover and refrigerate for at least 2 hours or until very cold.

NOTE: For a crunchier, more typical salsa, put tomatoes through fine die of a food grinder.

(continued on next page)

18

JICAMA SALAD:

1/2 small jicama, peeled and cut into fine julienne strips

1/2 small red bell pepper, seeds and membranes removed, cut into fine julienne strips

1/2 small yellow bell pepper, seeds and membranes removed, cut into fine julienne strips

1/2 small zucchini (only part that has green skin attached), cut into fine julienne strips

1/2 small carrot, peeled and cut into fine julienne strips

4 tablespoons cold-pressed peanut oil

2 tablespoons lime juice

Salt to taste

Cayenne pepper to taste

Combine vegetables, oil, lime juice, salt, and cayenne to taste and toss to mix well.

ADVANCE PREPARATIONS: Lobsters may be boiled up to a day ahead. Remove tail meat and slice. Store, covered and refrigerated. Yellow Tomato Salsa must be prepared at least 2 hours (but no more than 8 hours) ahead and refrigerated, covered, until cold. Adjust seasoning. Jicama Salad may be prepared several hours ahead and refrigerated. In that case, omit salt until almost ready to serve. Cheese and spinach for tacos may be shredded several hours ahead. Wrap tightly and refrigerate. Wine Suggestion: Sauvignon Blanc, Arbor Crest, 1985.

The Mansion on Turtle Creek
Dallas, TX

Appetizers

Seafood Mousse

1 can cream of shrimp soup
8 ounces cream cheese,
   softened
1 envelope unflavored gelatin
1 medium catfish fillet

1/2 cup finely chopped celery
1/4 cup finely chopped onion
1 cup mayonnaise
1 tablespoon Worcestershire
1 tablespoon lemon juice

Combine soup and cream cheese; bring to a boil, stirring until smooth. Sprinkle gelatin over mixture; refrigerate 15 minutes. Place catfish in boiling, salted water. Cover and simmer 10 minutes or until fish flakes easily. Drain and flake catfish. Combine cooked catfish, cooled soup mixture, celery, onion, mayonnaise, Worcestershire and lemon. Chill until thickened. Pipe with pastry bag onto crackers or vegetable slices or serve as a dip with crackers or corn chips. Preparation Time: 30 minutes.

Ann S. Ball

Sausage and White Bean Dip

1 head garlic
2 (15 ounce) cans small
   white beans, drained and
   rinsed
1/2 cup pure olive oil
1 (12 ounce) package Jimmy
   Dean sausage, cooked
   and crumbled

1 tablespoon fresh chopped
   thyme
2 teaspoons lemon juice
1/2 teaspoon salt
1/4 teaspoon black pepper

Slice top of garlic head off, exposing cloves. Wrap in aluminum foil and bake at 350° for 40 minutes, or until cloves are very soft. Squeeze cloves of garlic out of skin into the bowl of food processor. Add 1 can of white beans and olive oil and puree until smooth. Add sausage, the rest of the white beans, thyme, lemon juice, salt and pepper. Blend well. Serve with toasted bread or your favorite crackers.

George Bryan

20

Sausage Crostini

1 pound Jimmy Dean
  sausage (your favorite
  flavor) cooked, crumbled
  and drained
1/2 cup Monterey Jack
  cheese

1 cup Cheddar cheese
1/3 cup mayonnaise
1/4 cup sliced almonds
1 cup red onion, chopped
1 (1 pound) loaf of honey
  wheat cocktail bread

Mix together sausage, cheeses, mayonnaise, almonds and onion. Spread mixture onto cocktail bread. Place on baking sheet. Bake at 350° for 20 minutes. Makes about 40 appetizers. (This mixture can be made ahead of time and refrigerated, or spread on bread ahead of time and frozen until ready to bake.)

George Bryan

Brie and Bacon Pizza
Great for light supper.

2 tablespoons olive oil
1 medium onion, chopped
2 cloves garlic, minced
2 cans "Italian Style" stewed
  tomatoes, drained and
  chopped
1 teaspoon dried basil
1 teaspoon dried red pepper
  flakes

1 ounce wedge brie, (cut in 1/2
  horizontally and chopped
  into small pieces)
5 to 6 slices bacon, cooked
  crisp and crumbled
1 large thin crust Boboli
  pizza shell

Preheat oven according to Boboli or pizza shell instructions. Heat oil in large skillet over medium heat; add onions and garlic. Sauté for three minutes or until tender. Add next 3 ingredients and turn heat up to medium high. Cook sauce until thick and chunky and all liquid has evaporated, about 15 to 20 minutes. To assemble, place pizza shell on cookie sheet and cover with hot pizza sauce. Cover with Brie pieces and sprinkle bacon over top. Cook in oven 8 to 10 minutes or until all cheese is fully melted. Remove and serve. Servings: 4. Pan Size: 16-inch round cookie sheet. Preheat: According to package instructions. Preparation Time: 30 to 40 minutes. Cooking Time: 8 to 10 minutes.

Suzy Carpenter

21

Appetizers

Sweet and Sour Sausage Bits

2 pounds smoked sausage,
   fully cooked

1 small jar peach preserves
1 small bottle Russian dressing

Cut sausage into bite size pieces. Mix preserves and dressing. Add sausage. Put in chafing dish and heat, or cook in microwave 3 to 5 minutes. Servings: 12 to 24. Pan Size: 3 quart baking dish. Preparation Time: 15 minutes.

Sheila Freudenbergh

Party Meat Balls

MEATBALLS:
2 pounds lean ground beef
1 cup corn flake crumbs
1/2 cup dried parsley
1/4 teaspoon black pepper

2 beaten eggs
2 tablespoons dried minced onion
1/2 teaspoon garlic powder
1/3 to 1/2 cup ketchup
2 tablespoons soy sauce

SAUCE:
2 cans cranberry jelly roll
2 bottles chili sauce

4 tablespoons brown sugar
2 teaspoons lemon juice

MEAT BALLS: Combine all ingredients, mix well, form into quarter size balls and place on a cookie sheet with sides lined with foil. Do not allow balls to touch. Bake at 400° for 10 minutes. After cooking, allow to cool in pan. Tilt pan so grease will go to edge. (Can make ahead and freeze, take out on day to serve.) Servings: Makes about 100 balls.

SAUCE: Melt cranberry sauce, add all others, mix well and simmer together for 20 to 30 minutes, add balls to sauce and serve in chafing dish. Can refrigerate and/or freeze. Preheat: 400°. Preparation Time: 45 minutes to 1 hour. Cooking Time: 10 minutes.

Dee Gibson

Mexican Cheesecake Olé

16 ounces cream cheese, softened	3 eggs
2 cups sour cream, divided	4 ounce can chopped green chilies
2 cups (8 ounces) sharp Cheddar cheese, grated	8 ounces medium picante sauce
1½ packages Lawry's taco seasoning	

In a medium bowl combine cream cheese, 1 cup of the sour cream, Cheddar cheese and taco seasoning. Beat in eggs one at a time. Add chilies and stir to combine. Pour into a springform pan spayed with cooking spray. Bake at 350° for 45 to 50 minutes or until almost brown. Spread remaining 1 cup of sour cream on top. Refrigerate overnight. Just before serving spread picante sauce on top. Serve with tortilla chips.

Lou Martin

Cabrito Torta

16 ounces cream cheese, softened	1 cup oil packed sundried tomatoes, drained and chopped (reserve several for garnish)
2 (1x3½-inch) logs French goat cheese, softened	
1 cup good quality pesto	

Line a round cake pan with plastic wrap. Spread one package of cream cheese on bottom. Spoon half of the pesto on top. Carefully spread one log of goat cheese over pesto. Top with chopped sundried tomatoes. Repeat to form two layers. Cover and freeze. When ready to serve remove from freezer and allow to soften to room temperature. Uncover and invert onto serving plate. Garnish with reserved sundried tomatoes and serve with crackers.

Nancy Lewis Welsh

23

Appetizers

Roasted Garlic with Feta Cheese Spread

*This recipe was modified from an appetizer
served at Anna Lee's in Roswell, GA.*

16 tablespoons olive oil
Oregano, ground
Fresh basil, chopped
8 whole heads of garlic
8 ounces feta cheese

8 ounces cream cheese
Cavender's Greek seasoning
Small can black olives, chopped
Crackers (garlic rounds
   suggested)

In a muffin pan, fill each cup with 2 tablespoons olive oil, 1/2 teaspoon oregano, 1/4 teaspoon basil. Cut the tops off heads of garlic, and place one in each cup upside down (cut size down). Bake at 250° for 20 to 30 minutes or until each head is tender. While garlic is baking mix 8 ounces of crumbled feta cheese with 8 ounces of cream cheese. Add 1 1/2 teaspoons of Cavender's Greek seasoning and olives. Spread feta mixture on crackers; take garlic from oven, place one clove on each cracker and serve. Servings: 64 crackers. (Depends on size of garlic pod.) Pan Size: Muffin tin (8 spaces). Preheat: 250°. Preparation Time: 15 minutes. Cooking Time: 20 to 30 minutes.

Dick R. Gourley

Roquefort Cheese Spread

This is wonderful and simple to make, my most requested recipe!

8 ounces Roquefort cheese
   or blue cheese, softened
8 ounces cream cheese,
   softened

1/2 cup butter, softened
2 tablespoons lemon juice
1 cup chopped ripe olives
1 tablespoon minced green onion

Beat Roquefort (or blue cheese) and cream cheese with lemon juice on low speed. Add butter and mix well. Add olives and onions. Mold into mound, cover with paprika or parsley and chill. Serve with crackers.

Mrs. Roane Waring, Jr.

Best Homemade Pimento Cheese

This is a sweet, creamy pimento cheese, always a big hit!

1 pound Velveeta cheese
1/4 cup sugar
3/4 cup mayonnaise

8 ounce jar pimentos,
chopped and drained

Melt cheese in double boiler. Add sugar, mayonnaise and pimentos. Mix thoroughly. Serve hot as dip or cold for sandwiches and celery.

Mary Ruth Witt

Black Olive Roquefort Cheese Ball

8 ounces cream cheese,
room temperature
4 ounces Roquefort cheese,
crumbled
1/4 cup butter, room
temperature
2 heaping tablespoons
minced chives, fresh or
frozen

4 1/2 ounce can chopped ripe
olives
1/2 cup finely chopped
pecans

Blend cheeses and butter with your hand, then mix in olives and chives and chill for easier shaping. When thoroughly chilled, form into ball or log and pat nuts over the surface, including the bottom. Chill until ready to serve. When serving, decorate the base of the ball with whole ripe olives and sprigs of parsley. Can be frozen. Servings: 10 to 12. Preparation Time: 15 minutes.

Ray and Betty Ashley

25

Appetizers

Cheese Straws

1 (5 ounce) jar Kraft Old
  English cheese
1 stick butter or margarine

1/4 teaspoon red pepper
Dash salt
1 1/2 cups all-purpose flour

Mix above ingredients well. Press through cookie press on cookie sheet. Bake at 375° until light brown.

Marie Holley Anderson

Curried Vegetable Dip

1/2 teaspoon dry mustard
1/2 teaspoon curry powder
3/4 teaspoon Worcestershire
  sauce

1/4 teaspoon grated onion
3/4 teaspoon paprika
2 cups mayonnaise
8 drops hot sauce

Combine ingredients in large bowl. Add salt and pepper to taste. Mix thoroughly. Let stand at least 24 hours. Serve with fresh vegetables.

Charlotte Wolfe

The Big Dipper

1 (16 ounce) jar Vlasic
  medium hot peppers,
  drained
2 eggs

2 tablespoons milk
16 ounces sharp Cheddar
  cheese, shredded
Tortilla chips

Remove seeds and ends from drained peppers and chop. Put chopped peppers into a 9-inch pie plate (may divide into 2 plates for smaller portions). Beat eggs and milk slightly and add shredded cheese. Pour over peppers. Bake in a 325° oven for 20 to 30 minutes. Serve warm with chips. Servings: 12. Pan Size: 1 or 2 9-inch pie plates. Preheat: 325°. Preparation Time: 10 minutes. Cooking Time: 20 to 30 minutes until set.

Barbara J. Riley

Vegetable Spread

You'll seldom taste anything this good! On bread, on crackers, generously stuffed in a tomato, or by the spoonful every time you pass the refrigerator, it gets better with every bite.

2 tomatoes	**¼ cup cold water**
1 cup celery	**¼ cup boiling water**
1 small onion	**1 pint mayonnaise**
1 cucumber	**1 teaspoon salt**
1 envelope plain gelatin	

Finely chop all vegetables and drain well on paper towels. Soften gelatin in cold water, add boiling water and cool. Fold in mayonnaise and salt. Add vegetables and spread on bread rounds or use as dip with crackers. Servings: 12 to 16. Preparation Time: 20 to 30 minutes.

Myra Harding

Asparagus Sandwiches

Great for parties and luncheons.

1 can asparagus, drained	**1 loaf thinly sliced sandwich**
8 ounces cream cheese,	**bread, crusts trimmed**
softened	**(wheat or white)**
2 boiled eggs	**Parmesan cheese**
1 teaspoon Lawry's seasoned	**Butter**
salt	

Mix first four ingredients in food processor. Spread on bread slice and roll up. Place on cookie sheet. Brush with melted butter and sprinkle with Parmesan cheese. Bake at 350° for 15 minutes or until lightly browned.

NOTE: You can freeze these ahead of time. Add butter and Parmesan when ready to bake.

Stacey Folk

27

Appetizers

Herb Pinwheels

5 bunches green onions, finely chopped
2 cloves garlic, minced
3/4 cup fresh parsley, minced
1½ teaspoons oregano
½ teaspoon salt
1 package refrigerator crescent rolls, chilled
½ cup Parmesan cheese

Sauté onions, garlic, parsley, oregano and salt in butter for 2 minutes. Using a floured surface, press four crescent rolls together to make a square. Join remaining rolls in same fashion. Roll out dough to flatten. Spread with one half of onion mixture, sprinkle with ¼ cup Parmesan cheese. Roll up jelly roll style. Repeat with remaining rolls. Chill until firm enough to slice in ½-inch slices. Bake slices on cookie sheet at 375° for 8 minutes. Slices freeze well. Preparation Time: 1 hour.

Elizabeth Gillespie

Martha's Tortilla Pinwheels

16 ounces sour cream
8 ounces cream cheese, softened
2 tablespoons picante sauce
1 can green chilies, drained and chopped
1/3 cup black olives, chopped
1 bunch green onions, chopped
1 (18 ounce) package flour tortillas (10 tortillas)

Blend sour cream, cream cheese and picante sauce together. Add green chilies, black olives and green onions. Spread one rounded tablespoon of mixture onto each tortilla. Roll up tortilla. Place in airtight plastic bag and chill 1½ to 2 hours. When ready to serve, slice each tortilla into 1-inch slices. Serve with salsa. Servings: Approximately 50.

Nancy Williams

Mushroom Tarts

24 thin slice
Plain sandwich white bread
4 tablespoons butter
3 tablespoons finely
  chopped shallots
1/2 pound mushrooms, finely
  chopped
2 tablespoons flour
1 cup cream or ~~half-and-half~~
1/2 teaspoon salt

1/8 teaspoon cayenne
  pepper
1 tablespoon finely chopped
  parsley
1 1/2 tablespoons chopped
  chives
1/2 teaspoon lemon juice
2 tablespoons Parmesan
  cheese

4"   *375°*

Cut out small circles of bread with biscuit cutter and press into tiny muffin tins. Preheat oven to 400°. Bake 10 minutes and cool. For filling, sauté shallots and mushrooms in butter. Then add flour, cream, and other ingredients. Fill cooled bread shells and bake at 350° for 10 minutes. Servings: 20. Pan Size: Tiny muffin tins. Preparation Time: 30 minutes. *(Roll flatish ε rolling pin)*

Janet Canale

Burgundy Mushrooms

4 pounds mushrooms
1 pound butter
1 quart burgundy
1 1/2 tablespoons
  Worcestershire
1 teaspoon dill seed

1 teaspoon black pepper
1 tablespoon Accent
1 tablespoon garlic powder
2 cups boiling water
4 beef bouillon cubes
4 chicken bouillon cubes

Combine all ingredients in a pot and bring to a boil. Reduce heat and simmer 5 to 6 hours, covered. Remove lid and simmer 3 to 5 hours or until liquid barely covers mushrooms. Refrigerate and serve in chafing dish. Freezes well.

Marilyn Newton

29

Appetizers

Mushrooms Cayman Arms

3½ tablespoons butter, divided	4 teaspoons minced onion
2 tablespoons flour	1 pound mushrooms, thinly sliced
1½ cups milk, scalded	1 tablespoon soy sauce
½ cup dry white wine	2 tablespoons brandy, heated
Nutmeg, to taste	4 slices toasted French bread
Salt and pepper, to taste	Grated Cheddar cheese

In a medium saucepan, melt 1½ tablespoons of butter and stir in flour. Cook over low heat, stirring for 3 minutes. Remove from heat and add scalded milk and wine, whisking vigorously until sauce is thick and smooth. Add nutmeg, salt and pepper to taste and simmer the sauce for 15 minutes. In a skillet, sauté onion in 2 tablespoons butter over moderately high heat for 2 to 3 minutes or until browned. Add mushrooms and sauté for 1 to 2 minutes or until they are just tender. Remove from heat and add soy sauce. Add heated brandy, ignite, and shake the pan until the flames go out. In each of 4 ovenproof bowls, put 1 slice of toasted French bread, divide mushroom mixture among the bowls, and top with the sauce and grated Cheddar cheese to taste. Bake at 350° for 12 to 15 minutes or until cheese is bubbly. Servings: 4.

Charles P. Brown

California Caviar

Everyone loves this dip and rarely do you have any left over.

1 (4 ounce) can green chilies, chopped	1 (4 ounce) package crumbled feta cheese, tomato basil flavor or plain
1 (3¼ ounce) can black olives, sliced	½ cup Italian salad dressing
4 green onions, chopped	¼ cup fresh cilantro, chopped
1 tomato, chopped	

Blend all ingredients and serve with corn chips. Preparation Time: 10 minutes.

Mary P. Garrett

Country Caviar

2 (14 ounce) cans black-eyed
   peas
15 ounce can white hominey
2 medium tomatoes,
   chopped

4 green onions, chopped
1 medium green pepper,
   chopped
8 ounce bottle Zesty Italian
   Dressing

Combine all ingredients, mix well. Pour salad dressing over mixture. Cover and refrigerate overnight. Drain and serve with tortilla chips.

Charlotte Wolfe

Black-Eyed Pea Dip

1 package frozen black-eyed
   peas, cooked according
   to directions
1/2 cup chopped onion
1/4 cup bacon drippings
1 can diced Rotel tomatoes,
   drained

Dash Tabasco
Lawry's seasoned salt to taste
Salt and pepper to taste
Sour cream
Cilantro

Sauté onion in bacon drippings. Mix with tomatoes and black-eyed peas. Let simmer in pan for 5 minutes. Season with Lawry's seasoned salt, salt, pepper and dash of Tabasco. Serve warm with sour cream and top with chopped fresh cilantro and corn chips for dipping.

Scott Sellers

Appetizers

Winkles Mexican Dip

This recipe originally came from Houston.
Loren's favorite snack after a long day on the golf course.

1 (4 ounce) can chopped
   green chilies, drained
1 (4 ounce) can sliced black
   olives, drained
3 green onions, chopped
1 medium tomato, chopped

Salt to taste
Pepper to taste
2 tablespoons red wine
   vinegar
3 tablespoons olive oil

In a small bowl mix together all ingredients. Serve with tortilla chips.

Loren and Kim Roberts

Hot Pizza Dip

8 ounces cream cheese,
   softened
3 teaspoons Italian
   seasoning
2 cups (8 ounces) shredded
   mozzarella cheese
1 cup (4 ounces) shredded
   Parmesan cheese

1 jar pizza sauce
1 (3 ounce) package
   pepperoni, chopped
1/4 cup chopped peppers
   (pepperoncini)
1/4 cup chopped onions
1/4 to 1/2 cup chopped black
   olives

Combine cream cheese and Italian seasoning. Spread into bottom of 9-inch pie plate. Combine mozzarella cheese and Parmesan cheese; sprinkle 2/3 on top of cream cheese. Spread pizza sauce over cheese. Sprinkle pepperoni, pepperoncini peppers, onions and black olives on pizza sauce. Top with remaining cheese. Serve with crunchy garlic toast or Melba rounds. Pan Size: 9-inch pie plate. Preheat: 350°. Cooking Time: 20 to 25 minutes, until bubbly.

Sara Cunningham

Jalapeño Spinach Dip

3 celery stalks, chopped
   medium fine
1/2 large onion, chopped
1 (6 ounce) can mushroom
   pieces
1 small can water
   chestnuts, chopped
5 tablespoons butter, divided

1 (10 ounce) package frozen
   chopped spinach, slightly
   thawed
Garlic salt to taste
8 ounces jalapeño
   processed cheese
1 (10¾ ounce) can cream
   of mushroom soup

Sauté celery, onion, mushrooms, and water chestnuts in 3 tablespoons butter. Drain and set aside. Cook spinach in remaining 2 tablespoons butter until no liquid is left in pan. Season with garlic salt. Melt cheese in microwave and add mushroom soup. Combine all, and serve in chafing dish as a dip. Serve with Melba rounds or scoop corn chips.

NOTE: This may be served as a vegetable in buttered ramekins, topped with crushed, canned French fried onion rings. Bake at 350° until hot.

Peggy Emrich-Simmons

Appetizers

Spinach Dip with Pita

1 tablespoon chopped
   jalapeños
3/4 cup chopped onions
2 tomatoes, chopped (about
   2 cups), drained
10 ounce package frozen
   chopped spinach, thawed
   and squeezed dry

8 ounces cream cheese,
   softened
2 cups (8 ounce) shredded
   Monterey Jack cheese
1/3 cup half-and-half

Mix all ingredients together and pour into buttered oven-proof dish. Bake at 400° for 20 to 25 minutes. Serve warm with pita toasts.

PITA TOASTS:
2 teaspoons lemon pepper
2 teaspoons ground cumin

1/4 cup butter, melted
6 pita bread loaves

Stir pepper and cumin into melted butter. Halve pita breads. With tip of knife, open up each into 2 pieces. Cut into triangle shapes. Brush with butter mixture and place on broiler pan or cookie sheet. Broil until crisp. Servings: 8 to 10.

Ann Page

Black Bean Salsa

1 can black beans
1 can crisp corn, drained (or
   3 ears of fresh corn)
1 medium tomato, chopped
1/2 cup red bell pepper,
   chopped
1/4 cup red onion, chopped
2 tablespoons white wine vinegar

1 tablespoon vegetable oil
1/2 teaspoon salt
1 bunch of cilantro, chopped
Several Serrano peppers
   (mild), seeded and
   chopped

Mix all together and chill. Servings: 6.

Anne H. Piper

34

Spicy Salsa

6 cups tomatoes, red ripe,
    peeled and chopped
2 cups onions, chopped
1/2 cup hot peppers, minced
8 cloves garlic, minced
1 teaspoon oregano,
    crumbled
1 teaspoon cumin powder
6 tablespoons parsley,
    chopped

4 tablespoons lemon juice
1 tablespoon filé powder
1 cup vinegar
3 teaspoons salt,
    non-iodized
1 tablespoon black pepper,
    freshly ground

Wear rubber gloves. Wash, cut peppers in half, remove seeds, and chop peppers finely. Wash tomatoes. Blanch in boiling water for 1 minute, place tomatoes into cold water. Remove skins, core and coarsely chop tomatoes. Put tomatoes, chopped onions, minced garlic, and the other ingredients into a large stock pot. Heat to boil and then simmer for 30 minutes. Pour salsa into hot prepared pint jars, leaving a 1/2-inch head space. Put on lids and process jars in a hot water bath with 2-inches of water covering the tops of the jars. Process for 20 minutes. Remove jars from the bath and let cool in a dark, draft-free place. Store jars in the refrigerator after they have been opened.

Tricia Seubert

Appetizers

Ohman House Salsa

Named after my father, who was in the Memphis restaurant business for over 25 years.

1 large avocado, ripe
2 (28 ounce) cans whole
  tomatoes
1/2 chopped large purple onion
1 tablespoon minced garlic
2 tablespoons chopped parsley
1 teaspoon chopped oregano

1 1/2 tablespoons olive oil
1 tablespoon red wine vinegar
1 to 2 tablespoons cracked
  pepper
1 (4 ounce) package crumbled
  Athenos feta cheese (basil and
  tomato flavor)

Peel and seed avocado. Drain and rinse tomatoes. Chop avocado and tomatoes, and place in a large bowl. Add onion and next six ingredients, tossing to coat. Fold in cheese. Serve with tortilla chips. Servings: 2 to 4 cups. Preparation Time: 20 minutes.

Billie Ohman McKee

Brenda's Salsa

I invented this recipe after sampling salsa in many different countries.

4 medium sized firm
  tomatoes
4 green onions, chopped
1 cup thick and chunky
  picante sauce

4 or 5 sprigs fresh cilantro,
  chopped
Garlic salt to taste

Chop tomatoes and drain in colander. Mix with other ingredients and serve with low fat chips. Great low-cal appetizer.

NOTE: This is especially good in the spring when Vidalia onions and vine-ripe tomatoes can be used.

Brenda Harris

SOUPS ON

RICH SOUPS

SPONSORED BY

Turner & Nan Askew

Cream of Artichoke Soup
Delicious! Can be served hot or cold.

1 bunch green onions
1 rib of celery
1 medium carrot
2 tablespoons fresh
  parsley, chopped
1 clove garlic, minced
1/2 stick butter
1 bay leaf
Pinch of thyme
1 quart chicken stock
1/4 cup dry white wine
  (French vermouth)

1 cup sliced, cooked
  artichoke hearts
Juice of 1/2 lemon
Dash Tabasco
1 cup heavy cream
Salt and white pepper to
  taste
Thinly sliced lemon or thyme
  sprigs

Chop green onions, celery, carrot, parsley, and garlic in food processor until very fine. Sauté the vegetables, bay leaf, and thyme in butter. Add chicken stock and wine and simmer 10 to 15 minutes. Chop artichoke hearts in food processor until fine; add artichokes, lemon juice and Tabasco to chicken stock mixture; simmer 5 to 10 minutes. Remove from heat and blend in heavy cream. Season to taste. Serve with a garnish of thinly sliced lemon or sprig of fresh thyme. (Reheat in double boiler.) Yields: 11/2 to 13/4 quarts.

Margaret Ann Eikner

Asparagus Rosemary Cream Soup

1 onion, chopped
1/4 cup butter
1 pound potatoes, sliced
26 ounces vegetable broth
2 pounds asparagus,
   trimmed and sliced

1 cup half-and-half
1/2 teaspoon salt
1/2 teaspoon white pepper,
   freshly ground
2 tablespoons fresh
   rosemary, chopped

Sauté onion in butter in a large saucepan until translucent. Add potatoes and broth, salt and pepper. Bring to boiling. Cover and lower heat. Simmer until potatoes are tender. Add rosemary and asparagus. Cook until the asparagus is tender. Remove from heat. Stir in half and half. Process soup in food processor in batches until entire batch is smooth. Serve hot or chilled. Servings: 12.

Tricia Seubert

Curried Carrot Soup

2 large onions, diced
1 bunch celery, diced
4 pounds carrots, chopped
2 tablespoons garlic, minced
2 tablespoons red curry powder

1 gallon chicken stock
2 bay leaves
1 cup rice
1 quart heavy cream
Salt and pepper to taste

Sauté onion until softened. Add celery and carrots and sweat for 5 to 10 minutes. Do not let onions brown. Add garlic and cook one minute more. Stir curry powder into vegetables and cook for 2 to 3 minutes. Add chicken stock and bay leaves. Bring to boil. Lower heat and simmer for 15 minutes. Add rice and continue cooking for 25 to 30 minutes. Add cream and heat through. Puree and season to taste with salt and pepper. Makes 2 gallons.

Folks in the Kitchen wine recommendation: Cambria Katherine's Chardonnay.

Bistro 110
Chicago, Illinois

Soups

San Francisco Corn Chowder

4 ounces diced bacon
2 cloves garlic, minced
1 medium onion, chopped
1 green pepper, chopped
2 stalks celery, chopped
1 (4 ounce) can diced green
   chilies
1 (2 ounce) jar diced pimento
3 cups whole kernel corn,
   fresh or frozen

3 tablespoons butter
3 tablespoons flour
1/2 gallon milk
1/4 cup chopped cilantro
1/4 teaspoon red pepper flakes
1/2 teaspoon cumin
1/2 teaspoon ground coriander
Salt to taste
1/2 cup diced ham

Sauté bacon. Remove all but 2 tablespoons bacon fat and sauté garlic, onion, pepper and celery. Add the mild green chilies, pimento and corn. Separately, make a roux with the butter and flour. Add milk, blending it into the roux. Add sautéed vegetables and remaining ingredients. Simmer until flavors blend. Makes 5 quarts or about 20 one-cup servings.

Nancy Lewis Welsh

Famous Corn and Crabmeat Soup

Great first course for any elegant occasion.

1 cup fresh yellow corn,
   canned or frozen can be
   substituted
1/4 cup butter
1/4 cup all-purpose flour

2 cups chicken stock
2 cups half-and-half
1 pound lump crabmeat
Salt and pepper to taste
1/8 teaspoon garlic salt

Cut fresh corn from cob, saving scraping and milk from cob. Set aside. Melt butter in saucepan, add flour and blend well. Add chicken stock, stirring constantly. Cook until thick and smooth. Stir in cream, crabmeat, corn, corn scrapings and seasonings. Cook on low heat until corn is tender. Servings: 4 to 6. Preparation Time: 45 minutes. Cooking Time: 30 minutes.

Beth Rooks

Cantaloupe Soup

1 cantaloupe	1/2 teaspoon cinnamon
2 cups freshly squeezed orange juice	2 teaspoons lime juice

Purée cantaloupe in a food processor. Combine all ingredients and chill.

Margaret McNeil

Cucumber Soup

3 cups unpeeled cucumbers, puréed in food processor	3 tablespoons white wine vinegar
3 cups chicken stock or broth	2 cloves garlic, minced
3 cups sour cream	2 teaspoons salt
	1/2 teaspoon white pepper

Mix all ingredients and refrigerate 2 to 3 hours before serving.

Mrs. Lina P. Karlson

41

Soups

French Onion Soup
Nothing better for a cold or in the cold!

3 pounds peeled onions
1 stick butter or margarine
1½ teaspoons pepper
2 teaspoons salt
2 tablespoons paprika
1 bay leaf
¼ cup flour

3 quarts canned beef
  bouillon
1 cup white wine (optional)
Kitchen Bouquet (optional)
French bread, sliced
Shredded Parmesan cheese
  or sliced Swiss cheese

Slice onions ⅛-inch thick. Melt butter in a large saucepan, add onion and sauté slowly 1½ hours. Add the next five ingredients and sauté over low heat 10 minutes more. Add bouillon and wine. Simmer for 2 hours. Adjust color darker with Kitchen Bouquet. To serve, put hot soup in bowl. Top with a slice of French bread that has cheese melted on top. Servings: 8 1-cup. Pan Size: Large. Preparation Time: 2½ hours. Cooking Time: 2 hours.

John and Barbara Moore

Favorite Potato Soup

8 to 10 pounds potatoes,
  cubed
1 small onion, diced
1 can chicken broth
1 can cream of chicken soup
1 can Cheddar cheese soup
1 can evaporated milk

Pepper to taste
1 small can Veg-All
  (optional)
2 teaspoons dried parsley
  flakes
Milk, about 1 quart

Boil potatoes and onion in chicken broth for 30 minutes. Mash potatoes with a potato masher. Add both soups and stir to combine. Add canned milk, pepper, parsley flakes and Veg-All. Mix well. Add enough milk to reach the desired thickness. Heat thoroughly. Servings: 6 to 12. Pan Size: Large pot.

Louise Callahan

The Potato Soup
Serve this soup hot or cold!

3 medium potatoes, partially
   peeled and cubed
1 stalk celery, chopped
1 green onion, chopped
1/4 to 1/2 teaspoon salt
1 cup water
1 (12 ounce) can evaporated
   milk

2 to 4 tablespoons butter or
   margarine
1 tablespoon dried parsley
   or 2 tablespoons fresh
   chopped parsley

In large pan combine prepared potatoes, celery, onion, salt and water. Cover and simmer until potatoes are done. Add butter, evaporated milk and parsley. Cook about five minutes longer. Slightly mash potatoes leaving some in cubes. Servings: 4 to 6. Preparation Time: 30 minutes. Cooking Time: 30 minutes.

ADDITIONS:
1 can whole kernel corn,
   drained or 1 can cream
   corn

Chopped ham
Crumbled bacon

GARNISHES:
Black pepper
Parsley

Chopped onion
Shredded carrots

Barbara J. Riley

43

Cream of Wild Rice Soup

*A wonderful way to warm up in the winter
when you are not counting calories.*

3 cups cooked wild rice	1 cup flour
1/2 cup butter	8 cups chicken broth
1 large onion, finely diced	Salt and pepper to taste
1 carrot, finely diced	(white pepper)
1 rib celery, finely diced	1 cup light cream or
1 cup finely diced ham	half-and-half

Prepare the wild rice. In a 4 to 5 quart soup kettle, sauté the onion, carrot, celery and ham in butter about 3 minutes, or until the vegetables have softened slightly. Sift in the flour, a little bit at a time, stirring and cooking until the flour is blended in well, but do not let it brown. Slowly add the chicken broth, stirring until mixture is well blended. Add the cooked wild rice, adjust seasonings as desired. Heat thoroughly. Add the cream (or half-and-half) and reheat gently, but do not boil. May garnish with thinly sliced fresh mushrooms. Servings: 10 to 12. Preparation Time: 45 minutes (to cook wild rice). Cooking Time: 30 minutes (plus time to cook wild rice).

Lois M. Ketcham

Cream of Tomato and Dill Soup

1 small Spanish onion, finely
   chopped
2 stalks of celery, finely
   chopped
3 pounds steak tomatoes
1 ounce fresh dill
1/2 pound fresh basil
1 clove garlic

2 quarts of chicken stock
10 ounces of V-8 juice
1 ounce Worcestershire
   sauce
2 pints heavy cream
1/2 cup butter
1/2 cup all-purpose flour
Salt (optional)

Sauté the celery and onion until they are nice and crisp. Add the concasse tomatoes, seeded and chopped. I'll explain this! To concasse a tomato simply bring a pot of water to a boil. Make an X mark at the base of the tomatoes with a knife and submerge the tomatoes in the water for about 15 to 20 seconds. This will release the skin of the tomato and make it easy to peel. Once peeled, cut tomatoes in half and squeeze the seeds out. Chop. Now you have concasse tomatoes. Reduce flame and add the finely chopped fresh herbs and garlic. Stir. Add the chicken stock, V-8 juice and Worcestershire. Bring to a boil. Once it comes to a boil, reduce to a simmer and add the heavy cream. Now, to make the roux. All roux is, is equal parts of butter and flour. You can substitute margarine or oil, but I prefer butter. It gives the roux a nuttier flavor and will enhance the soup. Melt butter, lower the heat and slowly add the flour stirring often. You will notice it start to thicken. Stir and lower heat. The mixture will brown a little and start to smell like a piecrust. At this point, remove from heat and add slowly to the soup until it is thickened. At this point, the soup is finished and so are you! Sit down and enjoy a great bowl of a hearty tomato and dill soup.

James R. Alarie
Executive Chef
The Chef's Garden
Naples, Florida

Soups

Roasted Red Bell Pepper Soup

2 quarts chicken stock
6 whole potatoes, cubed
Dash nutmeg
1/2 teaspoon white pepper

8 whole red bell peppers,
   roasted and peeled
2 cups heavy cream

Simmer the potatoes in the chicken stock with the seasonings until tender. Add the roasted red bell peppers (canned can be used). Simmer for several minutes and then process in a food processor. Add cream and keep hot until ready to serve. Servings: 12.

Chef Stan Gibson
University Club
Memphis, Tennessee

Old Fashioned Ham and Bean Soup

1 pound dried kidney beans
1 meaty ham bone or ham
   hock
1/2 cup chopped onion
1/2 cup chopped celery

1/2 cup chopped carrots
4 whole cloves
1 bay leaf
1 teaspoon salt
1/4 teaspoon pepper

Place beans and 3 quarts water in a large kettle. Bring to a boil. Remove from heat; cover. Let stand 1 hour. Add ham bone, onion, celery, carrots, cloves, bay leaf, salt and pepper. Simmer for 2 hours or until beans are tender. Remove ham bone from soup. Cut ham from bone. Return ham to soup. Remove bay leaf. Servings: 10 to 12.

Laquita Price

46

New Year's Ham and Bean Soup

For an old Southern New Year's Day party, serve this soup with cornbread, cabbage, barbeque ribs and black-eyed peas.

1 package dried Great
  Northern beans
1 large meaty ham bone or
  ham hock
1/4 cup gravy powder mix
1/2 cup flour
1 onion, chopped
2 bay leaves
1 teaspoon chili powder
Red pepper, to taste
Salt and pepper, to taste

1/4 teaspoon chopped
  parsley
Dash Tabasco
1 teaspoon Worcestershire
  sauce
1 teaspoon dried basil
2 cloves garlic, chopped
4 stalks celery with leaves,
  chopped
2 carrots, chopped
2 jalapeño peppers, minced

Use a big pot! Soak beans overnight in water. Pour off water, rinse and add enough fresh water to cover. Add ham bone. Mix together the gravy mix and flour with water until creamy. Add flour mixture, onion and seasonings to the beans. Cook over low heat for one hour. Let cool and skim off grease. Cut meat from ham bone. Return the bone and meat to the pot. Add garlic, celery, carrots and jalapeño peppers. Continue to cook until the beans are soft. A lot of servings!

Susan Sandor

47

Soups

Bab's Navy Bean Soup
Very low in fat.

3 (16 ounce) cans navy
   beans
1/4 cup green pepper,
   chopped
1/2 cup onion, chopped
1 cup carrots, chopped
1 clove garlic, minced

2 tablespoons olive oil
1 (10 ounce) can Rotel
   tomatoes, diced
1 cup water
1 tablespoon salt
1/2 tablespoon sugar
2 tablespoons parsley flakes

Sauté green peppers, onion, carrots and garlic in the olive oil. Cook 5 minutes. Add tomatoes and water, stir in navy beans along with the salt and sugar. Simmer for 30 minutes to 1 hour. Add parsley flakes, cook for 5 additional minutes. Even better made the day before. Servings: 6. Pan Size: Dutch oven. Preparation Time: 30 minutes. Cooking Time: 1 hour.

Babs Ducklo

Cheese Soup

2 tablespoons minced onion
4 tablespoons butter
Garlic powder, to taste
4 1/2 tablespoons all-purpose
   flour

2 cups milk
2 cups beer
1/2 pound Cheez Whiz
1/2 cup cooked carrots,
   minced

Sauté onion in butter until tender, but not brown. Sprinkle with garlic powder. Blend in flour and heat until bubbly. Add milk and beer and cook until sauce boils and thickens, stirring constantly. Remove from heat and add Cheez Whiz. Stir until melted. Add carrots and cook until heated through.

Barbara Martin

48

Egg Drop Soup

1 quart vegetable broth
1 can creamed corn
3/4 teaspoon salt
1/2 teaspoon white pepper,
 freshly ground

3 tablespoons cornstarch
3 tablespoons cold water
1 egg
2 green onions, sliced thin

Bring broth and corn to a boil. Mix the cornstarch and water together and mix well. Add this to the boiling broth and allow the soup to thicken. Reduce heat to medium. Whisk the egg into the hot soup. Add salt and pepper to taste. Garnish with green onion slices. Servings: 4.

Tricia Seubert

Tortilla Soup

Family favorite, very easy to make and can be frozen to be used later.

1 cup chopped onions
2 fresh jalapeño peppers,
 seeded and chopped
4 garlic cloves, minced
1/2 cup vegetable oil
2 (14 1/2 ounce) cans stewed
 tomatoes
2 (10 ounce) cans Rotel
2 (10 1/2 ounce) cans beef
 bouillon
2 (10 3/4 ounce) cans chicken
 broth, undiluted

2 (10 3/4 ounce) cans tomato
 soup, undiluted
3 cups water
1 tablespoon cumin
1/2 to 1 teaspoon red pepper
4 tablespoons chopped fresh
 cilantro
10 to 12 flour tortillas, cut in
 1/4-inch strips
1 cup (4 ounces) shredded
 Cheddar cheese

Sauté onions, peppers and garlic in oil in large Dutch oven until tender; add next 9 ingredients. Bring to boil, cover, reduce heat and simmer for 45 minutes to one hour. May be frozen at this time. To serve add 2/3 of the tortilla strips and cheese. Simmer 5 minutes. Garnish with remaining tortilla strips that have been toasted. Servings: 10 cups. Pan Size: Dutch oven. Cooking Time: 45 minutes to 1 hour.

Sara Cunningham

Soups

Mexican Tortilla Soup
So easy and so good!

1 can zesty tomato soup
1 can chicken broth
1 can whole kernel corn
1 can pinto beans or cut
   green beans, drained
1 can Mexican style tomatoes

1 can Rotel chilies
1 package taco seasoning
1 cup Monterey Jack
   cheese, grated
6 tortillas (corn), cut into
   small squares

Heat first seven ingredients together with three cups water. Just before serving, add Monterey Jack cheese and corn tortillas, cut into small squares. Heat until cheese melts into soup.

Mary Ellen Plyler

White Chili

1 pound large white beans
6 cups chicken broth
2 cloves garlic, minced
2 medium onions, chopped
1 tablespoon oil
2 (4 ounce) cans mild green
   chilies, chopped

2 teaspoons ground cumin
1 1/2 teaspoons oregano
1/4 teaspoon ground cloves
1/4 teaspoon cayenne
   pepper
4 cups cooked chicken,
   chopped

TOP WITH:
Grated Monterey Jack
   cheese

Salsa
Sour cream

Combine beans, broth, garlic and half the onions in a large soup pot. Bring to a boil. Reduce heat, simmer about 3 hours or more until beans are soft, adding more broth if necessary. In a skillet, sauté remaining onions in oil until tender. Add chilies and seasonings and mix thoroughly. Add to bean mixture. Add chicken and simmer one hour. Serve topped with grated cheese, salsa and sour cream. Servings: 8 to 10. Cooking Time: 4 hours.

Anne Billings

Chili

This is really better the second day.

1 pound ground beef
1 clove garlic, minced about
   1 teaspoon
1 large onion, finely
   chopped, about 1 cup
1 medium green pepper,
   finely chopped, about 2/3
   cup
4 tablespoons chili powder
1 tablespoon cider vinegar

1/4 teaspoon allspice
1/4 teaspoon coriander
1 teaspoon cumin
1/2 teaspoon salt, or to taste
1/2 cup water
2 cups (16 ounces) canned
   crushed tomatoes
1 (16 ounce) can red kidney
   beans with liquid

Cook beef, garlic, onion, and green pepper in a heavy skillet over medium-high heat, stirring frequently to break up meat. Cook until onion is soft and meat has lost its pink color. Add remaining ingredients. Bring to a boil. Cover and reduce heat. Simmer the chili for 45 minutes, stirring frequently.

BEANLESS CHILI: Follow the basic recipe. Omit the beans, use 2 pounds of lean ground beef and 3/4 teaspoon salt.

MEATLESS CHILI: Follow the basic recipe. Omit the beef and water. Use 1 tablespoon vegetable oil to sauté the garlic, onion and pepper. Add one (16 ounce) can of garbanzo beans and one (16 ounce) can of pinto beans.

MINOR VARIATIONS: To make the chili hotter, add cayenne pepper or Tabasco sauce. For a thicker sauce and fuller flavor, add masa (corn flour). To improve the flavor, let the chili simmer longer. Chili often tastes even better the second day, after its ingredients have had a chance to blend overnight. Servings: 6. Pan Size: 4 quart cooker. Preparation Time: 30 minutes. Cooking Time: 30 to 45 minutes.

Carol Wandling

Soups

Mexican Cheese Chicken Soup

4 chicken bouillon cubes
3 cups diced peeled
   potatoes
1 carrot, grated
1 onion, finely chopped
1 bunch broccoli, chopped
2 cloves garlic, chopped
6 cups water
3 boneless, skinless
   chicken breasts

1/4 cup flour
1/4 cup butter or margarine
2 cups milk
2 chicken bouillon cubes
1 pound Mexican Velveeta
   cheese (mild)
1 small jar diced pimento
   (optional)

Place first seven ingredients in a large pot and cook until potatoes are tender, about 20 to 25 minutes. Meanwhile, in a separate pot, boil the chicken breasts until tender about 20 minutes and cut into bite-size pieces. Add chicken to the vegetables. In a small saucepan combine flour, butter and milk. Add 2 bouillon cubes and heat. Add cubed cheese and stir until melted. Combine cheese mixture with chicken and vegetables. Stir in pimentos. Heat to desired serving temperature. Servings: 1 gallon. Pan Size: Large pot. Preparation Time: 20 minutes. Cooking Time: 30 to 40 minutes.

Shirley S. Hardin

Mississippi Hot Stuff

2 cans Cheddar cheese
   soup
1 can stewed tomatoes
2 cans chili hot beans

1 can Rotel tomatoes
1 1/2 pounds ground beef,
   brown and drain
Corn chips

Combine all ingredients in large saucepan, heat for 5 minutes. Serve over corn chips. Servings: 8 to 10. Pan Size: Large saucepan. Preheat: Medium heat. Preparation Time: 20 minutes. Cooking Time: 5 minutes.

Shirley Lawrence

Butternut Shrimp Bisque

3 tablespoons butter
2 cups diced yellow onions
1 bay leaf
4 cups butternut squash,
    peeled, de-seeded, and
    diced into 1/2-inch cubes
2 cups peeled fresh shrimp
2 1/4 teaspoons salt

3/8 teaspoon ground
    cayenne pepper
1/8 teaspoon ground white
    pepper
1/2 cup shrimp stock (see
    note)
6 cups heavy whipping
    cream

Heat the butter in a heavy-duty saucepan over medium-high heat. Add the onions and bay leaf and cook, stirring constantly, until the onions become soft and clear, 3 to 4 minutes. Reduce heat to medium and add the butternut squash. Cook this mixture, stirring occasionally, until the squash begins to soften, 6 to 8 minutes. Reduce heat to low and add the shrimp, salt, cayenne, and white pepper. Cook, stirring occasionally, until the shrimp turn pink, 2 to 3 minutes. Add the shrimp stock and cook, stirring occasionally, for 6 to 8 minutes. If the mixture begins to stick to the pan, scrape it with a spoon and continue cooking. This will intensify the taste of the bisque. Transfer the squash mixture to a food processor and purée. Return the puréed squash to a saucepan, add the cream, and bring to a boil. Reduce heat to low and simmer for 2 to 3 minutes. Serve immediately. Servings: 6.

Folks in the Kitchen wine recommendation: Buena Vista Sauvignon Blanc.

NOTE: To make shrimp stock, place shrimp heads and shells into a saucepan and cover with cold water. Bring to a boil, simmer for 5 minutes, and strain.

Frank Brigtsen's
Brigtsen's Restaurant
New Orleans, LA

Soups

Zuppa di Cozze

20 mussels
2 tablespoons light olive oil
1 teaspoon red pepper
2 cloves of chopped garlic

1 cup of light tomato sauce
Salt and pepper, to taste
1/2 cup of white wine
Chopped Italian parsley

Heat the olive oil in a medium saucepan and add the red pepper and garlic. Add the mussels and sauté for a few minutes. Add the salt and pepper. Add the white wine. Continue to cook for two minutes. Add tomato sauce and cook for five more minutes or until the mussels are open. Toss in a small handful of parsley and serve. Note if the sauce is too thick, add some fish stock at the end.

Folks in the Kitchen wine recommendation: Brolio Vino Santo.

Cafe Roma
San Luis Obispo, CA

Ducks Limited

2 ducks
2 tablespoons butter
2 stalks celery, coarsely
   chopped
2 carrots, coarsely chopped
1/4 cup burgundy
1/4 cup lemon juice
1 tablespoon Worcestershire
   sauce

1 clove garlic
1 tablespoon marjoram
1/4 teaspoon pepper
1 teaspoon seasoned salt
4 or 5 drops hot pepper
   sauce
Cooked rice
Sausage or shrimp
   (optional)

Brown ducks in butter. Place celery and carrots in bottom of pot; place duck on top. Combine remaining ingredients. Pour 1/2 of mixture over duck; cover and cook in crock pot on low for 7 to 9 hours. Add remaining mixture and cook on high for 30 minutes. Serve over rice.

Lea Manhein

54

Quince and Duck Soup

2 tablespoons salad oil
1 cup yellow onion, peeled and chopped
3 each fresh garlic cloves, peeled
1 teaspoon fresh ginger, peeled and minced
1 1/2 cups white wine
1 1/2 gallons rich duck stock
1 1/2 cups heavy cream
2 ounces brandy
5 ounces apple juice
1 small carrot
1 3/4 tablespoons salt
2 1/2 teaspoons Tabasco
2 1/2 teaspoons ground cardamom
3 tablespoons honey

1 1/2 tablespoons lemon juice
1 1/2 tablespoons Dijon mustard
2 teaspoons green peppercorns
1 teaspoon poppy seed
1 teaspoon ground white pepper
1/2 teaspoon ground allspice
1/2 teaspoon basil leaf
1/4 teaspoon celery seed
Pinch saffron
3/4 cup unsalted butter
1 1/2 cups flour, all-purpose
1 1/2 pounds quince meat, diced
1 pound boneless roast duck, diced

Sauté the onion, garlic and ginger in the oil. Add the wine and bring to a boil. Add the stock, cream and brandy with all seasonings and bring to a boil. Make the roux by melting butter and cooking the flour while whisking until it turns an amber color. Cool. Add the cooled roux to the soup and whisk. Purée the soup with a hand blender or strain out the solids and purée in an food processor and return to the soup. Add the diced duck and quince and simmer, tasting carefully and adjusting seasoning if necessary. Garnish with cut chives or other fresh herbs. Yields 2 gallons.

Folks in the Kitchen wine recommendation: Au Bon Climate Pinot Noir.

Keystone Ranch
Keystone, CO

Favorite Duck Gumbo

2 mallard ducks
3 quarts water
1½ sticks butter or margarine
1 cup flour
1 small stalk celery,
   chopped
3 cloves garlic, minced
4 medium onions, sliced
1 large bell pepper, chopped
1 bunch green onions,
   chopped
1 small can tomato paste
2 teaspoons Accent

1 teaspoon oregano
2 tablespoons salt
2 tablespoons gumbo filé (or
   put ½ teaspoon over rice
   instead)
2 tablespoons dried parsley
1 teaspoon thyme
1 tablespoon black pepper,
   or to taste
½ teaspoon red pepper, or
   to taste
2 small cans tomatoes
1 pint sliced okra

Cook ducks in water until tender. Reserve the broth. Remove meat discarding skin and bones. Melt the butter in an iron skillet. Slowly blend in flour to make the roux. Stir constantly until golden brown. Strain two quarts of the reserved broth. Add the roux and stir until well blended. In a larger pot combine the duck meat, broth and remaining ingredients. Simmer for three hours, stirring about every 10 to 15 minutes. Serve over rice with hot cornbread on the side. Servings: 8 to 10.

Mrs. Dan Canale

Duck Gumbo

6 tablespoons flour
6 tablespoons oil
1 large onion, minced
1/2 cup diced celery
2 mallard duck breasts, cut
   from the bone

Salt and pepper, to taste
1/2 cup minced parsley
4 green onions, chopped
1 pound hot hickory smoked
   bulk sausage, crumbled
Cooked rice

In a 6 quart Dutch oven, make a roux with the flour and oil, stirring constantly over medium low heat until reddish brown. Add onion and celery and cook, stirring until slightly wilted. Add duck pieces and 6 cups of hot water. Mix well to dissolve the roux. Season with salt and pepper and bring to a boil. Lower heat, add parsley, green onions and sausage. Cook, covered until duck is tender about 1 1/2 to 2 hours, stirring occasionally. Skim the top before serving over hot rice. Servings: 6. Pan Size: 6 quart Dutch oven. Preparation Time: 30 minutes. Cooking Time: 2 hours.

Peggy Emrich-Simmons

Quick Gumbo

4 cups cooked diced
   chicken
1 large onion
1 slice Mar-Tenn country ham
   or Bryan hickory crest
   ham
1/2 pound shrimp
1 (28 ounce) can tomatoes,
   undrained
1 small can tomato purée
1 large package frozen okra

1 tablespoon chopped
   parsley
1/2 teaspoon thyme
Several dashes of Cajun
   seasoning
1 package Bryan Cajun
   flavored smoked
   sausage, sliced
1 quart Sweet Sue chicken
   broth
1/2 teaspoon filé powder

Trim and chop ham into bite-size pieces. Sauté lightly with chopped onion. Combine remaining ingredients, except shrimp and cook about 20 minutes. Add shrimp and cook for 5 to 10 more minutes. If planning to freeze gumbo, do not add filé powder until ready to serve. Servings: 6 to 8.

George Bryan

Shrimp Gumbo

6 onions, chopped
4 green peppers, chopped
1 bunch celery, chopped
4 garlic cloves, chopped
1 bunch parsley, chopped
2 to 3 tablespoons bacon
  grease
1 (1 quart, 14 ounce) can
  tomato juice
2 (1 pound, 12 ounce) cans
  tomatoes
2 (6 ounce) cans tomato
  paste

1 package crab and shrimp
  boil
5 tablespoons
  Worcestershire
1 tablespoon salt
12 pinches gumbo filé
6 drops Tabasco, or to taste
1/2 tablespoon pepper
1 (16 ounce) bag chopped
  frozen okra
3 pounds peeled shrimp
1 pound lump crabmeat
Cooked rice

Cook onions, peppers, celery, garlic and parsley in bacon grease until transparent. Add tomato juice and tomatoes broken into pieces with their juice. Add tomato paste and seasonings. Stir well and cook slowly for 2 hours. Remove crab and shrimp boil pouch. Add shrimp and cook for 5 minutes. Add okra and continue to cook slowly for another hour. Stir in crabmeat, mix thoroughly and heat through. Serve over a bed of rice. If gumbo is too thick, add 1 can of consomme. Servings: 12. Pan Size: Large pot. Cooking Time: 3 hours.

Mrs. J. Hal Patton

SALADS

VEGETABLES

TOSSED SALAD

DRESSING

SPONSORED BY

Willard & Rita Sparks

Salads

Parker Salad

1/4 cup red wine vinegar
3/4 cup olive oil
1 teaspoon salt
1/4 teaspoon white pepper
1 tablespoon dijon-style
   mustard

4 ounces crumbled bleu cheese
5 cups mixed greens
1/2 cup chopped red onions
1/2 cup toasted slivered almonds
1 small can mandarin
   oranges, chilled

Mix first five ingredients by whisking together in a mixing bowl. Stir in bleu cheese immediately before serving. Toss salad greens, red onions, almonds and oranges together in large salad bowl. Toss salad again with bleu cheese vinaigrette and serve. Servings: 6. Pan Size: Large salad bowl. Preparation Time: 20 minutes.

Toni Campbell Parker

Butter Lettuce Salad "Mother's Style"

6 heads butter lettuce (bibb
   lettuce)
3 large Granny Smith
   apples, peeled, cored,
   and sliced
1/2 cup walnuts, coarsely
   chopped
Salt and white pepper to taste

1/8 cup sugar
1/3 cup champagne vinegar
   (you may substitute with
   tarragon vinegar)
11/2 cups heavy cream
2 bunches chives, chopped
   fine
3 shallots, chopped fine

In a medium-size mixing bowl, stir together the salt, pepper, and the sugar. Add the champagne vinegar and stir. Next, add the heavy cream, shallots, and chives. Place the butter lettuce, apples, and walnuts into a large mixing bowl. The final step is to pour the dressing onto the butter lettuce and toss. Servings: 12. Enjoy!

Folks in the Kitchen wine recommendation: Beringer Chenin Blanc.

Wilhelm Hoppe
Hoppe's at 901
Morro Bay, CA

60

Charlotte's Salad

Iceberg lettuce and Romaine
  lettuce
6 to 8 strawberries, sliced
2 green onions, chopped fine
Celery, chopped
Red pepper, sliced fine
1 apple, peeled and chopped
1 tomato, julienne, do not
  use seeds

Snow peas, steamed and
  shocked under cold
  water
Pecans, chopped
Alfalfa sprouts, pickled
  ginger, feta cheese for
  garnish

Toss the above, and when ready to serve, put in bowls and top with a piece of pickled ginger, alfalfa sprouts and sprinkle with feta cheese. Pour on just enough dressing to coat. Serve.

DRESSING:
1 bottle 7 Seas Italian
  dressing

½ cup powdered sugar
2 tablespoons poppy seeds

Mix dressing and powdered sugar together until sugar is dissolved and add poppy seeds. Refrigerate. Oil rising to top may be skimmed off and discarded.

Charlotte Wolfe

Salads

Spinach Salad

3 or 4 bunches spinach
3 or 4 hard boiled eggs

6 strips bacon, cooked

SALAD DRESSING:
1½ cups vegetable oil
¼ cup vinegar
¼ cup lemon juice
1½ teaspoons salt
1 teaspoon dry mustard

4 tablespoons sugar
1 teaspoon paprika
2 teaspoons Worcestershire
⅓ cup ketchup
1½ teaspoons garlic powder

Combine all dressing ingredients. Toss spinach greens with dressing, add eggs and crumbled bacon. Toss again and serve immediately.

DRESSING: Mix all ingredients in a jar and shake until well mixed. Makes enough for about eight servings.

Betty Ingram

Caesar Salad

2 cloves garlic, 1 crushed and
   1 one to rub the bowl
2 heads Romaine lettuce,
   washed and torn into
   bite-size pieces
Anchovies, mashed
¾ cup olive oil

¼ cup vinegar
1 tablespoon lemon juice
Salt and pepper, to taste
1 egg, coddled
Parmesan cheese
Croutons, if desired

Salt bottom of large wooden salad bowl, rub garlic on bottom and sides. Place washed lettuce into bowl. Make dressing of oil, vinegar, crushed garlic, lemon juice, mashed anchovies and coddled egg. Pour over lettuce. Top with Parmesan cheese and croutons. Servings: 4 to 6. Pan Size: Large wooden bowl. Preparation Time: 15 minutes.

Jessica Crouch

Caesar Salad with a Zing

Adapted from a Northern Canadian family recipe.

2/3 cup olive oil
2 teaspoons wine vinegar
3 cloves garlic
3 dashes Worcestershire
  sauce
3 dashes Tabasco
1/4 teaspoon dry mustard

1 tablespoon lemon juice
2 eggs (optional)
2 rolled anchovies (one inch
  anchovy paste)
Head of Romaine lettuce
Grated Parmesan cheese
Croutons

Place first nine ingredients in blender. Blend on medium power for 30 to 45 seconds until thick and creamy. Refrigerate mixture for at least 6 hours, preferably overnight. Wash lettuce in ice water; tear into bite-size pieces and dry. Place into large wooden bowl. Remove mixture from refrigerator and blend again 15 to 20 seconds; the dressing should be the thickness of pancake batter. Pour over lettuce. Shake cheese onto lettuce and toss until all pieces of lettuce are coated. Add more cheese and croutons and serve while still cold. Taste the zing! For more adventurous diners, increase garlic, Worcestershire and Tabasco. Servings: 6 to 8. Preparation Time: 15 minutes at most.

Bruce Alpert, M.D.

Greek Salad

Great with grilled meat or alone as a meal!

2 medium tomatoes, quartered
1 medium zucchini, julienned
1 medium cucumber, sliced
1 cup ripe olives
1 medium purple onion, sliced
3/4 cup feta cheese

1 (6 ounce) jar marinated
  artichoke hearts,
  reserving marinade
1/4 cup red wine vinegar
1/4 teaspoon ground pepper
Red lettuce leaves

Combine first 6 ingredients and toss. Drain artichokes. Save marinade and add artichokes to first mixture. Combine reserved marinade, vinegar and pepper. Pour over tomato mixture. Toss and cover. Chill for 8 hours. Serve on lettuce and top with additional feta if desired. Servings: 4 to 6

John and Barbara Moore

63

Salads

Asparagus Mousse with Caper Sauce

May be served as luncheon salad or appetizer in smaller portions.
Delicious served simply or with addition of seafood and Caper Sauce.

2 envelopes plain gelatin
1/2 cup cold water
2 (14 ounce) cans asparagus
Reserved liquid from
  asparagus
8 ounce package cream
  cheese, softened

1 cup mayonnaise
Dash Worcestershire sauce
Dash Tabasco sauce
1/2 teaspoon salt
Juice of one lemon
1/4 cup sliced almonds
  toasted and chopped fine

Soak gelatin in cold water. Bring reserved asparagus juice to a boil. Remove from heat and add gelatin to dissolve. Place drained asparagus in blender with about half the gelatin and juice mixture and purée. Add softened cream cheese and blend. Pour into large mixing bowl and stir in remaining gelatin/juice mixture, mayonnaise, Worcestershire sauce, Tabasco, salt, lemon juice and toasted chopped almonds. Grease Pyrex dish or molds with mayonnaise and fill with mixture. Cover container with plastic wrap and refrigerate overnight. Serve on crisp salad greens with garnish. Garnish can be as simple as a dollop of mayonnaise, or boiled shrimp with caper sauce, or for a special luncheon salad, thin slices of smoked salmon with caper sauce on bed of crisp mixed salad greens. Servings: 6 to 8 luncheon, 12 appetizer. Pan Size: 8x13x2-inches. Preparation Time: 30 minutes. Cooking Time: Refrigerate overnight, assemble to serve in ten minutes or less.

CAPER SAUCE:

1/2 cup mayonnaise
1/2 cup cream cheese
1 tablespoon capers
1 teaspoon caper liquid
1 teaspoon fresh lemon juice
1/2 medium red onion,
  finely chopped

Thin slices smoked salmon
  (optional)
Shrimp, small can, rinsed
  (optional)
Crabmeat, small can, rinsed
  (optional)

(continued on next page)

Blend mayonnaise and cream cheese in blender or with mixer until smooth. Gently, stir in capers, liquid, lemon juice and onion. If desired, add shrimp or crabmeat. Should you choose to serve with smoked salmon, spread sauce on crackers and top with salmon slice. Pan Size: 2 cup mixing bowl. Preparation Time: 10 minutes.

Dorothy D. Thurman

Asparagus Salad

Wonderful served at Christmas with beef tenderloin. Color is excellent.

1/2 cup cold water	**1/2 cup cider vinegar**
2 envelopes unflavored gelatin	**1 cup diced celery**
1/2 cup hot asparagus juice	**1/4 cup chopped onion**
1 cup sugar	**2 small jars pimento**
1/2 cup lemon juice	**1 large can asparagus tips**
	1/2 cup pecans toasted

Mix together cold water and unflavored gelatin. Add hot asparagus juice. Mix sugar, lemon juice and vinegar. Mix together with the gelatin then fold in remaining ingredients. Refrigerate until firm.

Blythe Patton Orr

Salads

Delta Green Bean Vinaigrette

*This is a recipe used in a buffet of the finest
dinner party every given in Greenville, MS.*

3 pounds tender young
   green beans
1 cup vinaigrette
1/2 pound Gruyere cheese,
   coarsely grated

1/2 pound white mushrooms,
   thinly sliced

FOR VINAIGRETTE - Use 3 parts to 1:
3 tablespoons olive oil
1 tablespoon balsamic
   vinegar

Fresh garlic
2 teaspoons coarse brown
   prepared mustard

Blanche and chill green beans. Toss with vinaigrette and top with cheese
and mushrooms. Use 1 cup vinaigrette for 3 pounds beans. Servings: 16.

Marilyn A. Newton

Blythe's Picnic Butter Beans

*This is a family favorite and a tradition for family
gatherings at Easter, 4th of July and birthday dinners.*

1 package frozen baby lima
   beans
1 can shoe peg corn,
   drained

1 scant cup real mayonnaise
1 bunch of green onions,
   chopped
Salt and pepper, to season

Cook lima beans according to package directions in salted water. Do not
overcook. Drain and set aside to cool. Once cool, add to shoe peg corn.
Gently stir in mayonnaise. Add green onions and salt and pepper.
Season well for zip. Less mayonnaise can be used according to
preference. If doubling recipe, do not double mayonnaise.

Caroline Orr/Blythe Patton Orr

66

Broccoli Salad

1 large bunch broccoli,
  stems peeled, chopped
  and flowerets removed
  for salad

16 ounces bacon, fried crisp
  and crumbled
1 cup raisins

DRESSING:
1/2 cup mayonnaise
1/4 cup sugar

2 tablespoons vinegar

Make dressing by mixing mayonnaise, sugar, and vinegar. Toss remaining ingredients together with dressing. Chill. Pack in water proof container. Servings: 4 to 6.

Mrs. John B. Apple

Broccoli Crunch

1 head cauliflower, broken
  into flowerets
1 pound broccoli, broken
  into flowerets
1/2 cup onion
3/4 cup mayonnaise

1 tablespoon sugar
3 tablespoons evaporated milk
1 teaspoon vinegar
1/2 teaspoon salt
1 teaspoon pepper

Combine cauliflower, broccoli, and onion, toss well. Combine mayonnaise and remaining ingredients, mixing well; pour over vegetables. Toss gently; cover and chill 4 hours. Servings: 10.

Charlotte Wolfe

Salads

Country Slaw

1 medium head cabbage	2 tablespoons pickle juice
2 cucumbers, peeled and diced	Mayonnaise
1 small package radishes, diced	Salt and pepper, to taste
	Fresh dill weed (optional)

Chop (do not grate) cabbage. In large mixing bowl, combine cabbage, cucumber, radishes and pickle juice. Add enough mayonnaise to hold mixture together. Salt and pepper to taste. Add fresh dill if desired.

Jean "Granny" Gray

Napa Cabbage Salad

1 Napa cabbage, chopped	1 package sliced almonds
1 bunch green onions, diced	2 tablespoons sugar
2 packages Ramen noodles (Oriental chicken soup), crushed	2 packages soup seasoning (from noodles)
2 tablespoons sesame seeds	1/2 cup water
	1 teaspoon soy sauce
	3/4 cup olive oil

Mix cabbage and green onions, set aside. In broiling pan, broil soup noodles, sesame seeds and almonds. Cool. Set aside. For dressing, heat sugar and soup seasoning in water until dissolved. Add soy sauce and oil. Pour into dressing container and shake. Toss cabbage and onions in dressing. Add noodles, sesame seeds and almonds. Gently toss and serve. Servings: 8. Preparation Time: 30 minutes.

Ann Leatherman

68

Garden Deviled Eggs

6 eggs, hard cooked
1/4 cup garlic and herb
   cheese spread
2 tablespoons mayonnaise
2 tablespoons finely
   chopped scallions

1 tablespoon finely chopped
   pimentos
1 tablespoon dijon mustard
48 wheat wafers
Parsley and tomato for garnish

Cut each egg crosswise in slices. Scoop yolks out into small bowl; mash well. Set egg whites aside. Stir cheese spread, mayonnaise, scallions, pimentos and mustard into yolks until smooth and well blended. Top each wafer with an egg white slice. Spoon or pipe yolk mixture onto egg whites. Garnish with parsley and tomato if desired. Servings: 48. Preparation Time: 20 minutes.

Shirley Lawrence

"New-Blue" Potato Salad

2 pounds new potatoes
1/2 green pepper, cut in
   1-inch cubes
1/2 red pepper, cut in 1-inch
   cubes

1/2 cup black olives, cut in
   half
1 ounce blue cheese,
   crumbled

Cut potatoes in large cubes and boil until tender. Drain and cool slightly. Add other ingredients. Servings: 3.

DRESSING:
Juice of 1/2 lemon
4 tablespoons olive oil

1 teaspoon dijon mustard

Ann Page

Mama Cita's Perfect Potato Salad

My grandmother (affectionally called Mama Cita) is a true down home cook. So we put our thoughts together and came up with the Perfect Potato Salad recipe.

5 red skin potatoes in their original jackets
3 medium size eggs
1 cup mayonnaise
1/2 cup sour cream
1 tablespoon parsley, chopped
2 tablespoons finely grated onions
2 tablespoons finely chopped celery

2 tablespoons finely chopped sweet pickles
2 tablespoons pimentos
2 tablespoons chopped green peppers
A few grains of cayenne pepper
1/4 teaspoon salt

Boil 5 medium-size red skin potatoes for 10 to 15 minutes (do not overcook). Boil 3 medium-size eggs (approximately 5 to 7 minutes). Peel and dice potatoes while they are still warm. When potatoes have cooled, add mayonnaise, sour cream and then mix these ingredients gently with a wooden spoon. Then, add the eggs, parsley, onion, celery, sweet pickle, pimento, cayenne, salt, and green pepper. Chill and serve. Servings: 4 to 6. Bowl Size: Large mixing bowl. Preparation Time: 30 minutes.

ADVICE: Potato salad is best made from red skin potatoes cooked in their jackets and peeled while still warm. Red skin potatoes hold their shape and will not crumble when sliced or diced.

Dr. Denise Mustiful-Martin

Curried Potato Salad

3 cups water
1½ teaspoons curry
  powder
1 teaspoon salt
4 cups diced raw potatoes
2 tablespoons French dressing
2 tablespoons lemon juice
2 tablespoons grated onion

1½ teaspoons salt
¼ teaspoon black pepper
¼ teaspoon garlic powder
1½ cups diced celery
½ cup diced green pepper
  (optional)
3 hard cooked eggs, diced
¾ cup mayonnaise

Combine water, curry powder and 1 teaspoon salt. Add potatoes and cook, covered, until tender. Drain. Combine French dressing, lemon juice, onion, 1½ teaspoons salt, pepper and garlic powder. Mix lightly with the potatoes and let stand for 30 minutes. Add celery, green pepper and eggs. Toss lightly, then blend in mayonnaise. Servings: 6. Preparation Time: 1 hour.

Ray and Betty Ashley

Wild Rice Salad

1 cup uncooked wild rice
2¾ cups chicken stock
2¾ cups water
1½ cups pecan pieces
1 cup currants
Rind of one orange, grated

10 ounces frozen tiny peas, thawed
¼ cup vegetable oil
⅓ cup fresh orange juice
1 teaspoon salt
Freshly ground pepper, to taste

Rinse rice in strainer under cold water. Combine with chicken stock and water in saucepan. Bring to boil. Reduce heat and simmer uncovered 35 to 45 minutes. Rice should not be too soft. Drain. Combine rice with remaining ingredients. Mix well. Let stand 2 hours. Serve at room temperature. Servings: 6. Pan Size: 3 quart saucepan. Preparation Time: 30 minutes. Cooking Time: 35 to 45 minutes.

Nancy Morrow

Shell Salad

A quick, easy summer salad.

3 cups cooked, chopped
   boneless chicken
1/2 cup Italian dressing
6 ounces shell pasta,
   cooked and drained
1/2 cup mayonnaise
3 tablespoons lemon juice
1 tablespoon prepared
   mustard

1 small onion, chopped
1 cup chopped cucumber
1 cup chopped celery
3/4 cup ripe olives, chopped
1 teaspoon pepper
1 teaspoon salt

Mix chicken and dressing with hot shell pasta. Let cool. Mix mayonnaise, lemon juice and mustard. Stir in vegetables and seasonings. Add to cooled pasta. Chill. Servings: 8 to 10.

Nancy Williams

Cybill Shepard's Tomato Aspic

2 cups spicy V-8 juice
12 ounces cottage cheese
1 rib celery, chopped
4 to 6 spring onions, chopped
1 small cucumber, chopped

1 tablespoon lemon juice
Dash of Worcestershire
   sauce
Salt, to taste
2 packages gelatin

Dissolve gelatin in 10x6-inch casserole. Heat 1 cup V-8 juice with lemon juice, Worcestershire sauce and salt. Pour over gelatin and add remaining V-8 juice. Refrigerate. Add cottage cheese and vegetables. Return to refrigerator. When firm, serve on lettuce leaf and top with mayonnaise.

Patty S. Micci

Curried Chicken Salad

2 to 3 cups cooked chicken,
  cubed
1 (4 ounce) can water chestnuts
1 pound seedless grapes or
  1 (11 ounce) can mandarin
  oranges
1½ cups chopped celery

1 cup mayonnaise
1 teaspoon soy sauce
2 tablespoons curry powder
½ cup sour cream
2 teaspoons lemon juice
Salt and pepper, to taste

Combine chicken, water chestnuts, fruit and celery. Mix all remaining ingredients and add to chicken mix. Toss well. Chill several hours or up to a day ahead. Serve on lettuce leaf. Servings: 6 or more.

Helen Hardin

Artichoke Chicken Salad
Perfect ladies' luncheon dish.

1 package Uncle Ben's 5
  minute wild rice
3 (3½ ounce) jars marinated
  artichokes, drained
4 green onions, chopped (no
  tops)

2 (4 ounce) cans sliced ripe olives
3 whole chicken breasts,
  cooked and diced
1 to 2 cups mayonnaise
Parsley

Prepare rice according to directions. Combine all ingredients except mayonnaise. Add 1 cup mayonnaise to chicken mixture, adding more until you reach desired consistency. Garnish with parsley. Servings: 10 to 12.

Colleen Cowles Capstick

Steak Salad with Mustard Vinaigrette

Something different for a summer luncheon.

DRESSING:

1 egg, beaten
1/3 cup olive oil
2 teaspoons Dijon mustard
1 1/2 teaspoons lemon juice
3 tablespoons tarragon
   vinegar

1 teaspoon Worcestershire
3 dashes Tabasco
1 teaspoon salt
1/4 teaspoon fresh pepper

SALAD:

2 pounds cooked steak,
   cubed
1/2 pound mushrooms,
   sliced
6 green onions, sliced
1 small can hearts of palm,
   sliced
2 tablespoons chopped
   chives

2 tablespoons fresh
   parsley, chopped
2 tablespoons fresh dill,
   chopped
Assorted greens
Tomato wedges

Mix dressing ingredients together thoroughly; set aside. Combine all salad ingredients except greens and tomatoes. Mix carefully. Refrigerate overnight. Toss dressing and salad with chilled, crisp greens and garnish with tomato quarters or cocktail tomatoes. Servings: 8 to 10. Preparation Time: 10 minutes then 15 minutes.

Ann Clark Harris

74

Shrimp and Snow Pea Pasta Salad

1 pound shrimp, cooked, peeled
   and deveined
3³/4 cups uncooked pasta
   (fusilli or rigatoni)
1 (6 ounce) package frozen
   Chinese pea pods
1/2 cup sliced water
   chestnuts, drained

1/2 to 1 cup mayonnaise
2 tablespoons chopped fresh
   parsley
1¹/2 tablespoons chopped
   pimento
1/8 teaspoon salt
1/8 teaspoon pepper

Cook pasta, rinse with cold water and drain. Cook pea pods and drain. Combine all ingredients in a large bowl and toss lightly. Chill for 4 to 6 hours. Servings: 6 to 8.

Beth Worley

Shrimp Salad Masterpiece

1 (6 ounce) package curried
   rice mix
2 cups shrimp, cooked,
   halved lengthwise
1 cup diced celery
1/2 cup diced green pepper
4 slices bacon, cooked and
   crumbled

1/2 cup whipping cream
1/2 cup salad dressing
1 teaspoon curry powder
Lettuce leaves for serving
Coconut, cashews and
   chutney for garnishing

Cook rice mix according to package directions. Cool. Reserve 6 shrimp halves for garnish. In bowl, combine shrimp, rice, celery, green pepper and bacon. Whip cream and combine with salad dressing and curry. Stir into rice mixture. Cover and chill. To serve, scoop salad into lettuce-lined bowl, garnish with shrimp halves, coconut, cashews and chutney. Servings: 6.

Sharon S. Kelso

Warm Salmon Salad with Potatoes and Shiitake Mushrooms

1¹/₄ pound salmon fillet, without skin
5 small red bliss potatoes, about 12 ounces
8 ounces mixed green lettuce leaves or mesclun
1 large shallot, chopped
1 pound fresh shiitake mushrooms

1 ounce minced fresh herbs (tarragon, chives, chervil, Italian parsley)
1 tablespoon grated ginger
6 tablespoons extra virgin olive oil
¹/₂ tablespoon lite soy sauce
2¹/₂ tablespoons sherry wine vinegar

Cut salmon fillet into 20 slices, ¹/₄-inch thick, about 5 slices per serving. Boil the potatoes with skin in salted water. Peel and slice them. Mix ginger and chopped shallot. Place the sliced potatoes on a plate, season with salt, pepper, 1 tablespoon sherry wine vinegar, and 2¹/₂ tablespoons olive oil. Add shallot-ginger mixture, toss without breaking the potato slices and keep warm. Remove the stems of the mushrooms, clean and wash them. Slice the caps ¹/₄-inch thick. In a hot teflon pan, quickly sauté the mushrooms in 2 tablespoons olive oil. Add salt, pepper, and ¹/₂ tablespoon fine herbs. Toss salad with 1¹/₂ tablespoons olive oil, ¹/₂ tablespoon sherry wine vinegar, salt, pepper and ¹/₂ tablespoon fine herbs. Place salad in center of plate with sliced potatoes encircling it. Quickly sauté salmon slices in a hot teflon pan with a few drops of olive oil (about 15 seconds each side), deglaze with 1 tablespoon sherry wine vinegar and 1 tablespoon lite soy sauce. Arrange salmon slices on top of the potatoes, then pour some sauce on top of the salmon. Sprinkle shiitake mushrooms on top of salad and serve.

Folks in the Kitchen wine recommendation: Columbia Crest Merlot.

René Pujol Restaurant
New York City, NY

76

Salmon Pasta Salad

2 tablespoons red onion, chopped
1/2 cup chopped celery
1/2 cup mayonnaise
1 to 2 tablespoons Dijon mustard
2 tablespoons fresh lemon juice

3 tablespoons fresh dill
6 to 8 ounce salmon fillet, broiled
6 to 8 ounces pasta (bow tie or fusilli) cooked al dente, drained and cooled

Combine the first 6 ingredients in large serving bowl. Toss in the pasta until coated. Crumble pieces of the salmon over salad and toss gently. Preparation Time: 20 to 30 minutes.

Beth Worley

Spiced Peach Salad

Great with wild game, chicken, or pork

1 (6 ounce) lemon or peach gelatin or 1 (3 ounce) of each
1 (28 ounce) can spiced peaches, drained, reserving juice
1/2 cup water
1/2 cup orange juice

Juice of 1 lemon
1 (8 ounce) can white cherries or grapes, drained, reserving juice
1/8 teaspoon salt
1 cup chopped pecans (optional)

Chop peaches. Combine 1/2 cup water with 1 cup peach juice and bring to a boil. Dissolve gelatin in boiling liquid, stirring until dissolved. Add orange juice, lemon juice and 1 cup of fruit juice (making 1 1/2 cups total). Add the fruit and nuts. Mix and pour into a 6 to 8 cup mold. Chill and serve on lettuce. Servings: 8 to 10. Pan Size: 6 to 8 cup mold or flat casserole 9x9x2-inches. Preparation Time: 15 minutes.

Ann Clark Harris

77

Salads

Mandarin "Stand-Up" Salad

Name "Stand-Up" because each square stands alone perfectly, no quiver, no weeping. Taste and appearance make it a superb salad! It is our favorite summer salad to enjoy at home, share with neighbors, and take to church potluck suppers.

2 (6 ounce) packages orange
    gelatin
3 cups boiling water
3 cups miniature
    marshmallows
1 (16 ounce) can crushed
    pineapple in its own juice

2 (11 ounce) cans mandarin
    oranges
2 cups Cool Whip
Red cherries and mint tips
    (optional)

Mix gelatin with boiling water. Drain juice from oranges. Do not drain pineapple. Add oranges, pineapple and marshmallows to gelatin. Fold in Cool Whip and pour into a flat container, approximately 12½x8½-inches. Refrigerate overnight, or at least 6 hours. Cut into squares. Decorate each square with a teaspoon of Cool Whip, red cherry and mint top. Will keep 4 to 5 days in refrigerator. Servings: 15. Pan Size: 12½x8½-inches. Preparation Time: 25 minutes.

Mrs. Patricia P. Cox

Mandarin Orange Salad

2 cans apricot nectar
2 small or 1 large box lemon
    gelatin
1 small can frozen orange
    juice

2 cans mandarin oranges,
    drained
1 can grapefruit sections,
    drained
¼ cup almonds, sliced

Heat apricot nectar until hot, not boiling, add gelatin and frozen orange juice. Stir until dissolved. Add drained fruit and almonds. Refrigerate until firm. Serve on bed of lettuce.

Blythe Patton Orr/Caroline Orr

78

Frozen Fruit Salad

2 (3 ounce) packages cream
   cheese, softened
1 cup mayonnaise
1 cup whipping cream,
   whipped
1/2 cup red maraschino
   cherries, chopped

1/2 cup green maraschino
   cherries, chopped
1 can (21/2 cups) crushed
   pineapple, drained
21/2 cups miniature
   marshmallows

Combine cream cheese and mayonnaise. Blend until smooth. Fold in whipped cream, fruit and marshmallows. Pour into a one-quart refrigerator tray. Freeze firm. Take out of refrigerator about 15 minutes before serving time. Servings: 8 to 10.

Mrs. William M. Frazee

Cranberry Nut Salad
"My own creation."

2 small packages cranberry
   gelatin
3 ounces cream cheese
1 can rhubarb pieces
14 ounces crushed
   pineapple

1 cup pecans, chopped
1/2 cup light mayonnaise
1/2 cup plain yogurt
1 teaspoon sugar

Mix gelatin and cream cheese. Add boiling water according to package directions. Pour into 9x13-inch dish. Add rhubarb, pineapple and pecans. Refrigerate overnight. Mix mayonnaise, yogurt and sugar. Cover and refrigerate overnight. Cut gelatin into squares and top with yogurt mixture. Servings: 8 to 10. Preparation Time: 20 minutes.

W. L. Cox

79

Salads

Congealed Cranberry Salad
So easy to prepare and is absolutely delicious!

6 ounce package cherry gelatin
1 small can crushed
   pineapple, drained

1 jar cran-orange relish
1 cup finely chopped nuts
   (pecans)

Dissolve gelatin in 2 cups boiling water. Add drained pineapple, cran-orange relish and nuts. Mix well. Refrigerate to jell. Servings: 9 to 12. Pan Size: 9x9x2-inch glass dish. Preparation Time: 20 minutes.

Carol Wandling

Come Back Salad Dressing
From Elite Cafe, Dyer, TN.

2 cloves garlic, finely chopped
1 cup mayonnaise
1/2 cup ketchup
1 teaspoon prepared
   mustard
1/2 cup vegetable oil
1 tablespoon Worcestershire

1 teaspoon pepper
1/2 cup chili sauce
Dash paprika
Juice of one grated onion
Juice of 2 lemons
2 tablespoons water
Salt, to taste

Mix all ingredients together and refrigerate 3 to 4 hours before serving. Servings: 2¾ cups. Preparation Time: 10 to 15 minutes.

Jerry Thomas

80

Charlotte Too Dressing

Charlotte Too is the name of our boat and this is a dressing that we have used many times when entertaining aboard.

1 cup mayonnaise	2 tablespoons safflower oil
1/2 cup Dijon mustard	3/4 teaspoon cider vinegar
1/4 cup honey	1/8 teaspoon onion salt
	1/4 teaspoon pepper flakes

Combine all ingredients in blender, process until smooth. Cover and chill thoroughly. Servings: 1 1/4 cups.

Charlotte Wolfe

Ember's Restaurant House Dressing

The original dressing from the old restaurant.

6 ounces Gorgonzola cheese	2 or 3 green onions, chopped, tops included
3 ounces Roquefort cheese	2 teaspoons Worcestershire sauce
8 ounces mayonnaise	Salt and pepper, to taste
8 ounces sour cream	Ketchup
Juice of one lemon	
1 clove garlic, minced	

Crumble the two cheeses in small pieces. Mix all of the ingredients together. Add enough ketchup to give a pink tint to dressing. Serve on your favorite green salad.

Sara Cunningham

"Honey" French Dressing

1/2 scant cup sugar
1 teaspoon celery seed
1 teaspoon salt
2 tablespoons vinegar
2 tablespoons lemon juice
1 teaspoon Worcestershire

1/3 cup bottled chili sauce
1 tablespoon grated white
  onion
3/4 cup vegetable oil
1 garlic clove, minced

Combine in glass jar. Shake well. Refrigerate. Good on green salad or fruit salad. Servings: 1 cup. Preparation Time: 5 minutes.

Nancy Thomas

BREADS AND

BRUNCHES

WAFFLE

FRENCH BREAD

Apples

FRUIT

SPONSORED BY

Sara Lee Meat Group

Mama Jones' Rolls

The ones everyone asks about.

1 cup shortening	2 eggs
1 cup boiling water	1 1/2 teaspoons salt
3/4 cup sugar	6 cups flour
1 cup lukewarm water (more warm than cool)	1 stick butter, melted
2 packages yeast	Flour for rolling out rolls

Melt shortening in boiling water over medium heat. Add sugar, stir and let cool. Transfer to large mixing bowl. Using large measuring cup, dissolve yeast in lukewarm water. Add to shortening mixture. Add eggs, salt and flour. Stir. Refrigerate overnight (or up to 3 days). Roll out using very little flour. Use a glass to cut into circles. Dip each roll in butter and fold and pinch closed with finger tip to make pocketbook shape. Place rolls on baking sheet and let rise for 3 to 4 hours. Bake at 400° to 425° for 8 to 10 minutes. Can be frozen before rising. Servings: 60. Preheat: 400° to 425°.

Kelly Wells

Quick Rolls

Quick to prepare. Great for breakfast or dinner. Easy to halve recipe.

2 cups self-rising flour	1 cup milk
1/4 cup mayonnaise	1 teaspoon sugar (optional)

Mix well, but not too much. Spoon into greased muffin pan. Servings: 12. Pan Size: 12 cup muffin pan. Preheat: 450°. Cooking Time: 10 minutes.

Sara Cunningham

Popovers

1 cup flour, sifted
3/4 teaspoon salt
1 cup milk, cool
1 tablespoon oil or clarified
    butter

2 to 3 eggs, room
    temperature, not mixed

Preheat oven to 415°. Mix flour and salt together. Add milk and oil together. Add to flour mixture, stir until well combined. Add eggs, one at a time, and mix well after each addition. Beat mixture for 2 minutes more. Warm popover pans. Season with vegetable shortening. Portion batter 3/4 full into each cup. Bake for 30 to 40 minutes or until deep golden brown and sides are very crisp. After baking, remove from oven, slit with knife, to let steam out and crisp popovers inside. Dust with powdered sugar. Serve hot with butter and jam. Servings: 7 to 8. Preheat: 415°. Cooking Time: 30 to 40 minutes.

Folks in the Kitchen wine recommendation: Iron Horse Brut.

Paulette's Restaurant
Memphis, TN

Granny's Homemade Biscuits

1/2 cup shortening
2 cups self-rising flour

3/4 cup milk

Using a pastry knife, blend shortening and flour until texture is coarse and crumbly. Add milk and stir until mixed. Pat out dough on a floured surface and cut with a round biscuit cutter. Bake at 300° for 12 minutes. Servings: 4. Pan Size: 8x8-inches. Preheat: Yes. Preparation Time: 20 minutes. Cooking Time: 12 minutes.

Janet Farris Henderson

85

Homemade Biscuits

2 cups self-rising flour   **3/4 cup milk**
1/4 cup cooking oil

Mix all ingredients until blended. With floured hands, pinch off small amounts, about 2-inch ball. Make round ball and pat to flatten about 1/2-inch. Arrange biscuit dough on pan. Bake at 450° until biscuits start to brown, about 20 minutes.

Louise Callahan

Corny Bread

*Good Christmas Eve cornbread traditionally
served with Brunswick Stew.*

2 packages Jiffy cornbread   **2 eggs**
mix   **1 (16 ounce) can cream style**
1 (8 ounce) container sour   **corn**
cream   **Butter**

Mix all ingredients by hand or mixer until well mixed. Pour into greased iron skillet and bake at 350° for 40 minutes or until lightly brown. Cool for 10 minutes. Cut pieces like you would cut a pie. Butter and enjoy. Servings: 12. Pan Size: Iron skillet. Preheat: 350°. Preparation Time: 5 minutes. Cooking Time: 40 minutes.

Mrs. Joseph Morrison

"No-Waist" Cornbread

For a great snack or light meal, crumble hunk of cornbread in tall glass,
cover with milk, salt and pepper to taste, enjoy!

1 1/2 cups cornmeal
1/2 cup all-purpose flour
1 teaspoon baking soda
1 teaspoon baking powder

1 egg, beaten
2 cups nonfat cultured
   buttermilk
Cooking spray

Combine cornmeal, flour, baking soda and baking powder in medium bowl. Stir well. Add egg and buttermilk stirring until smooth. Pour batter into 9-inch square pan coated with cooking spray. Bake at 400° for 35 minutes or until cornbread is golden brown. Servings: 9. Pan Size: 9-inch square. Preheat: 400°. Preparation Time: 5 minutes. Cooking Time: 35 minutes or until golden brown.

Barbara J. Riley

Breads and Brunches

Mama Rosa's Italian Loaves

2 packages active dry yeast
3 cups warm water
3 tablespoons oil
3 eggs

1 teaspoon salt
1¼ cups sugar
10 to 11 cups flour

Dissolve yeast in warm water (105° to 115°). After yeast is dissolved, add oil, eggs, salt and sugar. In a large bowl, put the flour in, using 10 cups. Add yeast mixture to flour and stir until all flour is mixed in. Turn the dough out onto a lightly floured surface and knead until dough is smooth and elastic, about 10 minutes, adding more flour if needed. Place in a greased bowl, turning once to grease top. Cover with cloth and let rise in a warm, draft-free spot until double in size, about 1½ to 2 hours. After first rising, punch down and turn over; let rise again until almost double, 30 to 45 minutes. Punch down again and cut into 6 portions, about the size of grapefruit. Let rest, covered for 10 minutes. Flatten dough, pressing out all air. Form into long, thin loaves. Place on greased baking sheets. Cover and let rise 50 to 60 minutes. Bake at 350° for 30 to 35 minutes or until lightly browned. Cool on wire rack. Servings: 6 loaves, 24 servings. Pan Size: Largest cookie sheets. Preheat: 350°. Preparation Time: About 5 hours. Cooking Time: 30 to 35 minutes.

Roz Grage

Whole "Wheat Germ" Jalapeño Cheese Bread

1 cup shortening	2 packages yeast, dissolved
3/4 cup sugar	in 1 cup lukewarm water
1 1/2 teaspoons salt	6 cups whole wheat flour
3/4 cup Kretschmer honey	1 cup sliced jalapeño
wheat germ	peppers
1 cup boiling water	1 cup sliced Cheddar
2 eggs, well beaten	cheese

Cream shortening, sugar and salt. Add boiling water; stir until dissolved. Set aside until lukewarm. When lukewarm, add beaten eggs and yeast. Sift flour and add wheat germ. Gradually, add flour mixture to liquid mixture. Put in warm area to proof. After first rising, turn onto floured board and knead. Divide dough into half. Roll out into rectangle, dough should be about 3/4-inch thick. Spread half of jalapeño peppers on dough and sprinkle half of cheese on top of peppers. Carefully roll dough jelly roll fashion. Seal edges and put into greased loaf pan. Let rise again until doubled in size. Servings: 2 loaves. Bake for 45 minutes at 400°. Pan Size: Greased loaf pan. Preheat: 400°. Cooking Time: 45 minutes.

Charlotte Wolfe

Breads and Brunches

Cheese Braid

2 packages yeast	**4 tablespoons lukewarm water**
6 tablespoons sugar	

Mix yeast in water, add sugar and set aside.

CREAM TOGETHER:

1/2 pound butter	**1 cup thick sour cream**
3 whole eggs	

ADD:
5 cups sifted flour

Add melted yeast mixture. Mix well and let stand in refrigerator overnight. Take out of refrigerator 1 hour before ready to use. Divide into 4 parts. This recipe makes 4 braids. Roll into rectangle 9x12-inches. Place on greased baking sheet. Mix together the following filling and spoon down the center.

CHEESE FILLING FOR EACH ROLL:

1 large (8 ounce) package	**2 1/2 tablespoons sugar**
cream cheese	**1 teaspoon vanilla**
1 egg yolk	

Beat well in mixer. With scissors, cut dough along either side of filling into inch wide strips; fold from side to side at an angle, across filling. Cover. Let rise in warm place free from draft, until doubled in bulk, about 1 hour. Bake at 350° for 25 minutes. While still warm, frost with the following icing.

ICING RECIPE FOR 2 BRAIDS:

2/3 cup powdered sugar	**2 tablespoons orange juice**
1 tablespoon lemon juice	

Drizzle over top. Freezes well.

Aileen T. Burson

90

Alice's Holiday Challa

A recipe that has been in our family for generations.

3 cups warm water (105° to
  115°)
5 large eggs, room
  temperature
1/2 cup oil
11/2 to 2 cups sugar (2 cups
  for a sweeter bread)
1 tablespoon plus 1
  teaspoon salt

3 packages quick rise yeast
14 cups all-purpose flour
1/4 teaspoon saffron
  (optional)
1 to 2 eggs, beaten
Poppy seeds (optional)

In a large bowl, combine first six ingredients in the order listed, liquid first, dry ingredients last. Add flour and work in until well combined. Knead into rounded shape. Cover with towel. Keep in a warm place to rise for one hour or until double in bulk. Punch down and let rise again for one hour. Divide dough into three parts. Braid into three strips after rolling each part by hand. Fold ends under. Let rise uncovered for about one hour, then brush top thoroughly with beaten eggs. Sprinkle with poppy seeds if desired. Bake in a preheated 375° oven for 35 to 45 minutes until lightly browned. Servings: 4 loaves. Pan Size: Cookie sheet. Preheat: 375°. Preparation Time: 4 hours. Cooking Time: 35 to 45 minutes.

Alice Wexler

Breads and Brunches

Banana Nut Bread

1/4 pound buter or margarine
1 cup sugar
2 eggs

1/2 cup chopped nuts
2 cups self-rising flour
3 large ripe bananas

Let bananas get almost black in ripeness. Whip bananas until light, 3 to 5 minutes. Cream butter and sugar together; add eggs one at a time. Mix flour into this mixture; batter will be stiff. Add bananas and nuts. Bake in greased pan at 350° for 60 to 75 minutes until toothpick comes out clean. Pan Size: 2 pound loaf pan. Preheat: 350°. Preparation Time: 20 to 30 minutes. Cooking Time: 60 to 75 minutes.

Charlotte Griffin

Sidney's Banana Nut Bread

1 1/4 cups plain flour
1 teaspoon baking powder
1/4 teaspoon salt
1 cup sugar
1/2 cup vegetable oil
2 large eggs

3 (ripe) mashed bananas
1 cup finely chopped nuts
  (pecans or walnuts)
1/2 cup raisins (optional)
1/2 teaspoon cinnamon
  (optional)

Sift together: flour, baking powder, salt and sugar. Work in vegetable oil. Add and mix well by hand: eggs, bananas, nuts, raisins (optional) and cinnamon (optional). Pour into well-greased and floured loaf pans. Bake at 350° for 30 to 40 minutes. Pan Size: 1 large or 2 small loaf pans. Preheat: 350°. Cooking Time: 30 to 40 minutes.

Sidney Connell

92

The Best Banana Bread

This recipe was given to me 26 years ago while visiting a friend in Buffalo, New York. She said it was the best banana bread ever made and she was right.

1½ cups sugar
2 eggs
½ cup vegetable oil

½ cup milk
1 teaspoon vanilla

SIFT:
2 cups flour
1 teaspoon baking soda

2 teaspoons baking powder

½ cup chopped pecans

3 ripe bananas, mashed

In large bowl, mix all the ingredients in order listed. One of the most important directions to follow is the pan size; always make 6 muffins and then pour remaining batter in a loaf pan. It will always turn out perfect if you do this. Servings: 15 slices and 6 muffins. Pan Size: 1 loaf pan and 6 muffins. Preheat: 350°. Preparation Time: 10 to 15 minutes. Cooking Time: Leave muffins in oven 25 to 30 minutes and the loaf pan in oven one hour.

Linda and Rick Quinn

Cranberry Orange Nut Bread

³/₄ cup sugar	3 cups Bisquick
1 egg	³/₄ cup chopped nuts
1¹/₄ cups orange juice	1 cup fresh cranberries,
1 tablespoon grated orange rind	chopped medium

Preheat oven to 350°. Mix sugar, egg, orange juice, rind and Bisquick. Beat vigorously 30 seconds. Batter may still be lumpy. Stir in nuts and cranberries. Pour into well-greased loaf pan, 9x5x3-inches or larger. Bake 55 to 60 minutes or until toothpick stuck into center comes out clean. Crack in top is typical. Remove from baking pan. Cool before slicing. Pan Size: 2 pound loaf pan. Preheat: 15 minutes at 350°. Preparation Time: 20 minutes. Cooking Time: 1 hour to 1 hour 15 minutes.

Gail Sepich

Banana Strawberry Nut Bread
*Classic banana nut bread with added strawberries
makes this bread a special treat!*

1 stick butter, softened	¹/₂ cup chopped pecans
1 cup sugar	3 ripe bananas, well mashed
2 eggs, well beaten	1 (10 ounce) box sliced
1 teaspoon baking soda	strawberries, thawed and
2¹/₄ cups sifted flour	drained

In a large bowl, cream butter and sugar. Add eggs. In a separate small bowl, combine baking soda and flour. Gradually add flour mixture to butter mixture. Toss chopped pecans in a little flour. Add mashed bananas, drained strawberries and pecans to butter mixture. Mix together until just combined. Pour into a greased and floured pan. Bake at 350° for 50 minutes. Pan Size: 9x5-inches. Preheat: 350°. Preparation Time: 25 minutes. Cooking Time: 50 minutes.

Sandy Nichols

Strawberry Nut Bread
Great for Christmas gifts!

3 cups all-purpose flour
1 teaspoon salt
1 teaspoon soda
3 teaspoons cinnamon
2 cups sugar
3 eggs, well beaten

2 (10 ounce) packages
   frozen strawberries,
   thawed
1¼ cups oil
1¼ cups chopped pecans

Sift dry ingredients in large bowl making a well in center of mixture. Mix remaining ingredients and pour into well. Stir enough to dampen all ingredients. Pour into greased loaf pan. Bake at 350° for 1 hour 15 minutes. Pan Size: 2 loaves or 6 mini-loaves. Preheat: 350°. Preparation Time: 15 minutes. Cooking Time: 1 hour 15 minutes.

Lynda McReynolds

Sausage-Cheese Muffins
Simple and great.

1 pound pork sausage, mild
   or hot
¼ cup minced onion

1 (11 ounce) can Cheddar cheese
   soup mixed with ½ cup water
3 cups Bisquick

Brown sausage with onion, cook through but do not get too brown. Drain thoroughly on paper towels. Mix sausage with soup and water. Stir in Bisquick until just moistened. Spray mini-muffin pans well with cooking spray. Fill muffin tins to top, mounding slightly as they only rise a little. My "modern" adaptation: use Chorizo sausage and nacho cheese soup. Servings: 3 dozen. Pan Size: mini-muffin pans. Preheat: 400°. Preparation Time: 15 minutes. Cooking Time: 12 to 15 minutes.

Nancy Thomas

Pizza Bread

1½ teaspoons oregano	1 tablespoon butter or margarine
1½ teaspoons chili powder	2 teaspoons salt
1 teaspoon garlic powder	3 tablespoons sugar
2 tablespoons parsley flakes	5 cups flour
1 teaspoon fennel seed	1¾ cups warm water
(optional)	3 cups Cheddar cheese, grated
3 teaspoons yeast	4 ounces pepperoni

Blend first nine ingredients together with 1¾ cups flour. Blend with a mixer until it resembles coarse meal. Slowly add water until all water is used. Remove mixer; add remaining flour. Knead until all flour is used. Should be a little tacky. Place into a greased bowl to rise until doubled in size. Remove from bowl; knead a second time. Cut into 2 pieces. Roll the bread about ¼-inch thick in a rectangular shape. Spread 1½ cups of cheese onto the bread and press into the dough. Layer 2 ounces of sliced pepperoni in 2 rows about 4-inches apart. Roll the dough into a loaf and pinch the seams well. Brush with water to get excess flour off bread. Let rise for 20 minutes. Bake at 400° until golden brown, about 20 minutes. Makes two loaves. Servings: 30. Pan Size: Cookie sheet. Preheat: 400°. Preparation Time: 20 minutes. Cooking Time: 20 minutes.

Steve Weisenhorn

Mrs. "T's" Strawberry Preserves
"My mother always made them when the local berries came in and gave them to her friends, minister and doctors."

2 quarts strawberries, hulled	**6 cups sugar**
Boiling water	

Cover strawberries with boiling water and let stand for 5 minutes. Drain well. Add 2 cups of the sugar, bring to a boil over medium high heat and boil for 5 minutes. Add remaining 4 cups sugar, bring back to a boil and continue to cook for 15 minutes, skimming the top frequently. Pour into a shallow pan, cover and let sit overnight. In the morning pack in sterilized jars. To retain color, store in freezer. Be sure to use local berries that are not water soaked.

Jessie (Jet) Thomas Leyman

Granny's Concord Grape Jelly
*Wonderful for the breakfast table and for
peanut butter and jelly sandwiches.*

**1 cup juice (see Concord   1 cup sugar
    Grape Juice below)**

Bring the juice to a boil, then add the sugar. Continue a rolling boil for approximately 5 to 10 minutes, constantly dipping a spoon in to test for readiness. The jelly is ready when the spoon is raised and the liquid from the edges of the spoon runs together and hangs from it. Pour into hot sterilized 1/2 pint jars and seal. Servings: 2 half-pint jars. Pan Size: Medium saucepan. Preparation and Cooking Time: 15 minutes total.

CONCORD GRAPE JUICE: 1 gallon Concord grapes

In a large heave stockpot, pour just enough water over the grapes to cover them. Simmer until they burst, stirring a little to prevent sticking. Remove from heat and strain into a large bowl. (For a clear jelly, do not mash.) This may be stored in the refrigerator in a half gallon glass container and will keep several months.

NOTE: Be careful not to overcook, because the jelly will become stretchy. Also, do not double the recipe, the result is better when using the above measurements.

Nancy Worley

Breads and Brunches

Becky's Pancakes

For 28 years of marriage, this is Sunday breakfast at our house.

12 ounces of buttermilk   **2 tablespoons cooking oil**
1 egg   **1 overripe banana (optional)**
1 cup flour   **or 1/2 cup blueberries**
1 tablespoon sugar

Put all ingredients in a blender and mix. Pour on greased hot griddle in 2 1/2-inch diameter circles. When bubbles pop, flip and cook about 30 seconds on second side. Serves 4 people, 7 to 8 pancakes each. Makes a thin, light pancake. Servings: 4. Preheat: 15 minutes on medium high. Preparation Time: 5 minutes. Cooking Time: 15 minutes.

Becky Wilson

Pancakes

Quick, tasty, and better for you.

1 1/2 cups all-purpose flour   **1 1/4 teaspoons baking soda**
1/4 cup quick oatmeal   **1 tablespoon corn oil**
1 tablespoon brown sugar   **1 whole egg**
1/2 teaspoon salt   **1 1/2 cups 2% milk**

Lightly mix flour, oatmeal, sugar and salt with baking soda. Add corn oil, whole egg and fold in milk until egg breaks. Stir lightly. Let set a minute or more while you heat griddle. Makes 8 5-inch pancakes. Turn pancakes on hot griddle when you see bubbles come through mix. Servings: 8 pancakes. Preheat: Griddle until water drop sizzles. Preparation Time: 3 minutes. Cooking Time: 4 minutes.

J. D. Kinney

98

Sour Cream Pancakes

1 cup milk (2% may be used)	1 tablespoon sugar
1 egg	1/4 teaspoon salt
1/4 cup sour cream (low fat may be used)	2 tablespoons butter or margarine, melted
1 cup all-purpose flour	1/2 cup fresh blueberries
1 tablespoon baking powder	(optional)

Combine milk, egg, sour cream; beat well. Stir together flour, baking powder, sugar and salt. Add to milk mixture. Beat just until large lumps disappear. Stir in butter. Fold in blueberries, if desired. For each pancake, use about 1/4 cup batter. Servings: 12 (4-inch) pancakes. Pan Size: Griddle/skillet.

Cecile Skaggs

Potato Pancakes

I grew up on these pancakes, but my Italian mother was never good at sharing her recipes (or at least correct recipes). It wasn't until I married a WASP that she shared it with my husband.

2 large potatoes, grated	1/4 teaspoon baking powder
2 tablespoons flour	1 small onion, grated
1/4 teaspoon salt	1 egg

Squeeze water out of potatoes after grating. Combine all ingredients and mix well. Drop by tablespoon onto greased frying pan. Brown on both sides. Can be served with apple butter, sour cream or cottage cheese and butter for brunch. As a side dish, serve plain or with butter. Servings: 2 for brunch; 4 for side dish.

Gloria Qualls

99

Breads and Brunches

Bread Pudding Brunch Casserole

Everyone loves it! Easy to serve for a bunch at brunch!

1 loaf sourdough or French bread, cubed
8 ounces cream cheese, softened
2 cups whipping cream

1 dozen large to extra large eggs
1/2 cup maple syrup
1/2 teaspoon vanilla

Grease casserole well. Place cubed bread in casserole. Mix remaining ingredients together and pour over bread, cover and refrigerate overnight. Remove 1 hour before cooking. Bake at 375° for 50 minutes (cover with foil after 25 minutes). Serve with syrup and mixed fruit or berries. Servings: 6 to 12. Pan Size: 9x13-inch (3 quart). Preheat: 375°. Preparation Time: 15 minutes. Cooking Time: 50 minutes.

Ann Clark Harris

Orange Upside Down Toast

Great for fancy breakfast or brunch.

1/4 cup butter, melted
1/3 cup sugar
1/4 teaspoon cinnamon
1 teaspoon orange zest

4 large eggs, slightly beaten
2/3 cup fresh orange juice
8 slices of bread

Melt butter in jelly roll pan. Combine sugar, cinnamon and orange zest. Sprinkle on top of melted butter. Mix eggs and orange juice, soak bread. Arrange on top of butter. Bake at 325° for 20 minutes or until done. Servings: 4 to 8. Pan Size: Jelly roll. Preheat: 325°. Preparation Time: 15 minutes. Cooking Time: 20 to 30 minutes.

Ann Clark Harris

The Best Ever Brunch Dish

6 eggs	8 ounces cottage cheese
1 teaspoon salt	1 1/2 pounds Muenster
2 teaspoons sugar	cheese, grated
1 cup milk	2/3 cup butter, softened
3 ounces cream cheese,	1 teaspoon baking powder
softened	1/2 cup flour

In a small bowl mix together eggs, salt, sugar and milk. In a separate bowl, cream remaining ingredients. Add egg mixture to creamed mixture. Pour into 9-inch quiche dish or a 9-inch square Pyrex dish. Bake for 1 hour at 350°. Serve with fresh fruit and muffins. Pan Size: 9-inches. Preheat: 350°. Cooking Time: 1 hour.

Loren and Kim Roberts

Cheese Pouf
"Mock cheese soufflé."

8 slices white bread	3 eggs
1 (8 ounce) package American	1 teaspoon salt
cheese	1/2 teaspoon pepper
4 slices processed Swiss	3/4 teaspoon dry mustard
cheese	2 cups milk
1/4 cup melted butter or	
margarine	

Trim and cut bread into 1 inch cubes. Cut cheeses into bite-size squares. In greased shallow casserole dish, alternate layers of bread and cheeses. Pour melted butter on top. Beat eggs, stir in salt, pepper, mustard and milk, pour over bread. Bake covered at 350° for 30 minutes, then uncovered for an additional 30 minutes. Let cool before cutting. Servings: 4 to 6. Pan Size: Soufflé pan. Preheat: 350°. Preparation Time: 20 minutes. Cooking Time: 1 hour.

Gail Sepich

Broccoli-Cheese Strudel

Great for brunch, light lunch or appetizer.

1 stick butter or margarine	4 ounces Swiss cheese, shredded
1/4 cup all-purpose flour	1 (10 ounce) package frozen
1/2 teaspoon salt	chopped broccoli, thawed
1/8 teaspoon cayenne pepper	6 sheets phyllo pastry
1 1/4 cups milk	1/4 cup dried bread crumbs

Melt 4 tablespoons butter in a 2 quart saucepan and stir in flour, salt and cayenne pepper. Gradually add milk and cook stirring until thickened and smooth. Stir in cheese and broccoli. When cheese melts, remove from heat and set aside. Melt remaining butter. Unfold phyllo pastry. Cover with waxed paper and overlay with a damp cloth to prevent drying. Working quickly, brush one sheet with some of the melted butter and sprinkle with bread crumbs. Place another sheet on top of the first, then brush with butter and sprinkle with bread crumbs. Repeat until all six sheets are used. Spoon broccoli mixture down long side of phyllo pastry. Roll jelly roll fashion. Place seam side down on greased cookie sheet. Bake at 375° for 30 minutes or until golden brown. Can be baked in advance and reheated at 350°. Servings: 10.

Sharon S. Kelso

Spinach and Crab Quiche

3 eggs, beaten	1 can lump crabmeat
2 tablespoons flour	8 to 10 ounces grated Swiss
1/2 cup mayonnaise	cheese
1 (10 ounce) box frozen	1/2 onion, chopped and
spinach, cooked and	sautéed in butter
drained	1 tablespoon dijon mustard
	1 unbaked pie shell

Mix eggs, flour, mayonnaise, spinach, crab meat and cheese; set aside. Spread mustard on bottom of pie shell and bake at 350° for 3 to 5 minutes. Place cooked onions on bottom of shell and fill shell with egg mixture. Cook at 350° for 1 hour or until done. Servings: 6.

Miriam Smith

Squash Quiche

2 cups chopped, fresh
   squash
1 small onion, chopped
1/4 cup Bisquick mix
2 eggs, beaten

1/4 cup oil
1/4 heaping cup grated Cheddar
   cheese
5 to 6 slices bacon, crumbled
Salt and pepper, to taste

Combine all ingredients and pour into a greased pie plate. Bake 30 minutes at 350°. Servings: 4 to 6. Pan Size: 9-inch pie plate. Preparation Time: 10 to 15 minutes. Cooking Time: 30 minutes.

Pat Thomas

Sausage-Apple Quiche

1 pound Jimmy Dean
   sausage (your favorite
   flavor) cooked, crumbled
   and drained, divided into
   equal portions
2 (9-inch) pie crusts
3 medium apples, peeled,
   cored, sliced and divided
   into equal portions

2 eggs
3/4 cup heavy cream
1/4 cup brown sugar
1 teaspoon ground nutmeg
1 teaspoon ground cinnamon

Bake crusts for 5 minutes at 400°. Layer sausage and apples into two crusts. Mix remaining ingredients; pour over sausage and apples. Sprinkle lightly with additional brown sugar, nutmeg and cinnamon if desired. Bake for 1 hour at 375°. Let stand 10 minutes before cutting to serve. Servings: 6 to 8.

George Bryan

Breads and Brunches

The Jimmy Dean Country Breakfast Casserole

1 pound Jimmy Dean
   sausage, cooked,
   crumbled and drained
10 eggs, lightly beaten
3 cups light cream
   (half-and-half)
1 teaspoon salt
1 bunch green onions,
   chopped

1 teaspoon dry mustard
16 ounces day-old bread,
   cubed
1 cup Cheddar cheese,
   shredded
1 cup Swiss cheese,
   shredded

Grease pan well. Place bread in pan. Sprinkle with cheeses. Combine rest of ingredients together and mix well. Pour over bread. Refrigerate overnight. Bake for 1 hour at 350° or until golden brown. Servings: 6 to 8. Pan Size: 9x13-inches. Preheat: 350°.

George Bryan

Peppered Bacon

Thick cut bacon with rind
Cornmeal

Black pepper, to taste

Preheat oven to 400°. Dredge bacon in cornmeal and black pepper. Put in black skillet and bake for 20 minutes or until crisp. Drain on paper towels. Great for brunch or served with turnip greens or pinto beans.

Jean "Granny" Gray

Ham Delights

1/2 pound butter, melted	3 packages small party rolls
3 tablespoons prepared	(20 to package)
mustard	1 pound shredded boiled ham
3 tablespoons poppy seeds	1/2 pound shredded Swiss
1 small chopped onion	cheese
1 teaspoon Worcestershire	
sauce	

Combine first 5 ingredients to make a sauce. Split rolls in half, not separating them individually. Spread sauce over top half of rolls. Layer ham and cheese on bottom half of rolls. Cover ham and cheese with top half of rolls. Bake at 350° for ten to fifteen minutes or until cheese melts. Ham Delights may be frozen and thawed when ready to use. Servings: 60. Pan Size: Baking sheet. Preheat: 350°. Preparation Time: 30 minutes. Cooking Time: 15 minutes.

Toni Campbell Parker

Quick Country Ham and Red Eye Gravy

A consistent, easy way to cook sliced country ham with gravy.

1 cup Coca-cola	1 to 4 slices country ham
1 teaspoon instant coffee	

Pour cola and instant coffee into a skillet large enough to hold ham in a single layer. If available, use a non-stick, covered skillet. Do not trim fat from ham slices. Lay slices in skillet. Simmer, covered, for 30 minutes. Remove ham. Reduce liquid over high heat until desired consistency. Serve with grits!

Eph Wilkinson

Oysters Campbell

Italian bread crumbs
2 lemons, juiced
1 cup Parmesan cheese
Salt, to taste
1 tablespoon crushed red
  pepper
3/4 cup olive oil

3 tablespoons chopped dried
  parsley
1½ tablespoons minced
  garlic
1 quart oysters, shucked and
  rinsed

Mix first eight ingredients together. Lay oysters in single layer in baking dish. Layer dressing on top. Bake at 350° until heated through or done. Servings: 8. Pan Size: Rectangular baking dish. Preheat: 350°. Preparation Time: 30 minutes. Cooking Time: 20 minutes.

Toni Campbell Parker

Chicken Soufflé

Not as heavy as most! Serve with fresh fruit and rolls.

2 cups cooked chicken,
  finely chopped
4 egg whites
1/2 cup flour
1 pint milk, heated

4 tablespoons butter, melted
1/2 cup chopped mushrooms
1 tablespoon parsley,
  chopped
1/2 cup chopped celery

Combine flour, milk and butter. Beat egg whites until soft peaks form; fold into flour mixture. Add remaining ingredients. Pour into a soufflé dish and bake at 325° for 30 to 40 minutes.

Kathy Shannon

Fresh Apple Cake

2 cups sugar	2 teaspoons cinnamon
1¹/2 cups cooking oil	1 teaspoon nutmeg
2 teaspoons vanilla	2 teaspoons Worcestershire
2 eggs, beaten	sauce
1 teaspoon salt	3 cups chopped apples
3 cups flour	1 cup chopped, toasted
1¹/2 teaspoons soda	pecans

Combine sugar, oil, vanilla, eggs and salt. Beat well. In a separate bowl mix flour, soda, cinnamon and nutmeg. Add this to first mixture. Beat well, add Worcestershire sauce, apples, pecans. Mix well. Bake 1 hour 15 minutes at 325° in a bundt pan. Preheat: 350°. Preparation Time: 20 minutes. Cooking Time: 1 hour 15 minutes.

Dottie Weir

Cinnamon Coffee Cake

1³/4 cups sugar	3 cups sifted flour
³/4 cup butter	2 teaspoons salt
1¹/8 cups milk	4 egg whites, stiffly beaten

TOPPING:

2 cups chopped toasted	2 tablespoons cinnamon
pecans	³/4 cup flour
1¹/8 cups brown sugar	³/4 cup butter

Cream sugar and butter until smooth. Add milk alternating with the sifted dry ingredients. Fold in stiffly beaten egg whites. Pour into buttered baking dish. Cover with topping.

TOPPING: Mix together until crumbly and scatter over top. Bake at 350° for 40 to 50 minutes. Servings: 15 to 20. Pan Size: 9x13-inches. Preheat: 350°. Preparation Time: 20 minutes. Cooking Time: 40 to 50 minutes.

Dottie Weir

Poppy Seed Cake

A wonderful, moist, light cake, perfect for brunch or a light dessert.

¾ **cup vegetable oil**	**4 eggs**
½ **cup sugar**	**3 tablespoons poppy seeds**
8 ounces sour cream	**1 yellow cake mix**

Mix all ingredients except cake mix. Add cake mix. Do not overbeat. Spray pan with cooking spray. Coat well with sugar. Pour mixture in pan. Pan Size: Bundt pan. Preheat: 350°. Preparation Time: 10 minutes. Cooking Time: 40 to 45 minutes, do not overbake. Start watching and checking after 38 minutes.

Ann Floyd

Beano's Bloody's

2 (46 ounce) cans tomato juice	**4 tablespoons Old Bay seasoning**
6 ounces lemon juice	**3 teaspoons minced garlic**
12 ounces clam juice	**3 teaspoons coarse black pepper**
1 tablespoon Worcestershire	**2 teaspoons sesame oil**
1½ tablespoons hot sauce	**½ teaspoon cumin**
8 tablespoons horseradish	

In large container, mix all ingredients together and enjoy!

Christopher Folk

108

Mint Julep

Every self-respecting Southerner should know how to make a mint julep.

SIMPLE SYRUP:

1 cup sugar	**1 cup water**

5 or 6 sprigs of fresh mint	**1 ounce simple syrup**
1 large cup shaved ice	**Sour mash bourbon**

To make simple syrup, heat sugar and water. Bring just to a boil. Refrigerate to cool before serving. To make a mint julep, pour one ounce of simple syrup into a small (8 ounce) tumbler. Put 3 or 4 sprigs of mint into the glass. Using the back of a spoon, crush against the side of the glass to release the mint flavor. Remove crushed mint sprigs and discard. Do not remove syrup. Pack tumbler full of shaved ice. Pour bourbon into glass until full. Some of the ice will melt as you do this. Stir well. Garnish with one or two mint sprigs. Servings: 1.

Robert Qualls

Hot Buttered Rum

This is a wonderful drink for those cold Tennessee nights!

1 (16 ounce) box brown sugar	**1/2 teaspoon nutmeg**
1/2 cup butter	**1/2 teaspoon cloves**
1/2 teaspoon cinnamon	**Dash of salt**
	Rum

Combine all ingredients, except rum and refrigerate. To make individual serving, use 1 tablespoon of this mixture, 1 jigger of rum and boiling water. May be garnished with a lemon slice and a cinnamon stick.

Charlotte Wolfe

Bishop's Punch

*Great punch for a large crowd. It's easy and inexpensive
and can be done ahead!*

6 packages lemonade
   Kool-Aid, unsweetened
2½ cups sugar
2 quarts of hot tap water
2 (46 ounce) cans pineapple
   juice

3 large cans (frozen)
   lemonade, undiluted
3 (2 liter bottles) of lemon-lime
   soda

Dissolve Kool-Aid, sugar and water. Stir completely. Add pineapple juice
and lemonade. Freeze this mixture in pineapple juice cans or plastic
containers. Remove from freezer 1½ to 2 hours before serving and let it
begin to thaw. Pour in punch bowl, then pour lemon-lime soda over
slush. May use white wine champagne, vodka, or rum in place of soda.

Anne Ogden Plyler

110

MEAT AND GAME!

SPONSORED BY

Danny & Brenda Harris

Meat and Game

Beef Bourguignon

2 to 2½ pounds sirloin
8 slices bacon, cooked and
    crumbled, reserve
    drippings
Salt and pepper, to taste
1 can beef broth
1½ cups water
½ cup dry red wine

¼ teaspoon minced garlic
2 cups pearl onions
4 to 5 medium carrots,
    sliced thin
½ pound fresh mushrooms,
    sliced
¼ cup water
2 tablespoons flour

Trim sirloin and cut into 1½ inch cubes. In a large heavy pan, brown meat in reserved bacon drippings. Pour off fat. Sprinkle meat with salt and pepper. Add crumbled bacon, broth, water, wine and garlic. Cover and simmer over low heat for one hour, stirring occasionally. Add onions, carrots and mushrooms. Cover and simmer for an additional 30 minutes or until vegetables are tender. To thicken, gradually blend ¼ cup water into flour. Slowly stir flour mixture into pan. Cook, stirring until thickened. Servings: 4. Preparation Time: ½ hour. Cooking Time: 1½ hours.

Carole Ferrell

Braised Beef Tips over Rice

2 pounds stew meat, cut into
    1-inch cubes
2 tablespoons vegetable oil
1 can condensed beef
    consomme
⅓ cup red burgundy

2 tablespoons soy sauce
1 clove garlic, minced
¼ teaspoon onion salt
2 tablespoons cornstarch
¼ cup water
3 cups hot cooked rice, unsalted

In large skillet, brown meat on all sides in oil. Stir in consomme, wine, soy sauce, garlic and onion salt. Heat to boiling. Reduce heat; cover and simmer 1 hour or until meat is tender. Blend cornstarch and water; stir gradually into meat mixture. Cook, stirring constantly, until mixture thickens and boils. Cook and stir 1 minute. Serve over rice. Servings: 6. Cooking Time: 1 hour.

Margaret McNeil

Baked Beef Stew

2 pounds beef stew meat,
   cubed
1 cup celery, sliced
1 cup carrots, sliced
1 cup onion, sliced
1/2 green pepper, diced

28 ounce can tomatoes
3 tablespoons tapioca
1 tablespoon sugar
1 tablespoon salt
3 tablespoons sherry

Combine all ingredients in a Dutch oven or heavy ovenproof saucepan with tight fitting lid. Cover and bake in a 300° oven for 5 hours. Stir once. If dry, add water. Servings: 6. Cooking Time: 5 hours.

Blythe Patton Orr/Caroline Orr

Pepper Ragout

2 pounds beef or veal
1 tablespoon flour
2 tablespoons bacon grease
1 onion, diced
1 cup sliced mushrooms
2 tablespoons soy sauce
2 tablespoons sherry or
   marsala

1 cup beef broth
2 large tomatoes, chopped
6 green peppers, cut into
   strips
1/4 teaspoon ground ginger
2 bay leaves
1/2 teaspoon sugar
Salt and pepper, to taste

Cut meat in strips or cubes. Dust with flour and brown in bacon grease. Remove meat and add onions and mushrooms. Sauté for several minutes. Add remaining flour, soy sauce, sherry, and beef broth. Return meat to pan along with remaining ingredients. Simmer until tender.

Helen Hardin

113

Meat and Game

Anne's Meatloaf with Horseradish

I devised this years ago when oat bran was so "hot" and it does make the meatloaf light. The horseradish gives it a great flavor! Even people who don't like meatloaf like this one.

2 pounds ground chuck
1 onion, chopped
1 green pepper, chopped
2 stalks celery, chopped
2 cloves garlic, minced and
    sautéed
1 teaspoon plus salt (about 1
    teaspoon salt per pound
    ground beef)

1 tablespoon horseradish,
    powdered (generous
    measure)
3 eggs
1 cup oat bran
1/3 cup ketchup
1/4 to 1/2 teaspoon pepper
Bacon and extra ketchup

Brown beef and drain off drippings. Mix with rest of ingredients. You can sauté the vegetables if you like them softer or mix them in raw. Press into a shallow Pyrex baking dish, coat with a thin layer of ketchup and cover with bacon strips. Bake 1/2 hour covered and 1/2 hour uncovered. Servings: 8. Preheat: 375°. Cooking Time: 1 hour.

Anne Piper

114

Sweet and Sour Meatloaf

The most unlikely individuals will become meatloaf lovers overnight.

2 pounds ground beef
1/2 teaspoon dry mustard
2 teaspoons Worcestershire
1 egg

1 (8 ounce) can tomato sauce
1/4 teaspoon pepper
2 teaspoons salt
1/2 cup onion, chopped
3/4 cup bread crumbs

SAUCE:
3 tablespoons
   Worcestershire
1 tablespoon dry mustard

1/2 cup water
5 tablespoons brown sugar
4 tablespoons wine vinegar

Mix first nine ingredients with hands. Shape into square or rectangular loaf approximately 2 inches deep. Punch holes in loaf with fork. Mix sauce ingredients. Pour over loaf. Bake at 350° for one hour, basting throughout cooking time. Servings: 8 medium. Preheat: 350°. Preparation Time: 20 minutes. Cooking Time: 1 hour.

Mary Ruth Witt

Taco Surprise

1 pound ground chuck	2 bags small corn chips
1 pound pasteurized process cheese	Grated Cheddar cheese
1 pound stick chili	Chopped onions
1 pint whipping cream	Diced tomatoes
1 (10 ounce) can tomatoes and green chilies	Chopped lettuce
2 (16 ounce) cans chili hot beans	1 pint sour cream

SAUCE: Brown ground chuck in skillet. Drain and set aside. In Dutch oven, over medium-low heat melt processed cheese, chili, and whipping cream together. Purée tomatoes and green chilies in blender. Add tomato mixture and beans to cheese and chili mixture. Stir well to mix. Add ground chuck. Stir well. Cook over low heat until heated through.

TO SERVE: Line individual serving plates with corn chips. Spoon generous amount of sauce over corn chips. Top each serving with one to two tablespoons of cheese, onion, tomatoes and lettuce. Top with sour cream. Servings: 5. Pan Size: Dutch oven. Preparation Time: 30 minutes. Cooking Time: 15 minutes.

Clara Williams

Bleu Cheese Filet

1 (16 ounce) Prime filet	2 ounces premium bleu cheese
Salt and pepper, to taste	

Lightly salt and pepper filet. Broil for 15 to 20 minutes depending on desired doneness. Remove from grill and cut pocket in side of filet. Stuff bleu cheese in center of filet and return to grill for a few minutes, until cheese melts.

Folk's Folly Prime Steak House

Chutney Roast

3/4 cup unsweetened
   pineapple juice
1/2 cup steak sauce
1/3 cup Worcestershire
   sauce
1/3 cup port wine
1/4 cup lemon juice
2 teaspoons seasoned salt

1 teaspoon pepper
1 teaspoon lemon & pepper
   seasoning salt
1 teaspoon dry mustard
1 (3 to 4 pound) beef tenderloin
2 teaspoons cracked pepper
3 or 4 slices bacon
3/4 cup chutney

For marinade, combine the pineapple juice, steak sauce, Worcestershire sauce, wine, lemon juice, seasoned salt, pepper, lemon & pepper and dry mustard. Place meat in a large plastic bag; set in a baking dish. Pour marinade over meat, close bag. Refrigerate several hours or overnight, turning meat occasionally to distribute marinade. Drain, reserve marinade. Rub beef tenderloin with the cracked pepper. Place meat on rack in shallow roasting pan. Arrange bacon slices over tenderloin. Roast uncovered in a 425° oven for 30 to 45 minutes or until meat thermometer reaches desired temperature. Baste tenderloin twice during roasting with reserved marinade. Spoon chutney evenly over tenderloin. Bake 5 to 10 minutes more. Transfer meat to serving platter. Let stand 15 minutes before slicing. Servings: 12 to 16. Preheat: 425°. Preparation Time: 20 minutes. Cooking Time: 30 to 45 minutes.

Sally R. Halle

Meat and Game

Beef Tenderloin with Longboat Key Sauce

Beef tenderloin	1 cup burgundy or other dry
Salt and pepper	red wine
3/4 teaspoon fine herbs	11/2 cups beef broth
1/2 cup chopped onion	2 tablespoons tomato paste
1/2 cup chopped carrots	2 tablespoons cornstarch
1/2 cup chopped celery	1/4 cup Madeira or other dry
11/2 tablespoons vegetable oil	sweet wine

Place tenderloin in aluminum pan. Sprinkle with salt, pepper, and fine herbs. Sauté onion, carrots, and celery in oil until tender. Add red wine and pour mixture over tenderloin. Refrigerate at least two hours. Remove tenderloin and drain marinade into small sauce pan. Rinse aluminum pan and put tenderloin back in. Tenderloin should then be placed on the grill on low for one hour. Meanwhile, add beef broth and tomato paste to reserved marinade and simmer covered on low for an hour. Add the cornstarch to the Madeira. Stir and add marinade to thicken. Serve over sliced tenderloin. Servings: 6 to 8. Pan Size: 123/8x83/8-inches. Preparation Time: 2 hours. Cooking Time: 1 hour.

Susan M. Graf

The World's Best and Easiest Tenderloin

This was given to me by a caterer friend in Nashville. It's so easy, but never fails to receive raves. I think it's the garlic. Of course, this is made even more perfect if you use a tenderloin from the Folk's Folly Prime Cut Shoppe!

Beef tenderloin, entire	Garlic salt
tenderloin strip	Ground pepper

Preheat oven to 350°. With a sharp knife, peel off silverskin, if butcher has not already done for you. Rub tenderloin all over with garlic salt and fresh ground pepper. Place on a rack in the oven with a meat thermometer in the center. Cook approximately 10 minutes per pound. Carefully watch the meat thermometer and take tenderloin out before the needle reaches desired temperature, as it will keep cooking after you take it out. Preheat: 350°. Preparation Time: 5 minutes. Cooking Time: 30 minutes approximately.

Mary Loveless

118

The Editor's Mushroom and Red Wine Sauce

For beef steaks or rare roast beef for four from the book "The Redneck Guide to Wine Snobbery" by Mr. Victor L. Robilio, Jr.

2 tablespoons olive oil
1/4 cup chopped shallots or
    green onions
1 (4 ounce) can mushroom
    buttons, drained or 16 to
    20 fresh mushrooms,
    halved
8 to 10 Spanish olives, diced
1/4 cup red wine of your
    choice

1 tablespoon Dale's steak
    sauce or soy-based
    substitute
Lemon & pepper seasoning
    salt, to taste
2 to 3 tablespoons butter or
    butter substitute
1 tablespoon cornstarch

In a medium skillet, sauté shallots in olive oil over medium heat. Add mushrooms and olives. Add one-half of the wine, reserving the rest. Bring to a slow boil. Add seasonings and butter. Once a slow boil returns, stir cornstarch into remaining wine to dissolve and stir into skillet. Bring back to a low boil and stir until thickened. Turn off heat and cover skillet. Sauce will stay hot while you barbecue your steaks. Servings: 4. Preparation Time: 15 minutes. Cooking Time: 15 to 20 minutes.

Judge Kay Spalding Robilio

Spicy Steak Sauce

Similar to A-1, but better! Can be used with any grilled meat - steak, pork, chicken or lamb!

2 tablespoons olive oil
1/2 cup chopped onion
4 tablespoons honey
1/2 cup apple cider vinegar
1/2 cup balsamic vinegar
1/2 cup soy sauce
1/2 cup Ruby Red grapefruit
   juice
1/2 cup beef broth

1/2 cup Worcestershire
   sauce
6 tablespoons tomato paste
1 tablespoon minced garlic
4 tablespoons raisins
1 tablespoon black
   peppercorns
11/2 teaspoons dried thyme
3/4 teaspoon salt

Heat olive oil in pan and sauté onions until soft. Add honey and cook 2 minutes. Add remaining ingredients. Bring to a boil, then reduce heat to medium-low. Simmer 1 hour, stirring occasionally. Remove from heat and cool to room temperature. Purée in blender until smooth. Pour into jar with tight screw top. Will keep indefinitely in the refrigerator. Servings: 21/2 to 3 cups. Pan Size: Medium - large heavy saucepan. Preparation Time: 10 minutes. Cooking Time: 1 hour.

Nancy Thomas

Stuffed Leg of Lamb

5 to 6 pound leg of lamb, boned
11/4 to 11/2 pound pork
   tenderloin
1 clove of garlic, cut into slivers
3 cups brown prepared mustard

2 teaspoons horseradish
3 tablespoons vinegar
4 drops Tabasco
1 tablespoon Worcestershire
3 tablespoons olive oil

Insert pork tenderloin into boned leg of lamb and tie lamb with string. Insert garlic slivers into lamb. In a small bowl, mix together mustard, horseradish, vinegar, Tabasco and Worcestershire to form a paste. Place lamb on a rack in a large roasting pan. Pour olive oil into pan. Rub mustard paste over lamb to coat. Insert meat thermometer into lamb. Roast at 325° or until thermometer reaches 160° to 165° (pork will then be done). Slice and serve. Servings: 8. Preparation Time: 30 minutes.

Ray Podesta

Veal Picatta

1 pound veal round steak	1/2 cup white wine
Flour	1 lemon
4 tablespoons butter	2 tablespoons capers
1/2 cup water	

Pound veal until very thin and cut in serving size pieces (or you can use veal Parmesan which is already thin and sliced). Lightly dust veal pieces with flour. Melt 2 tablespoons butter in skillet and brown veal very quickly on both sides. Remove from skillet. Scrape bottom of pan and add remaining butter and melt. Add water, wine and juice of half of the lemon and cook about 10 minutes. Slice other half of the lemon in very thin slices. Return veal to skillet and add lemon slices and capers on top of veal pieces. Cook about 2 minutes. Put on serving platter and pour juices over veal. Servings: 4. Pan Size: 12-inches. Preparation Time: 5 minutes. Cooking Time: 12 minutes.

Gloria Qualls

Lombata di Vitello al Rosmarino

10 to 14 ounce veal chop	1/2 cup veal stock
Flour	1/4 cup brandy
Peanut oil	1 tablespoon butter
Fresh rosemary	Salt
8 cloves of peeled garlic	White pepper

Salt and pepper cleaned veal chop and lightly flour. Brown veal chop on both sides over high heat in a pan with peanut oil for 3 to 4 minutes. Put veal in 500° oven for 10 minutes. Add the cloves of garlic to the veal chop after it has been in the oven for 3 minutes. Remove the veal from oven and discard excess oil. Over high heat add the brandy, then add two sprigs of rosemary and the veal stock. Remove veal chop and turn heat down before adding 1 tablespoon of butter to sauce. Pour sauce over veal chop and serve immediately.

Folks in the Kitchen wine recommendation: Antinori Villa Riserva Red.

Cafe Roma
San Luis Obispo, CA

121

Meme's Veal Scallopini

This recipe was passed on to me from my mother. It was the first thing I ever prepared for my boyfriend, who soon after eating it became my husband. It must be pretty good.

1¹/2 pounds baby milk fed
   veal, cut into 6 thin slices
   across the grain
1/4 cup flour
1/2 cup Parmesan cheese
1 teaspoon salt
1/8 teaspoon pepper
1¹/2 tablespoons olive oil

3 tablespoons butter
3 tablespoons minced onion
1/4 cup dry white wine
2/3 cup beef bouillon
1/2 to 3/4 pound sliced fresh
   mushrooms
Parsley for garnish

Flatten each veal slice between sheets of wax paper by pounding gently with mallet until slices are 1/4-inch thick. Pat slices with paper towel until thoroughly dry. Sprinkle each slice with a mixture of flour, Parmesan cheese, salt and pepper. Gently press flour mixture into meat. Heat 2 tablespoons of the butter and 1 tablespoon of olive oil in a large non-stick skillet. Sauté veal slices for 4 to 5 minutes on each side (until lightly browned). Remove slices to a warm platter. In the same skillet, add half of the remaining butter and olive oil and sauté onion. Cook slowly for one minute. Pour wine and beef bouillon into skillet. Boil rapidly to reduce liquid to about 1/4 cup (stirring with a wooden spoon). Return veal slices to skillet and simmer 5 to 10 minutes. Meanwhile, sauté mushrooms in remaining butter and olive oil and then add to veal. Serve with rice pilaf, fresh asparagus and a good Chardonnay. This is also great with chicken instead of veal. Servings: 6.

Mary E. Katz

122

Oriental Barbequed Pork

Good with rolls at a cocktail buffet in lieu of the
predictable sliced beef tenderloin.

2 whole pork tenderloins
1/4 cup soy sauce
2 tablespoons dry red wine
1 tablespoon brown sugar
1 tablespoon honey

1/2 teaspoon red food
coloring (do not omit)
1/2 teaspoon fresh ground
ginger
1 large clove garlic, minced

Combine marinade ingredients in large glass bowl. Add pork tenderloins, turning to coat. Cover. Let stand at room temperature one hour (or refrigerate overnight) turning occasionally. Remove pork from marinade and place on wire rack over a baking pan. Bake at 350° 40 to 45 minutes, basting and turning frequently. Remove from pan. Cool to room temperature. Slice on diagonal for pretty, red-rimmed oval slices. Garnish with green onion tops. Servings: 8. Preheat: 350°. Preparation Time: 10 minutes plus marinating time. Cooking Time: 40 to 45 minutes.

Nancy Thomas

The Long Hot Tenderloin

This pork tenderloin was a $5,000 finalist in the Newman's Own, Inc./Good Housekeeping recipe contest. Paul Newman donates all profit from his food company to charity. I donated my $5,000 prize to Les Passees.

2 pork tenderloins,
approximately 1 pound each
8 to 10 cloves garlic, halved

Cracked pepper
8 ounces Newman's Own
Italian dressing

Cut 10 to 12 tiny slits in meat randomly and tuck a sliver of garlic in each opening. Sprinkle pork with cracked pepper and place in ziplock bag. Pour 1 cup Newman's Own Italian dressing over the pork tenderloins and turn to coat thoroughly. Seal bag and marinate in refrigerator overnight. Remove meat and bring to room temperature. Bake at 350° for 45 minutes. Also excellent cooked on grill. Servings: 4 to 6. Pan Size: Oblong baking dish. Preheat: 350°. Preparation Time: 20 minutes. Cooking Time: 45 minutes.

Pat Leary

123

Filet de Porc aux Abricots

Pork tenderloin with apricots.

2 pork tenderloins	1/2 teaspoon chopped mint
1 dozen sun-dried apricots	1/2 teaspoon crushed
2 cups red wine	peppercorns
10 ounces raisins	1 tablespoon olive oil
2 tablespoons honey	1/4 cup red wine vinegar
1/2 teaspoon crushed cumin	2 finely chopped shallots
1/2 teaspoon chopped dill	1/2 cup chicken stock

The day before you intend to prepare the pork, soak the apricots in water. Make a marinade by mixing together the red wine, honey, raisins, cumin, dill, mint, and peppercorns. Place the pork tenderloins in the marinade; refrigerate overnight. Take the tenderloins out of the marinade and pat dry. Save the marinade. Cut the meat into pieces 2-inches thick, then flatten them with the palm of your hand. Salt and pepper the meat. Put the olive oil in a skillet. Add the pork slices and sauté over high heat for 3 minutes on each side. Remove the pork from the skillet and set aside. Discard the excess fat from the pan and deglaze with vinegar. Add the shallots and reduce the liquid until almost dry. Add the chicken broth and the marinade. Bring sauce to a boil. Reduce for 5 minutes over low heat. Add the pork and the apricots. Simmer for 15 minutes. Serve with a turnip purée or with a rutabaga purée. (Prepare exactly as you would mashed potatoes.) This is an adaptation of a very old Roman recipe attributed to Apicius. I like pork, and this is a nice, different way of cooking it. Wine notes: A red Cote-du-Rhone, like a Gigondas or a Cornas, will be nice. Servings: 4.

Chanticleer Restaurant
Nantucket Island, MA

124

Fifth Avenue Pork Tenderloin

1 cup soy sauce
2 tablespoons honey
1/2 cup vodka
1/2 cup bourbon

1 (1 to 1 1/2 pounds) pork
   tenderloin
Chutney or pepper jelly

Combine soy sauce, honey, vodka and bourbon in shallow dish. Add pork and marinate for at least four hours or overnight, refrigerated. Pour off half of the marinade. Bake covered at 325° for 30 minutes. Serve with chutney or pepper jelly.

Caroline Orr

Faith's Pork Tenderloin

Doubles or triples easily.

1 pork tenderloin
1 teaspoon ground cinnamon
1/2 teaspoon ground cloves
1 stick bacon, cut into thirds

1 whole bay leaf
Approximately 1 cup apple
   juice

Place pork tenderloin in small baking dish. Sprinkle with cloves and cinnamon. Drape bacon slices over tenderloin (barber pole style). Pour apple juice in bottom of baking pan to about 1/4-inch. Float bay leaf in juice. Cover tightly with foil. Bake for 1 1/2 hours at 275° until tender. Servings: 4. Preparation Time: 15 minutes. Cooking Time: Approximately 1 hour 30 minutes.

Julia Johnson

Pork Tenderloin with Tangy Sauce

This sauce is an old recipe of my mother's.

SAUCE:

2 cups onions, chopped
1 1/2 cups sugar
1 teaspoon pepper
2 cups ketchup

1 1/2 cups vinegar
2 tablespoons plus 2
    teaspoons Worcestershire

1 pork tenderloin

MARINADE:

Soy sauce
Worcestershire sauce
Hot sauce, to taste

Ground pepper, to taste
Cavender's Greek seasoning, to
    taste
Seasoned salt, to taste

Sauce: mix first 6 ingredients in heavy saucepan and simmer for 15 minutes. Marinate tenderloin in soy sauce, Worcestershire, hot sauce, pepper, Cavender's and seasoned salt for approximately 30 minutes each side. Preheat oven 425°. Before cooking tenderloin, spoon generous amounts of sauce on tenderloin. Cook 20 to 25 minutes. Slice tenderloin in 1/2-inch slices. Pour remaining sauce on top. Servings: 3. Pan Size: Small Pyrex. Preheat: 425°. Preparation Time: 30 minutes. Cooking Time: 20 to 25 minutes.

Jenny Rose

John's Favorite Barbecue Pork Chops

8 to 10 boneless center cut
   pork chops
Flour
4 to 6 tablespoons vegetable
   oil

1/2 cup barbecue sauce
2 tablespoons brown sugar
1 small can mandarin
   oranges
Orange juice

Dredge pork chops in flour and sauté in oil until light brown. Drain and transfer to a baking dish. Combine barbecue sauce and brown sugar. Set aside. Drain mandarin oranges and pour the juice in an 8 ounce cup. Finish filling the cup with orange juice. Stir and combine with barbecue sauce mixture. Pour over pork chops. Cover with foil and bake at 350° for 1½ hours. Remove from oven, place mandarin oranges over chops, cover and return to oven for 5 minutes. Also great with chicken. Servings: 6 to 8. Pan Size: 9x13-inches. Preheat: 350°. Preparation Time: 20 minutes. Cooking Time: 1½ hours.

Carey Goodman

Marinated Pork Chops

1 stick butter
1/2 cup Worcestershire
   sauce
1/2 cup A-1 sauce
1/2 cup vinegar

1 onion cut in 6 pieces
Juice of 1 lemon
Crazy salt
Lemon & pepper seasoning
   salt

Melt butter in saucepan. Add remaining ingredients and bring to a boil. Cook over low heat for 5 minutes. Cool slightly. Pour over butterfly pork chops and marinate for 4 to 6 hours. Grill 10 minutes on each side for 1-inch thick chops, basting occasionally. Delicious!

Anne Keesee

Meat and Game

Honey Grilled Pork Loin

1 (3 pound) boneless pork
  loin
2/3 cup soy sauce
1 teaspoon ground ginger
3 cloves garlic, crushed

1/4 cup firmly packed brown
  sugar
1/3 cup honey
1 1/2 tablespoons sesame oil
Vegetable cooking spray

Trim fat from roast. Butterfly roast by making a lengthwise cut, cutting to within 1/2-inch of other side, and open roast. Place in shallow dish or large, heavy-duty plastic bag. Combine soy sauce, ginger, and garlic. Pour over roast. Cover or seal, and refrigerate at least 3 hours, turning occasionally. Remove from marinade, discarding marinade; set roast aside. Combine brown sugar, honey, and sesame oil in a small saucepan; cook over low heat, stirring constantly, until sugar dissolves. Coat grill rack with cooking spray. Place rack over medium-hot coals (350° to 400°). Place roast on rack and brush with honey mixture. Cook 20 to 25 minutes or until a meat thermometer reaches 160°, turning twice and basting frequently. Servings: 10 to 12. Cooking Time: 20 to 25 minutes.

Mrs. Leslie Price, Jr.

Sausage-Stuffed Pepper Cups

1 pound Jimmy Dean
  sausage (your favorite
  flavor)
6 medium bell peppers,
  green, red or yellow
1/2 teaspoon salt
1/4 teaspoon pepper

1 (14 1/2 ounce) can chopped
  tomatoes
1/2 cup Minute Rice
1/2 cup water
1 teaspoon Worcestershire
  sauce
1 cup Cheddar cheese

Brown sausage in skillet, crumble and drain. Add salt, pepper, tomatoes, rice, water and Worcestershire sauce to sausage. Mix together well; cover and simmer 15 minutes, until rice is tender. Cut tops off of peppers; remove seeds and membrane. Stuff peppers with sausage mixture. Place standing upright in baking dish. Sprinkle with Cheddar cheese. Bake, uncovered, at 350° for 25 to 30 minutes. Servings: 6.

George Bryan

128

Red Beans and Rice

1 pound dry red beans	1 teaspoon crushed red
5 to 6 pieces of bacon, cut	pepper
up	2 teaspoons salt
1 large onion, chopped	2 teaspoons sugar
4 cups cold water	1 package Polish sausage,
1 pound canned tomatoes	sliced
2 cloves garlic, chopped	Cooked rice

Soak dry beans overnight. Drain. In large Dutch oven, sauté bacon (but don't brown) and add chopped onions. Cook until onions are just tender. Add beans, water, tomatoes, and all seasonings. Cook on medium-high for 2 hours (covered), then reduce heat to low and let simmer for approximately 5 hours more (covered) until beans are done. During the last hour of cooking, add the sliced Polish sausage and stir well. Serve over cooked rice. Servings: 10. Pan Size: Large Dutch oven. Preparation Time: 30 minutes plus. Cooking Time: 7 hours approximately.

NOTE: Stir often - it is important to make sure the beans do not stick to the bottom of the Dutch oven. If the mixture gets too thick, it can be thinned with V-8 juice and water.

Sue Hays

129

Holiday Ham

Very easy, does not have to be a holiday to cook it.

14 pound country ham
   (uncooked), size varies,
   depending on how may
   you are serving
1.5 liter bottle of Burgundy
   wine

2 liters Coca-cola
1 seasoning packet
4 tablespoons whole cloves
4 tablespoons nutmeg
1 jar of honey

First, begin by scrubbing the ham well, then soak in lukewarm water for 6 hours. Second, rinse and soak ham in lukewarm water overnight. Third rinse and scrub again. Using your thumb, press firmly in the middle of the ham. If there is no "give", soak 3 more hours, if there is "give", you are ready to cook. Place ham in a large roaster. Cover the ham with Burgundy wine, and Coca-cola. Add seasoning packet, whole cloves, and nutmeg, making sure ham is totally covered by liquids. Cook slowly for 7 to 8 hours at 275° to 300° (depending on size of ham). Once ham is done, let cool completely. After cooled, strip off the outer layer of skin. Pour a thin layer of honey over the ham and return to oven for about 45 minutes to 1 hour, just long enough that the ham has a nice glaze. Preheat: 275° to 300°. Cooking Time: 8 to 9 hours total.

Sally Halle/Sharon Jones

Barbecued Duck

4 ducks
1/2 pint hot pepper jelly

1 (28 ounce) bottle
   barbecue sauce

Clean ducks carefully. Combine pepper jelly and barbecue sauce in saucepan and heat thoroughly. Baste the ducks with sauce and place on spits. Cook on a charcoal grill over a low flame and smoke until tender and golden brown, basting frequently.

Tripp Folk

Wild Ducks Orange

4 wild ducks
Flour
Salt and pepper
4 cups bacon grease or
  vegetable shortening
2 large stalks celery,
  chopped with leaves

1 onion, chopped
1 apple, chopped
2 oranges, chopped
1 (6 ounce) can frozen
  orange juice concentrate
1/4 cup Grand Marnier

Wash ducks and dry thoroughly. Flour ducks in sack with salt and pepper. In a large skillet, brown ducks in bacon grease. Lift from grease and drain well. Stuff cavities with celery, onion, apple, and oranges. Place ducks in roasting pan. Dilute orange juice concentrate with 1/4 cup water, and pour over ducks. Cook, covered, at 275° for 3 hours, basting frequently the last 45 minutes. Sprinkle with Grand Marnier. Servings: 8. Pan Size: Medium roaster with lid. Preheat: 275°.

Margaret Atkinson

Meat and Game

Pete's Italian Duck

3 wild ducks
Salt, pepper, garlic salt, to
taste
1/2 stick butter or margarine
2 large onions, chopped
2 cans Hunt's tomato herb
sauce
4 ounces Meyer's cream
sherry #44

2 ounces Kikkoman
marinade and barbecue
sauce
1 tablespoon Kitchen
Bouquet
1/4 Barzi spaghetti mix

Remove legs from duck and separate entire back from breast. Do not cook backs. Salt, pepper and garlic salt breast and legs to taste. Sprinkle 1/2 of chopped onions in bottom of aluminum pan then place ducks in pan, breast side up. Sprinkle remainder of chopped onions on top of breasts and legs. Sprinkle Barzi spaghetti mix on top of ducks. Pour Kikkoman sauce, Meyers cream sherry and Kitchen Bouquet over ducks. Then spread tomato herb sauce and butter over top of breasts and legs. Completely cover aluminum pan with foil, be sure to seal tightly. Place in 275° oven for 6 hours. Gravy may be served over rice, potatoes, etc. Servings: 6. Pan Size: 12x12-inches. Preheat: 275°. Preparation Time: 30 minutes. Cooking Time: 6 hours.

Pete Aviotti, Jr.

Smoked Duck Breasts

6 duck breasts
1 bottle Italian salad dressing
1/2 teaspoon salt
1/2 teaspoon pepper
1/2 teaspoon lemon & pepper
seasoning salt

6 strips of bacon
1 stick butter or margarine
3 tablespoons Worcestershire

Clean duck breasts. Place in plastic bag. Pour salad dressing over all, seal and marinate in refrigerator for 4 to 8 hours. Remove from marinade and season with salt, pepper and lemon & pepper. Wrap bacon around each breast and secure with toothpicks. In a small saucepan, melt butter and add Worcestershire. Place ducks on grill over low flame and close top of grill. Baste frequently with butter mixture. Cook until tender and golden brown.

Tripp Folk

132

John's Favorite Duck

My husband shouts that I cook the very best duck.

4 ducks	Worcestershire sauce
1 apple, sliced	Soy sauce
1 orange, sliced	Cavender's Greek seasoning or
1 onion, sliced	your favorite herb blend
Several celery stalks, sliced	8 ounces orange juice
8 ounces Italian dressing	

Soak ducks several hours in salted water. Rinse and place ducks in large roasting pan with breast side up. Stuff ducks with slices of apple, orange, onion and celery. Pour Italian dressing over ducks. Sprinkle generously with Worcestershire, soy sauce and herb blend. Marinate in refrigerator for several hours or overnight. When ready to bake, pour off marinade. Return ducks to roaster. Add one inch of water and orange juice. Bake at 500° or until breasts are brown (15 to 20 minutes). Turn ducks and continue baking until backs are brown. Reduce heat to 300° and bake for 3 hours, basting every 30 minutes. Serve on bed of brown and wild rice mix to which you've added sautéed onions, celery, mushrooms and steamed snow peas. Servings: 6. Pan Size: Large turkey roaster. Preheat: 500° then lower to 300°. Preparation Time: 1 hour divided. Cooking Time: 3 hours.

Pat Leary

133

Stuffed Venison Roast

1/2 can tomatoes, drained
   and chopped
1/4 cup green peppers, diced
1/4 cup celery, diced
1/4 cup onion, diced
2 teaspoons bacon fat
11/2 cups bread crumbs

1/4 cup fresh chopped parsley
1 teaspoon dry mustard
1 teaspoon white pepper
Dash of curry powder
Dash of garlic powder
1 large venison steak
   1/2-inch thick

Combine all stuffing ingredients and spread evenly over steak. Roll up and tie steak. Place in a baking dish and cook at 350° for 11/2 hours basting with the following sauce.

SAUCE:
6 tablespoons melted butter
3 tablespoons Worcestershire
   sauce

3 tablespoons soy sauce
1/4 teaspoon salt
Dash of garlic powder

Servings: 4. Preheat: 350°. Preparation Time: 30 minutes. Cooking Time: 11/2 hours.

Tripp Folk

Venison Marinade

4 cloves garlic, crushed
1 teaspoon salt
1 teaspoon cracked pepper
1/2 teaspoon Tabasco
1/2 cup vegetable oil

1 cup port wine
1 teaspoon dried whole
   thyme
1 bay leaf

Combine all ingredients. Stir well to blend. Pour marinade over venison (venison chops are best). Refrigerate overnight, turning occasionally. Presto! Your venison is marinated and ready for the grill.

Jim Patridge

Pigeon with Sweet Garlic

4 pigeons
24 garlic cloves
1 ounce butter
2 tablespoons white wine
1 cup chicken stock

¹/₂ ounce foie gras
  (optional)
1 teaspoon parsley, chopped
Salt and pepper

Have your butcher prepare and truss the pigeon. Reserve the liver. Separate the garlic cloves, but do not remove the skin. Lightly brown the pigeon in a sauté pan. Add the garlic cloves and cook at 450° for 20 minutes. Just before the pigeon and garlic are done roasting, add the liver. Remove the pigeon from the pot and discard the fat. Reduce the white wine in the pan with the garlic and liver. Pass through a food mill. (Include the foie gras with the above ingredients if it is preferred.)

FINISHING: Boil the chicken stock and blend with the purée, making sure not to let the sauce boil. Season with salt and pepper.

PRESENTATION: Warm the pigeon for two minutes in the oven. Arrange them on a serving dish and spoon the sauce over the pigeon. The dish can be accompanied with potato gratin dauphinois. Servings: 4.

Colonial Country Club
Memphis, Tennessee

135

NOTES

SEAFOOD AND POULTRY

SPONSORED BY

Mike & Nancye Starnes

Balsamic Chicken

4 boneless chicken breasts	**8 ounces porcini**
Salt and pepper	**mushrooms**
2 tablespoons flour	**1/4 cup balsamic vinegar**
2 tablespoons olive oil	**3/4 cup chicken broth**
3 cloves garlic, minced	**4 tablespoons white wine**

Wash chicken and pat dry. Sprinkle with salt and pepper and dredge in flour. Brown in olive oil for 3 minutes a side. Add garlic. Turn chicken and add mushrooms. Cook for an additional 3 minutes. Stir in vinegar, broth, and wine. Cook over low heat for 10 to 15 minutes, turning chicken occasionally.

Caroline Orr

Quick Coq au Vin

2 1/2 pounds boneless	**1 onion, chopped**
chicken breasts, cubed	**3 cloves garlic, minced**
Flour	**1/2 teaspoon thyme**
2 tablespoons vegetable oil	**1 bay leaf**
1 tablespoon butter	**Salt and pepper, to taste**
1/2 pound mushrooms,	**1 cup red wine**
sliced	**1/2 cup chicken broth**

Dredge chicken in flour. In a large skillet, brown chicken lightly in oil. Remove and set aside. Add butter, mushrooms and onion to skillet and cook over medium heat for 2 to 3 minutes. Add garlic and cook for an additional minute. Add remaining ingredients and stir, scraping up brown bits from bottom of pan. Cook for 3 minutes. Return chicken to skillet and simmer for 15 minutes.

Jack Powell

Chicken Picatta with a Lemon Caper Beurre Blanc

2 (4 ounce) boneless, skinless chicken breasts	Chopped shallots
	1 ounce heavy cream
Flour	6 to 8 capers
1 egg, beaten	1/2 lemon
1 ounce Chablis	1 ounce butter, room temperature

Dust chicken with flour, dip in egg wash and sauté in an oven-proof skillet until golden brown. Put skillet in oven and bake for 8 to 10 minutes at 425°. Remove chicken from skillet and keep warm. Deglaze pan with Chablis, chopped shallots and heavy cream. Reduce and add the capers, 6 to 8 depending on the size. Add the juice of half a lemon and stir slowly adding the butter. Pour sauce over chicken. Serve with fettucine noodles and a variety of sautéed garden vegetables. Enjoy!

James R. Alarie, Executive Chef
The Chef's Garden
Naples, Florida

Creole Blackened Chicken

6 boneless, skinless chicken breasts	1/2 cup finely minced Tasso
	1/4 cup finely chopped green onion
3 tablespoons Creole seasoning	
1/4 cup olive oil	2 cups heavy cream
3/4 roll garlic cheese	6 cups cooked rice

Coat chicken with Creole seasoning. Heat oil in oven-proof skillet and sauté chicken for 6 to 7 minutes on high, turning once. Place skillet in oven and cook for an additional 5 minutes at 350°. Meanwhile, in a saucepan, combine cheese, Tasso, onion and cream. Cook, stirring until cheese is melted and mixture is heated through. To serve, place chicken on a bed of rice. Spoon sauce over chicken and garnish with parsley.

NOTE: Tasso is a Cajun smoked ham. Order from your local grocery store. Finely mince and store in your freezer.

Marilyn Newton

Swiss Chicken Cutlets

4 boneless, skinned chicken breasts
1/2 teaspoon salt
2 eggs, beaten
1 cup fine dry bead crumbs
1/4 cup oil
3 tablespoons butter or margarine
1/4 cup flour

1/2 teaspoon salt
1/8 teaspoon pepper
2 1/2 cups milk
1/2 cup dry white wine
1 cup shredded Swiss cheese
Avocado slices (optional)
Tomato wedges (optional)

Place chicken breasts between wax paper and pound to about 1/4-inch thickness. Sprinkle lightly with salt. Dip in beaten eggs, then in crumbs. In skillet, heat 2 tablespoons of the oil. Brown cutlets a few at a time, about 2 minutes a side, adding oil as needed. Set chicken aside. In saucepan melt butter; blend in flour, salt and pepper. Add milk all at once; cook, stirring until thick and bubbly. Remove from heat; stir in wine. Pour half of sauce into bottom of baking dish. Arrange chicken on top of sauce and pour remaining sauce over the chicken. Cover and chill several hours or overnight. Bake, covered in 350° oven until heated through, about 50 minutes. Sprinkle with cheese and garnish with avocados and tomatoes, if desired. Return to oven to melt cheese, about 2 minutes. Servings: 4. Pan Size: 9x13-inches. Preheat: 350°. Preparation Time: 20 minutes. Cooking Time: 50 minutes.

Shannon Stevens

140

Susie's Mustard Chicken

MARINADE SAUCE:

3 cups vinegar

3¹/₂ teaspoons salt

1¹/₂ tablespoons dry mustard

4¹/₂ tablespoons ketchup

9 tablespoons lemon juice

¹/₄ teaspoon black pepper

BROWNING SAUCE:

6 tablespoons sugar

1¹/₂ teaspoons salt

9 tablespoons butter, melted

3¹/₂ tablespoons prepared
   mustard

3¹/₂ teaspoons
   Worcestershire sauce

¹/₄ teaspoon black pepper

8 boneless chicken breasts

Mix first six ingredients together for marinade sauce. Marinate chicken for one hour. Grill chicken and baste with marinade for first half of cooking time. Meanwhile, combine brown sauce ingredients and baste chicken for last half of grilling time. Do not overcook! Servings: 8. Preheat: Charcoal grill-medium coals. Preparation Time: 1 hour 30 minutes. Cooking Time: 15 minutes or cooked through, do not overcook.

Toni Campbell Parker

Flo's Chicken Breasts with Hearts of Palm
Elegant party dish and oh, so delicious!

8 whole boneless, skinless
   chicken breasts

Salt, pepper, thyme, to taste

8 canned hearts of palm

Butter

Hollandaise sauce

Salt, pepper and sprinkle thyme on chicken breasts. Roll each breast around a whole heart of palm. If palm is exceptionally large, cut in half lengthwise. Secure with toothpicks. Place chicken in baking dish large enough to hold chicken in a single layer. Dot generously with butter. Cover and bake at 350° for 35 to 45 minutes or until tender, basting frequently. Serve with Hollandaise sauce.

Mrs. Frank Campbell

141

Hazelnut Chicken in an Orange Thyme Cream Sauce

SAUCE:

3 cups heavy (whipping) cream

1½ cups orange juice, freshly squeezed

½ heaping tablespoon fresh thyme

¼ teaspoon salt

⅛ teaspoon ground white pepper

3 tablespoons Frangelico (or any other hazelnut liqueur)

FOR THE CHICKEN: 9 boneless, skinless chicken breasts, 6 to 8 ounces each

FOR THE CHICKEN BREADING:

1½ cups hazelnuts (filberts), raw, not blanched, medium chopped in processor, not pulverized

1½ cups fine dried bread crumbs

3 whole eggs, vigorously beaten

1 cup flour

FOR THE SAUTÉ:

1 cup clarified butter or margarine

1 cup soybean oil or olive oil

Combine all sauce ingredients except Frangelico in a deep saucepan so it will not boil over. Whisk together and reduce to 3 cups on high heat, whisking occasionally. Add Frangelico and remove from heat. This sauce can be made ahead and refrigerated. If it separates during refrigeration, simply stir it together before re-heating. If it separates during re-heating, just add a few drops of cream and whisk it together again. While sauce is reducing, trim the chicken breasts of all fat, place them on a cutting board under a doubled piece of food film and pound them to a uniform thickness of ¼-inch.

(continued on next page)

142

Cut each piece of chicken in thirds. Combine the hazelnuts and bread crumbs, mixing thoroughly. Dredge each piece of chicken first in flour, shake off the excess, then dip chicken in egg mixture and remove excess by pulling chicken between thumb and forefinger several times, and, lastly, dredge the chicken in the hazelnut-bread crumb mixture, again shaking off the excess. In a small sauté pan, heat the sauce, using 1/3 cup per portion, and remove from heat. Heat a little clarified butter and oil in an appropriate sauté pan and, on medium-high heat, sauté the chicken to a golden brown on both sides. Place the chicken on dinner plate with accompaniments. Whisk the heated sauce together one more time, and spoon the sauce over the chicken. Servings: 9.

Folks in the Kitchen wine recommendation: Duckhorn Sauvignon Blanc.

Victor Shepard, Executive Chef and co-owner
Le Bosquet Restaurant
Crested Butte, Colorado

Hungarian Chicken Paprika
The perfect pre-game meal.

4 tablespoons vegetable oil	**2 tablespoons sweet paprika**
1/2 onion, chopped	**3/4 cup water**
8 chicken parts	**3 tablespoons flour**
2 teaspoons salt	**1/2 cup sour cream**
1/4 teaspoon black pepper	

In a heavy skillet, sauté onions in oil over medium heat. Add chicken and brown. Add salt, pepper, paprika and water. Cover and simmer for 45 to 50 minutes or until chicken is tender. Mix enough water with flour to make a paste. Add to skillet and simmer, stirring until gravy thickens. Remove chicken. Add sour cream to skillet and stir until combined. Do not let it boil! Put chicken back in skillet and heat slowly. Serve over wide noodles or rice. Servings: 4.

Joe Theisman

143

Island Chicken

6 chicken breast halves
1/4 cup vegetable oil
2 tablespoons soy sauce
1 teaspoon garlic powder
1 teaspoon salt
1 teaspoon pepper
1 teaspoon dried rosemary

1 (1 pound 4 ounce) can
  fruit for salad
1 (1 pound 4 ounce) can
  pineapple chunks in juice
4 teaspoons cornstarch
1/4 cup sauterne wine
1/4 cup flake coconut

Place chicken bone side up in baking dish. Combine oil, soy and spices. Brush half over chicken. Bake at 350° for 25 minutes. Turn chicken and baste with remaining oil mixture. Bake an additional 40 minutes. Meanwhile, in a medium saucepan, stir juice from mixed fruits into cornstarch. Add wine and stir until sauce thickens, about 3 minutes. Add all fruits and heat through. Place chicken on serving platter, spoon sauce over and sprinkle with coconut. Servings: 4 to 6. Preheat: 350°. Cooking Time: 1 hour 15 minutes.

Mary E. Walker

Chardonnay Chicken

1/4 cup flour
1/2 teaspoon pepper
1 teaspoon seasoned salt
1 teaspoon basil
1 teaspoon Knorr aromat
  seasoning
8 chicken tenderloins
3 garlic cloves, minced

2 tablespoons olive oil
1/2 large bell pepper, cut into strips
4 green onions, cut into
  1-inch pieces
4 to 6 ounces fresh
  mushrooms, cut in half
1 tablespoon olive oil
3/4 cup chardonnay wine

Combine first five ingredients. Coat each tenderloin well and set aside. In large skillet, sauté garlic in 2 tablespoons olive oil. Add vegetables and heat just enough to coat with garlic. Remove from skillet and add 1 tablespoon of olive oil. When hot, add chicken and brown until golden brown on each side. Put the vegetables on top of the chicken, then pour 3/4 cup chardonnay over all. Cover and cook on low for about 10 to 15 minutes. Serve over wild rice. Oh, so very, very good!! Servings: 4. Pan Size: Large skillet. Cooking Time: 35 minutes.

Mrs. James Jobe Madison

"Looking for a Contest" Chicken

The first time I prepared this dish as an experiment, my husband said it should be entered in a contest.

2 whole boneless chicken
  breasts
Black pepper, to taste
Cavender's Greek
  Seasoning, to taste
2 tablespoons olive oil

2 tablespoons butter
1 onion, thinly sliced
1 cup sliced mushrooms
1/2 cup sliced red pepper
1/2 can cream of mushroom soup
1/2 cup vermouth

Pound chicken breasts until thin. Season with pepper and Greek seasoning. In a large skillet, brown chicken in olive oil and butter. Remove chicken and sauté onions, mushrooms and red pepper until wilted. Return chicken to skillet. Blend cream of mushroom soup with vermouth and add to skillet. Simmer until chicken and vegetables are tender. Serve over pasta or rice. Servings: 2 to 3. Pan Size: Large skillet. Preparation Time: 35 minutes. Cooking Time: 20 minutes.

Pat Leary

Golden Mushroom Chicken

An old family recipe.

4 whole boneless chicken
  breasts
Flour
1 tablespoon olive oil
1 bunch green onions, chopped

1/2 pound fresh mushrooms,
  sliced
1 can golden mushroom soup
1 cup dry white wine
1 cup chicken broth

Halve, wash, and pat chicken breasts dry. Dredge in flour. Sauté chicken in olive oil until brown on both sides. Add mushrooms and green onions. Sauté until limp. Combine mushroom soup, white wine and chicken broth. Add to chicken. Season to taste. Cover and simmer for 20 to 30 minutes.

Maggie Lee

145

Chicken Parmesan

A new twist on an old favorite, Veal Parmesan.

6 boneless, skinless	1 (8 ounce) can tomato sauce
chicken breasts	1 teaspoon dried oregano
3 tablespoons butter	1/2 teaspoon sugar
1/2 cup cracker crumbs	Onion salt, to taste
1/4 cup Parmesan cheese	1 cup shredded mozzarella
1/2 teaspoon salt and pepper	cheese
1 egg, beaten	1/2 cup grated Parmesan cheese

Melt butter in a small bowl. Add cracker crumbs, Parmesan cheese and salt and pepper and stir to combine. Dip chicken breasts in beaten egg, then in crumb mixture. Place in baking dish. Bake at 400° for 20 minutes. Turn chicken and bake 15 to 20 minutes more or until tender. Meanwhile, heat tomato sauce, oregano, sugar and onion salt in small pan. Pour sauce over chicken; top with mozzarella cheese, then Parmesan cheese. Return to oven to melt cheese. Servings: 6. Pan Size: 10x10x11/2-inches. Preheat: 400°. Preparation Time: 20 minutes. Cooking Time: 45 to 50 minutes.

Sandy S. Nichols

Hot and Spicy Barbecue Chicken

Chicken pieces	Black pepper
Garlic salt	Paprika

Wash chicken and pat dry. Sprinkle garlic salt over each piece, sparingly. Sprinkle black pepper over each piece, but BEWARE, the more pepper, the hotter the chicken. Last, lightly sprinkle paprika over the chicken. Cook over charcoal, a slow fire will result in tastier chicken about one hour. Chicken doesn't have to be fully cooked. Then, place chicken in an aluminum roasting pan and cover the pan tightly. Leave chicken steaming for another hour or hour and a half. When finished cooking, there should be plenty of juice in the bottom of the pan just right for over rice or sopping bread. Servings: 4. Cooking Time: 2 to 21/2 hours.

Jimmy Chancellor

Roulades of Chicken Florentine

6 boneless (skin on) chicken breasts	1 (4 ounce) package crumbled feta cheese, with tomato and basil
Salt and pepper, to taste	⅛ cup Parmesan cheese
1 (10 ounce) package frozen chopped spinach, thawed and drained	5 tablespoons olive oil

Place chicken between plastic wrap and flatten to ⅛-inch thickness. Season both sides with salt and pepper. Combine spinach, feta cheese, Parmesan and 2 tablespoons of olive oil and stir until well mixed. Brush chicken with 2 tablespoons olive oil. Place a small amount of spinach mixture in the middle of each chicken breast and spread to within ½-inch of edges. Roll breasts up tucking the loose ends under. Brush rolls with remaining 1 tablespoon olive oil. Place chicken skin side up in baking dish and cover with foil. Bake at 350° for 25 minutes. Uncover and place under broiler for 5 minutes or until chicken is browned. Serve with Hollandaise Sauce if desired. Servings: 6. Preheat: 350°. Cooking Time: 30 minutes.

Martha Kelsey Edwards

Light Chicken and Spinach Calzones

½ cup chopped onion	1 teaspoon Italian seasoning
1 tablespoon garlic powder	1 (15 ounce) carton fat-free ricotta cheese
½ teaspoon salt	1 cup fat-free mozzarella cheese
4 chicken breasts, cut into bite-size pieces	1 (16 ounce) loaf of frozen bread dough, thawed
1 (10 ounce) package frozen chopped spinach, thawed and drained	1 jar of light pasta sauce

Place first four ingredients in a skillet and cook until chicken is done. Add spinach, seasoning and cheeses. Mix well. Divide dough into 8 portions and roll each out to a 6-inch circle. Spoon chicken/spinach mixture onto each dough piece and fold over like a turnover, pinching edges to seal. Bake calzones at 350° for 20 minutes. Before serving, top with pasta sauce. Servings: 4. Preheat: Yes. Preparation Time: 40 minutes. Cooking Time: 20 minutes.

Janet Farris Henderson

Moroccan Chicken Pies with Daal

MOROCCAN SPICE MIX:

1/2 teaspoon aniseed
1 teaspoon fennel seed
10 whole all spice berries
1 teaspoon cardamom
10 whole cloves
20 whole black peppercorns
2 teaspoons ground cinnamon

1 tablespoon sesame seeds
1 teaspoon coriander seeds
1/2 teaspoon cumin
1/4 teaspoon red pepper flakes
1 tablespoon ground ginger
1 teaspoon ground nutmeg

Place all above spices in food processor and grind together until a nice powder form.

FOR CHICKEN FILLING:

4 breasts of chicken
1 can chicken broth
3 large eggs, beaten lightly
1/4 cup parsley flakes
2 tablespoons fresh parsley
1 1/2 tablespoons fresh lemon juice
20 sheets phyllo dough
1/4 teaspoon saffron threads, crumbled

2 tablespoons hot water
1 medium onion, chopped
1 tablespoon minced garlic
1 1/2 sticks unsalted butter
1 teaspoon ground ginger
1 1/2 tablespoons Moroccan spice mix
1 teaspoon salt
1/2 teaspoon ground black pepper

In small bowl, put hot water and saffron and set aside. In heavy large Dutch oven, sauté onion and garlic in 3 tablespoons of butter over medium-high heat, until golden. Reduce heat to medium, add ginger and 1 tablespoon Moroccan spice mix. Stir and cook for a couple minutes to release spice flavors. Add chicken, saffron (with water) and broth. Cook for 30 minutes. Turn off heat and let sit for 30 minutes.

(continued on next page)

148

Remove chicken to work surface and remove skin and bones. Shred chicken into thin flaky pieces. Place broth back on medium heat and reduce to about 1¾ cups. Reduce heat to low and add beaten eggs in a slow stream while whisking. Simmer until the eggs are solid. Let stand 10 minutes. Pour egg mixture through large strainer to remove any liquid. Transfer egg mixture to bowl, stir in chicken, parsley, lemon juice, 2 teaspoons Moroccan spice mix, salt and pepper. Melt remaining butter, and keep warm, not hot. On large wooden cutting board or counter top with wax paper, cut phyllo sheets in half lengthwise. Keep phyllo covered with damp towel. On another sheet of wax paper, place a sheet of phyllo and brush with butter. Add another sheet of phyllo and brush with butter, add two more layers. Put ⅓ cup of chicken mixture on phyllo three inches from edge. Fold the three-inch piece over the chicken mixture, then fold that over one more time. Now, fold side edges in and finish rolling the chicken until it forms a pillow. This should measure 3x5-inches. Brush top with butter and sprinkle a thin stripe design using the remaining Moroccan spice mix. Place on baking sheet. Finish other pies. Bake at 350° until golden brown and puffy, about 15 minutes.

DAAL:

1 cup dry yellow lentils	**½ teaspoon cumin**
¼ cup chopped onion	**½ teaspoon turmeric**
1 teaspoon garlic	**1 cup chicken broth or water**

Rinse lentils in cold running water. In saucepan, put lentils, water or broth, and all seasonings. Turn on low heat and simmer until lentils are tender (about 20 to 30 minutes). Pour Daal in center of plate (about ¼ cup). Place hot chicken pie in center and garnish with parsley or edible flowers. Serve at once.

Pamela J. Donovan

149

Quick and Easy Chicken Pot Pie

2 cups baked chicken
  breast
2 cans chicken gravy
1 can Veg-All, drained

1 teaspoon pepper
1 teaspoon salt (optional)
15 ounce box refrigerated pie
  crust

Preheat oven, 425°. Cut chicken into pieces. Mix chicken, gravy, drained Veg-All, salt and pepper in a large bowl. Prepare crusts for pie, according to instructions, in a deep dish pan. Pour chicken mixture into bottom crust and add second crust on top. Bake for 30 minutes or until nicely browned. Enjoy! Servings: 4 to 6. Pan Size: 9-inch pie pan. Preheat: 425°. Preparation Time: 10 minutes. Cooking Time: 30 minutes.

Elizabeth D. Bills

Mondo's Dumplings

1 small hen or large fryer
Celery
Garlic powder
Dried parsley
Salt and pepper

4 cups flour
4 teaspoons baking powder
1/2 teaspoon salt
3/4 cup reserved chicken
  broth

In a large pot, cover chicken with water, add seasonings and simmer until tender. Remove chicken, reserving broth and cool. Remove chicken from bone, cut into pieces and return to pot with the broth. To make dumplings, combine flour, baking powder, salt and reserved 3/4 cup chicken broth. Roll out thin and cut into two inch squares. Drop into chicken broth and boil for 45 minutes or until tender.

Patty S. Micci

Chicken and Dumplings

1 large hen and/or chicken
  breasts
Salt, pepper, seasoned salt
2 packages MBT instant
  chicken broth

1 large onion, quartered
Celery tops
2 medium carrots, cut into 3
  or 4 pieces

DUMPLINGS:
2 cups plain flour
1/4 teaspoon soda
1 teaspoon salt

5 level tablespoons shortening
1 cup buttermilk

Salt and pepper

1/2 cup milk

Place chicken, seasonings, broth and vegetables in large pot. Cover with water to half an inch above chicken. Simmer until tender. Let chicken cool in liquid. Remove vegetables. Debone chicken and cut into bite-size pieces. Return chicken to reserved broth, making sure broth is only half an inch above chicken. If needed, remove some broth and reserve for later use. Mix by hand flour, soda, salt, shortening, and buttermilk. Divide into three parts and roll each as thin as possible on a floured surface, using additional flour if needed. Slice into strips one inch wide. This may be done ahead and placed on layers of waxed paper. Refrigerate. To serve, heat chicken in broth. When hot, add strips of dumplings laying across top. Salt and pepper dumplings. Continue this until all dumplings are used. Pour 1/2 cup milk over all. Cover and cook for 15 minutes.

Vinita G. Hardgrave

151

Chicken in a Crescent Roll

3 or 4 chicken breasts,
  cooked and deboned
Salt and pepper
8 canned crescent rolls,
  separated

1 can cream of chicken soup
1 cup milk
Grated Cheddar cheese

Chop chicken, toss with salt and pepper. Spread chicken on each roll of dough, roll up and place in ungreased casserole. Mix soup with milk, pour over rolls. Cook for 25 minutes at 350°. Rolls will brown. Take out of oven, top with grated cheese. Cheese will melt without returning to oven. Serve hot. Servings: 8. Preheat: 350°. Preparation Time: 20 minutes. Cooking Time: 25 minutes.

Shirley Lawrence

Chicken Fajitas

3/4 cup Worcestershire
1/4 cup fresh lime juice
1 teaspoon minced garlic
1 teaspoon green onion,
  chopped
1/2 teaspoon salt
1/4 teaspoon crushed red
  pepper
1 tablespoon red wine vinegar

1 large onion, cut into
  medium-thick slices
1 red pepper, cut into
  medium-thick slices
8 chicken breast filets,
  skinned
2 tablespoons olive oil
12 flour tortillas
Salsa and sour cream, if desired

In a small bowl, combine first 7 ingredients. Chill, covered, for 4 hours to overnight. Thinly slice the longer side of the chicken breasts. In a large skillet, sauté the onion, red pepper and chicken in the olive oil over high heat for about six to eight minutes or until well browned. To serve, add the marinade to the chicken, onion, pepper mixture in the skillet. Heat for about three minutes more or until sizzling. Serve immediately with warm tortillas. Garnish with salsa and sour cream. Servings: 6. Pan Size: 18-inch skillet. Preheat: 5 minutes. Cooking Time: 15 minutes.

Kathy O'Connor

Chicken Enchiladas

16 ounces sour cream
1 can cream of chicken soup
1 can cream of celery soup
1/2 cup milk
1 tablespoon minced onion
1 teaspoon lemon & pepper
  seasoning salt
1/4 teaspoon celery salt

1/2 teaspoon salt
3 whole boneless, skinless
  chicken breasts, cooked,
  preferably boiled
11/2 cups shredded Cheddar
  cheese
1 (18 count) package soft tortilla
  shells

In a large bowl, combine first 8 ingredients. Spread 2 tablespoons of the mixture on the bottom of a 9x11-inch baking dish. Shred cooked chicken. Add chicken and Cheddar cheese to the soup mixture. Place a heaping tablespoon on tortilla shell and roll up. Place in baking dish. Continue this until baking dish is full. Spoon remaining mixture on top of the enchiladas. Cover with foil and bake at 350° for 45 minutes. Let stand 10 minutes before serving. This is great served with salsa!

Barbara Williamson

Mexican Chicken
This dish tastes better if made a day ahead.

8 to 10 boneless, skinless
  chicken breasts
Flour
2 to 3 tablespoons oil
1/4 cup chopped onion
1 (15 ounce) can tomato sauce
1/2 cup water
2 chicken bouillon cubes

1 (4 ounce) can diced chilies
1 (41/2 ounce) can chopped
  black olives
2 tablespoons wine vinegar
1 teaspoon cumin
1 teaspoon garlic salt
2 cups grated Monterey Jack
  cheese

Dust chicken with flour and brown lightly in oil. Remove and place in Pyrex dish. Mix remaining ingredients except cheese in saucepan and simmer for 5 minutes. Pour over chicken. Cover with foil and bake for 45 minutes to 1 hour at 350°. Remove foil and sprinkle with grated cheese. Bake 10 minutes or until cheese is melted. Servings: 8. Pan Size: 13x9x2-inch Pyrex dish. Preheat: Oven to 350°. Cooking Time: 45 minutes to 1 hour.

Warfield and Neville Williams

153

Cashman's Tennessee Brunswick Stew

There is an on-going feud dating back to the early 1900's about the origin of Brunswick Stew. Here's the recipe the Cashman family brought from native Savannah, Georgia, to Memphis, Tennessee, to enter into the fray.

4 (6 pound) stewing hens, cooked and deboned
1 (6 pound) Boston butt, baked, chopped and shredded
12 large white onions, process to fine cut
5 pounds potatoes, peeled and diced
2 gallons canned chopped tomatoes, undrained

2 gallons canned yellow niblet corn, drained
5 (16 ounce) bags frozen cut okra
5 (16 ounce) bags frozen butterbeans
2 (8 ounce) bottles chili sauce

ADD TO TASTE:
1/4 small (10 ounce) bottle Worcestershire sauce
1/4 small (5 ounce) bottle Tabasco sauce

3 tablespoons plus 1 teaspoon salt
1 1/2 tablespoons pepper

Allow about two hours one day and two hours the following day to prepare; sounds like a lot of time, but final product is worth it.

DAY ONE: Assemble ingredients. Cook stewing hens; cover with enough water to end up with 4 quarts stock. You may add a bouquet of onions, celery, and parsley for flavor. Bring water to boil, turn down heat and simmer until meat is tender enough to fall off the bone. Strain; put stock in refrigerator overnight and remove fat layer in a.m. Bake the Boston butt, well done; remove all visible fat, cool and chop or shred meat.

(continued on next page)

DAY TWO: Chop onions and dice potatoes. Mix in a 15 plus gallon stock pot the chicken stock, shredded chicken, chopped Boston butt, onions, potatoes, tomatoes, corn, okra and butterbeans. Cook on low heat stirring frequently for about two hours. Then, add chili sauce, Worcestershire, Tabasco, salt and pepper. Continue cooking, stirring frequently, for another two to four hours. (If stew burns on the bottom of pan, don't scrape the pan. Pour stew into another container, clean pot, pour stew back into pot and continue cooking.) Continue to stir frequently. When vegetables are tender, let stew cool. You can serve the same evening or next day. Best results are to let stand overnight to blend flavors. Heat and serve with BBQ, cole slaw and cornbread. Recipe is easy to halve or quarter. Can be frozen and used anytime. Servings: 40 to 50 (8 to 10 gallons). Pan Size: 15 plus gallons. Preparation Time: Collectively a day. Cooking Time: 4 to 6 hours.

Eugene K. Cashman, Jr.

Chicken Chili Bake

3/4 cup brown rice
13/4 cups chicken broth
3/4 cup chopped onion
Butter
3 cups chicken, cooked and
   chopped
1 (12 ounce) jar medium
   salsa
1 can cream of chicken soup

11/2 cups frozen whole
   kernel corn
2 tablespoons
   Worcestershire
2 teaspoons chili powder
1 teaspoon dried oregano
1/2 teaspoon curry powder
1/4 teaspoon pepper
1 teaspoon salt

Combine rice and chicken broth in a medium saucepan. Bring to a boil over high heat. Cover, reduce heat and cook until rice is tender. In a small skillet sauté onions in butter until tender but not brown. In a large bowl combine chicken with remaining ingredients. Stir in onions and rice. Spoon mixture into a 2 quart casserole coated with vegetable spray. Bake at 350° for 40 to 45 minutes or until bubbly and heated through.

Mrs. Harold E. Crye

155

Chicken and Rice Casserole

2 cups cooked rice
4 chicken breasts cooked
  and deboned
1 can cream of chicken soup
1/2 can water

3 tablespoons lemon juice
2 cups bread crumbs
1/2 cup butter, melted
11/2 cups grated cheese

Place cooked rice in a casserole dish, add chicken. Mix together soup, water and lemon juice, Pour over the rice and chicken. Top with bread crumbs. Drizzle with butter and top with cheese. Bake at 350° for 20 to 30 minutes. Servings: 6. Preheat: 350°. Preparation Time: 20 minutes. Cooking Time: 20 to 30 minutes.

Shirley Lawrence

Hot Chicken Salad Casserole

4 whole chicken breasts,
  cooked, cooled and diced
3 hard-boiled eggs, sliced
1/2 can cream of chicken
  soup
2 cups finely chopped celery
1 cup real mayonnaise
1 cup sour cream
1 (8 ounce) can sliced water
  chestnuts

1 (4 ounce) can mushrooms
2 teaspoons chopped onion
1/2 cup slivered almonds
2 teaspoons lemon juice
1 teaspoon salt
1 teaspoon pepper
1 cup shredded Cheddar
  cheese
1 can onion rings, crushed

Mix all of the above ingredients, except cheese and onion rings. Spoon into lightly greased baking dish. Sprinkle with cheese. Bake for 30 minutes at 350°. Top with onion rings and bake another 15 minutes or until lightly browned. Servings: 8. Pan Size: 9x13-inches. Preheat: 350°. Cooking Time: 45 minutes.

Bonnie Hartzman

Kay's Chicken Broccoli Casserole
A Folk family favorite.

2 packages frozen chopped broccoli	1/4 teaspoon curry powder 2 tablespoons lemon juice
2 cups chicken	1 cup sharp Cheddar
2 (10³/4 ounce) cans cream of chicken soup	cheese, shredded Bread crumbs for topping
1 cup mayonnaise	

Cook broccoli according to directions on package and drain well. Cook chicken and cut into bite-size pieces. Mix next five ingredients together. Place half the broccoli in casserole dish. Layer half the chicken on top. Pour half the sauce on top. Repeat. Sprinkle top with bread crumbs. Bake at 350° for 30 to 40 minutes.

The Folk Family

Thanksgiving Turkey at the Leary's
The cooking aroma is grand and cold turkey sandwiches are "the best".

1 (10 to 12 pound) turkey	4 stalks celery, cut in 1-inch
1 head garlic, separated	pieces
Salt and pepper	8 ounces Italian dressing
2 onions, quartered	

Rinse turkey and pat dry. Push fingers under skin to loosen. Insert 1/2 clove of garlic in each opening you've made under skin. Continue on until you have inserted 6 or 8 cloves of garlic under skin of breast, back and legs. Sprinkle salt and pepper in cavity and stuff with onion and celery. Turn turkey on end and drizzle Italian dressing under skin. Rub remaining dressing outside turkey. Sprinkle lightly with cracked pepper. Marinate overnight, refrigerated. Add water to marinade and cook turkey in covered roasting pan at 325° for approximately 3 hours. Baste every 30 minutes. Leg will move easily when done. During last 30 minutes; remove lid to brown. Pan Size: Large roaster. Preheat: 325°. Preparation Time: 40 minutes. Cooking Time: 3 hours.

Pat Leary

South African Roast Turkey
The juiciest turkey ever!

1 (14 to 16 pound) turkey	1 cup dry sherry or wine
4 stalks celery, coarsely	1 tablespoon paprika
chopped	2 tablespoons salt
2 large carrots, coarsely	1/4 teaspoon black pepper
chopped	4 cups water
2 cups tomato juice	

Wash turkey and pat dry. Place in a large deep roasting pan. Stuff with celery and carrots. Mix remaining ingredients together and pour over the turkey. Bake at 350° for 3 hours turning the turkey over every half hour. Use oven mitts or heavy rubber gloves to turn turkey. Skin will be crisp while the meat will be moist. Serve sauce separately. Servings: 10 to 12. Pan Size: Large. Preheat: 350°. Cooking Time: 3 hours.

Sue Ann Lipsey

Catfish Delta
A big hit at the Grace St. Luke's Bazaar lunch.

2 tablespoons butter or	1 small bell pepper, finely
margarine	chopped
2 tablespoons flour	2 cups grated Cheddar cheese
1 small onion, chopped	8 ounces fresh sliced
1 cup milk	mushrooms
1/4 teaspoon salt	3 pounds catfish fillets
1/8 teaspoon red pepper	1 cup Hollandaise sauce
1 tablespoon dried parsley	

Melt butter in 2 quart saucepan; add flour and mix well; add onion and cook over low heat for 2 to 5 minutes. Add milk and bring to a slow boil until it thickens. Stir in seasonings, bell pepper, cheese and mushrooms. Cook one minute more. Layer catfish in pan. Pour sauce mixture over top. Cover and bake at 350° for 30 minutes. Serve with Hollandaise sauce on top. Servings: 6 to 8. Pan Size: 9x12-inch pan or 2 quart. Preheat: Yes. Preparation Time: 1 hour. Cooking Time: 45 minutes.

Mrs. William Halliday

Spicy Grilled Catfish

Whole catfish fillet	1 lemon
La Martinique True French	Lemon & pepper seasoning salt
Vinaigrette salad dressing	Worcestershire sauce
Seafood Magic, blackened	
redfish seasoning	

Cover the base of a fish grill basket with aluminum foil. Crimp the edge to form a bowl. Place catfish in foil lined basket. Pour salad dressing over fillet until covered. Pour Worcestershire sauce around the edges of the fillet. Squeeze lemon over all. Season generously with blackened seasoning and lemon & pepper. Prepare charcoal grill. Grill fish in basket for approximately 25 to 30 minutes or until crisp around the edges.

Sellers Shy

Broiled Crappie Fillets
(or any white fish)

1 pound fish fillets	2 tablespoons lemon juice
4 tablespoons chopped	Lawry's seasoned salt
onions	Black pepper
3 tablespoons regular	Paprika
mayonnaise	Buttered bread crumbs
1/2 tablespoon butter	

In a small skillet, sauté onions in butter until clear. Add mayonnaise and then lemon juice and blend well. Remove from heat. Pat fillets dry and sprinkle both sides with Lawry's and lightly pepper. With pastry brush spread both sides with mayonnaise mixture. Place fillets on foil-lined Pyrex dish. Foil should be large enough to completely fold over and cover dish. Sprinkle fillets with bread crumbs and paprika. Cover loosely with foil. Preheat oven to 450°. Bake about 10 minutes covered and then an additional 5 minutes uncovered. Baking time really depends on thickness of fish, watch carefully. Servings: 2.

Helen Hardin

159

Grilled Juniper Ruby Trout

Over wilted greens with black quinoa pilaf and morel mushrooms.

FOR THE CURE:

2 teaspoons juniper berries

1 teaspoon whole white pepper

1/4 teaspoon crushed red pepper

1/2 teaspoon fresh ginger, minced

1/6 orange, zest only

2 teaspoons pickling spice mix

1/4 cup salt

1 cup granulated sugar

Mix all seasonings in a food processor. Add salt and sugar. Makes 2 cups.

TO CURE THE FISH: Trim the filets and cover with just enough of the cure to blanket the fish. After two hours, remove from the cure and grill skin side down. When the fish begins to cook, turn the fish and remove the skin. Serve with a quinoa pilaf:

QUINOA PILAF:

2 cups black quinoa, rinsed

2 cups chicken stock

1/2 onion, minced

1 tablespoon olive oil

1 teaspoon salt

1/4 teaspoon white pepper

Dash Tabasco

1 tablespoon honey

2 teaspoons white wine vinegar

3 tablespoons sliced almonds

Sauté the onion in olive oil and add the remaining ingredients and simmer for about 20 minutes until the quinoa is tender.

(continued on next page)

MORELS:

1 cup fresh morel
   mushrooms
1 tablespoon minced fresh
   garlic
1 tablespoon olive oil
1 tablespoon sherry wine
   vinegar

1 cup Madeira wine
1/2 teaspoon salt
1/8 teaspoon white pepper
Dash Tabasco

Sauté mushrooms and garlic in olive oil and add remaining ingredients.
Cook over high heat until most of the liquid is evaporated.

WILTED GREENS:

3 cups mixed baby lettuce
   or field greens
1 teaspoon minced fresh
   garlic
1/2 teaspoon grated fresh
   ginger
1 tablespoon olive oil

1 tablespoon balsamic
   vinegar
1 orange, juice and zest
1 teaspoon salt
1/4 teaspoon white pepper
Dash Tabasco

In a hot sauté pan, cook the garlic and ginger, then add the field greens
and remaining ingredients (measured out in advance) and quickly wilt
the greens without cooking them. Place them on the plate with the pilaf
and arrange the morels and fish nearby.

Folks in the Kitchen wine recommendation: Kermit Lynch Macon
Villages.

Keystone Ranch
Keystone, CO

Snapper Pecan Sandy

4 (4 ounce) skinless red snapper fillets
1 cup cold milk
2 cups pecan halves
4 tablespoons unsalted butter
1 tablespoon olive oil
1 egg
1/2 cup white wine
1/2 cup chopped shallots
1/2 cup red bell pepper, 1/4-inch dice

1/4 cup green bell pepper, 1/4-inch dice
1/4 cup celery, 1/4-inch dice
1/3 cup clam juice
24 large shrimp, peeled and deveined
Spice Mixture
Garlic mashed potatoes (see vegetable chapter)

Place fish in bowl and add milk to cover. Process pecans in a food processor until a texture similar to bread crumbs in attained. Add one tablespoon of the spice mixture to the pecans and pulse 3 or 4 times to blend. Pour into a pie plate. Heat 2 tablespoons of the butter and olive oil in a large skillet over medium heat. Remove fish from milk. Add the egg to the milk and whisk egg into milk until well blended. Return fish to bowl. When the butter starts to sizzle, remove fish, shake off excess milk and dredge in the pecan mixture. Place in skillet and cook until golden brown on both sides, about 3 minutes per side. Transfer to a cookie sheet that has been lined with paper towels and place in a warm oven. Deglaze the skillet with the white wine. Add remaining butter and shallots. Stir for one minute. Add bell peppers and celery. Stir for another minute and add the clam juice. Stir in one teaspoon of the spice mixture. Add shrimp and cook, stirring just until they turn pink and begin to curl. Remove from heat. Place each snapper fillet on a bed of garlic mashed potatoes. Top each fillet with the shrimp sauce, drizzling some of the remaining liquid over each serving. Serve immediately.

SPICE MIXTURE:
1 teaspoon ground white pepper
1 teaspoon sweet paprika
1 teaspoon dried thyme
1/2 teaspoon cayenne
1/2 teaspoon ground black pepper
1/2 teaspoon sea salt

Combine all ingredients.

John Pfund

162

Cod with a Crust of Herbs

4 (7 ounce) fillets of cod	4 ounces bread crumbs
5 ounces mushrooms	2 eggs
1 pound tomatoes	6 ounces butter
4 ounces parsley	2 tablespoons olive oil
4 shallots	1/2 cup fish stock
4 garlic cloves	1 lemon
1 branch of thyme	1 pinch sugar
	1 pinch salt

Melt the butter. Clean the mushrooms and chop with lemon juice. Chop two shallots and add to the mushrooms. Cook until the water is evaporated. Let cool. Mix in a bowl the chopped parsley, the butter, the bread crumbs and the eggs. Mix and add the mushrooms. Peel the tomatoes (boil them 20 seconds in boiling water). Seed tomatoes and chop them. Cook slowly with olive oil, a pinch of sugar and salt for 30 minutes. Heat the oven at 450°. Cut the garlic in julienne and the two other shallots. Take the flower of thyme. Cover each fillet of cod with the mix. Put in a dish the garlic, shallots, thyme and fish stock. Cook in the oven for about 10 minutes. Put under the broiler for 1 minute to color the crust. Transfer fish to a serving dish.

OPTIONAL: You may add different herbs.

Colonial Country Club
Memphis, Tennessee

Salmon Bake

4 medium salmon fillets	4 teaspoons olive oil
Sliced ginger	4 teaspoons white wine
1 Vidalia onion, sliced	Lemon juice
1 zucchini, grated	Salt and pepper, to taste

Place each fillet on a square of aluminum foil. Put 2 slices of ginger underneath each fillet. Top with onion and zucchini dividing equally. Drizzle each with 1 teaspoon oil, 1 teaspoon wine, a dash of lemon juice and salt and pepper. Seal foil packets and bake at 400° for 25 minutes.

Caroline Orr

Oriental Grilled Salmon

1½ tablespoons brown
   sugar
3 tablespoons water
1 tablespoon low-sodium
   soy sauce
2 teaspoons minced green
   onions
2 teaspoons lemon juice
½ teaspoon minced garlic
Dash of dried crushed red
   pepper
2 teaspoons peeled, minced
   ginger root

2 (4 ounce) salmon steaks,
   ½-inch thick
Vegetable cooking spray
2 tablespoons nonfat
   mayonnaise
1 tablespoon finely chopped
   Cilantro
½ teaspoon peeled grated
   ginger root
¼ teaspoon crushed garlic
Fresh cilantro (optional)

Combine first 8 ingredients in a large, heavy-duty plastic bag. Add salmon steaks. Seal bag and marinate steaks in refrigerator 2 hours, turning bag occasionally. Remove salmon steaks from marinade, reserving marinade. Coat grill rack with cooking spray; place on grill over medium hot coals (350° to 400°). Place steaks on rack; grill, uncovered, 5 to 6 minutes on each side or until fish flakes easily when tested with a fork, basting frequently with reserved marinade. Combine mayonnaise, cilantro, ginger root and garlic, stirring well. Top each salmon steak with 1 tablespoon mayonnaise mixture. Garnish with fresh cilantro if desired. 243 calories, 10.0 g fat (1.7 saturated fat), sodium - 449 mg. Servings: 2. Preparation Time: 2 hours (marinate). Cooking Time: Approximately 12 minutes.

Olin F. Morris

164

Grilled Salmon with Cilantro Butter

Make several batches of the Cilantro Butter and freeze.
It is wonderful with most any fish or grilled chicken.

SALMON FILLETS: Brush salmon with olive oil and lemon juice. Salt and pepper to taste. Grill over medium heat for 4 to 6 minutes a side depending on thickness of fillets. Remove from grill and immediately top with 1 teaspoon Cilantro Butter. Or cook in hot cast iron skillet 4 minutes per side.

CILANTRO BUTTER:

1/2 cup butter, softened
1/2 teaspoon grated lime
peel
2 tablespoons lime juice

1 to 2 tablespoons minced
cilantro
1/8 teaspoon cayenne
pepper, or to taste

Combine ingredients in food processor. Pulse several times to blend.

Kathy Pitts

Grilled Sesame Swordfish

A favorite fish entree from Captain Bilbo's Restaurant.

1 teaspoon Dijon mustard
1 tablespoon minced garlic
2 tablespoons soy sauce
1/2 teaspoon crushed red
pepper
2 tablespoons wine vinegar

3 tablespoons sesame oil
1/4 cup soy bean oil
1 tablespoon honey
4 to 8 (8 ounce) swordfish
fillets

Combine first 8 ingredients for marinade and mix well. Place marinade in plastic bag or shallow pan. Add swordfish. Marinate for 4 hours. Grill fish over low fire for 6 to 10 minutes. Do not overcook! Any fish that can be grilled may be substituted. Servings: 4 to 8. Preparation Time: 20 minutes. Cooking Time: 6 to 10 minutes.

Mike Warr

165

Grilled Lobster with Whiskey

2 live 2 pound lobsters	Chopped garlic
3 tablespoons melted butter	Salt and pepper
Whiskey	1 shallot, chopped
Salt and pepper	1½ ounces whiskey
3 tablespoons soft butter	8 ounces lobster stock
2 to 3 tablespoons fresh	Lemon juice, squeeze
bread crumbs	Salt
Chopped parsley	Butter

Remove claws from lobsters and boil for 5 minutes, remove meat from shells and set aside. Split lobsters in half. Remove sand sack and brain. Spoon liver and eggs into small bowl; set aside. Brush inside of lobster with melted butter and whiskey, sprinkle with salt and pepper. Place the lobsters open side down on a hot grill. Cook until shell is red half way up, turn over. In the small bowl with liver, add butter, bread crumbs, parsley, chopped garlic, salt and pepper. Mix and spoon into open cavity of lobsters on grill. If possible, cover grill and cook until stuffing is done, 5 minutes.

SAUCE: In sauté pan, cook chopped shallots in small amount of butter until soft, add whiskey and flame. When flame is out add lobster stock, lemon juice and salt. Reduce by half. Add butter and blend until fully mixed, add claw meat to heat right before serving. Servings: 2.

Folks in the Kitchen wine recommendation: Kistler McCrea Chardonnay.

Biba Restaurant
Boston, MA

Scallops Supreme

1½ pounds scallops
4 to 5 tablespoons unsalted
   butter
½ roll garlic cheese
2 teaspoons chardonnay
   wine

¼ can chicken broth
Cooked white rice
Fresh parsley for garnish

Melt butter in a large skillet. Add scallops and cook, stirring frequently over medium heat for 2 to 3 minutes or until scallops are opaque. To prepare sauce, mix together cheese, wine and chicken broth in a small saucepan. Heat until cheese is melted and mixture is bubbly hot. To serve, spoon rice onto serving plate. Arrange scallops on top and spoon sauce over. Garnish with parsley. Servings: 4.

Marilyn Newton

California Seafood

2 garlic cloves, finely diced
1 white onion, finely diced
1 green pepper, finely diced
3 tablespoons olive oil
8 ounce can tomato sauce
1 (10½ ounce) can peeled
   tomatoes, chopped
1 bottle clam juice

1 cup white wine
½ pound shrimp, shelled
½ pound bay scallops
1 pound monkfish or halibut,
   cut into pieces
1 (7½ ounce) can crabmeat
3 bay leaves

In an 8 quart pan, sauté garlic, onion, and green pepper in olive oil for 2 minutes. Add tomato sauce, tomatoes, clam juice and white wine. Bring to a boil, while stirring. Add remaining ingredients. Simmer for 20 to 30 minutes. Serve in soup bowls with crusty French bread. Servings: 4 to 6. Pan Size: 8 quart. Preparation Time: 15 minutes. Cooking Time: 45 minutes.

Charles E. White, M.D.

Crab and Shrimp Etouffe

*Originally published in Jambalaya, the official cookbook
for the 1984 Louisiana World Exposition.*

1¹/₂ sticks butter
1 cup finely chopped onion
¹/₂ cup finely chopped green pepper
¹/₂ cup finely chopped celery
4 cloves garlic, minced
4 teaspoons cornstarch
1 to 1¹/₂ cups chicken broth
¹/₂ cup white wine
4 teaspoons tomato paste
¹/₄ cup finely chopped green onions
¹/₄ cup finely chopped fresh parsley
1 tablespoon Worcestershire sauce
3 pounds fresh shrimp, shelled and deveined
Salt, pepper and Tabasco, to taste
1 pound crabmeat

In a large pot, melt butter. Add onion, green pepper and celery and sauté until tender. Add garlic. Dissolve cornstarch in 1 cup of chicken broth and add to vegetables. Add wine, stirring constantly. Add tomato paste, green onions, parsley and Worcestershire. Add shrimp and continue to stir until well combined. Cover and simmer for 10 minutes, stirring occasionally. If necessary, add remaining chicken broth. Add salt, pepper and Tabasco. Add crabmeat, stirring gently and continue to cook until heated through. Serve over steamed rice. Servings: 6 plus. Pan Size: Dutch oven. Preparation Time: 1 hour. Cooking Time: 45 minutes to 1 hour.

J. Mark Hansen

168

Easy Shrimp Stuffed Eggplant

This recipe has been handed down to me from three generations of fabulous cooks. Now, I pass the torch of my family recipe on to you!

4 medium eggplant
2 medium onions, diced
6 cloves garlic, diced
1/2 cup diced celery
1/2 cup diced green pepper
1/2 pound ground chuck
1/2 pound medium shrimp, chopped
1 cup chopped ripe tomatoes

2 eggs, beaten
2 cups cracker crumbs
2 tablespoons Cajun seasoning
Salt and pepper, to taste
Paprika
1 teaspoon olive oil (optional)

If ground chuck is lean, add 1 teaspoon olive oil to assist in sautéing. In a medium-size skillet, sauté onions, garlic, celery, green pepper and ground chuck until meat is browned and vegetables are wilted. Drain. Cut eggplants in half vertically. Scoop out pulp and set shells aside on a shallow baking pan. Put pulp in a large pot and cover with water. Cook over medium heat until tender, about 10 to 15 minutes. Drain well and place in a large bowl to cool. When cool, add shrimp, tomatoes, eggs, 1 cup cracker crumbs, Cajun seasoning, and meat mixture. Stir to combine. Add salt and pepper, to taste. Mound into eggplant shells. Sprinkle with remaining 1 cup cracker crumbs and paprika. Pour 1/4 cup water in bottom of pan to steam shells. Bake at 375° for 45 minutes or until shells are done.

Dr. Denise Mustiful-Martin

169

Feta Shrimp

1 cup finely chopped green
  onions
6 tablespoons olive oil
4 large ripe tomatoes,
  seeded and chopped
1 medium clove garlic,
  peeled and minced
2 tablespoons minced
  parsley, fresh if possible

1 teaspoon salt
Fresh ground pepper
1/2 teaspoon oregano
21/2 pounds raw medium
  shrimp, peeled
1/2 pound feta cheese,
  crumbled
1 cup chopped black olives
Cooked rice for 6

Sauté onions in olive oil until tender. Add tomatoes, garlic, parsley, salt, pepper, and oregano. Simmer mixture for 3 to 5 minutes, stirring constantly. Add shrimp and continue to cook until shrimp are pink in color. Stir in cheese and ripe olives. Serve over cooked rice, may garnish with additional parsley. Servings: 6. Pan Size: Large skillet. Preparation Time: 15 to 20 minutes. Cooking Time: 20 minutes (approximately).

Mabel McNeill

Shrimp Victoria

1 small onion, chopped
3/4 pound shrimp, peeled
  and deveined
2 tablespoons butter
21/2 ounces sliced mushrooms

11/2 teaspoons flour
1/2 teaspoon salt
1/2 cup sour cream
Cooking sherry, to taste
Cooked rice

Sauté onion and shrimp in butter for 10 minutes. Add mushrooms and sauté for 5 more minutes. Sprinkle in flour and salt. Cook over low heat stirring. Add sour cream. Cook 10 more minutes. Add sherry. Stir until well combined and heated through. Serve over rice. Servings: 4. Pan Size: Large sauté pan. Preparation Time: 25 minutes (if the shrimp have been peeled and deveined). Cooking Time: 25 minutes.

Dottie Weir

Oven Barbecue Shrimp

A different version! Messy and fun, lay out newspapers and serve lots of napkins!

1½ sticks butter (a must!)
1 cup and 4 tablespoons vegetable oil
2 teaspoons finely minced garlic
4 whole bay leaves, crushed fine
2 teaspoons washed and dried rosemary leaves
½ teaspoon dried basil
½ teaspoon oregano
½ teaspoon salt
½ teaspoon cayenne pepper
1 tablespoon paprika
¾ teaspoon black pepper
1 teaspoon fresh lemon juice
2 pounds fresh shrimp in shell

In a large ovenproof pan, melt butter and oil over medium heat. Add remaining ingredients except shrimp. Cook stirring constantly until mixture comes to a boil. Reduce heat and simmer 7 to 8 minutes stirring frequently. Remove pan from heat and let stand at room temperature for at least 30 minutes or until cool. Add shrimp to cooled mixture and cook over medium heat for 6 to 8 minutes or until shrimp turn pink. Put in preheated 450° oven and bake for 10 minutes. Serve in large bowls with sauce ladled over. French bread is a must for soaking up sauce. Serve with salad and stuffed potatoes for a great, fun meal.

Nancy Chandler

171

Shrimp Creole

1/3 cup vegetable oil
1/4 cup flour
1 bunch green onions, chopped
1/3 cup chopped celery
1 cup chopped onions
1/2 cup chopped green pepper
2 teaspoons minced garlic
3 tablespoons minced parsley
1 (1 pound) can chopped tomatoes, drained
1 (8 ounce) can tomato sauce
4 tablespoons dry red wine

4 bay leaves
6 whole allspice
2 whole cloves
1 teaspoon salt
3/4 teaspoon ground black pepper
1/4 to 1/2 teaspoon cayenne
1/4 teaspoon chili powder
1/4 teaspoon mace
1/4 teaspoon basil
1/2 teaspoon thyme
4 teaspoons fresh lemon juice
2 cups water
2 pounds shrimp, shelled
Cooked rice

Mix together oil and flour and cook in microwave for about 7 minutes or until the color of peanut butter. Put green onions, celery, onions, green pepper, garlic and parsley in a large pot. When roux is ready, pour over vegetables and cook over low heat stirring until they are soft. Add tomatoes, tomato sauce, wine, all seasonings and lemon juice. Add water and simmer for 45 minutes. Add shrimp and cook for 5 to 10 minutes or until shrimp are done. Serve over rice. Servings: 4 to 6. Pan Size: 5 quart. Preparation Time: 20 to 30 minutes.

Joel Cox

Easy Shrimp Curry

Great for a quick, fun dinner. Add salad and bread for a great meal!

2 medium onions, chopped
1 stick butter or margarine
1½ pounds medium
    shrimp, peeled and deveined
2 cans cream of shrimp soup

½ cup dry white wine
1 pint sour cream
½ teaspoon curry powder,
    or to taste

Sauté onions in butter until done. Add shrimp, heat through and mix in soup and wine. Cook over medium heat, stirring for about 10 minutes or until shrimp are done. Add sour cream and curry powder and stir until heated through. Serve over steamed white rice. Offer the following condiments on the side: chutney, coconut, white raisins and pine nuts. Servings: 6. Preparation Time: 20 to 30 minutes. Cooking Time: 15 to 20 minutes.

Charlane Lane

Crawfish Etouffee

2 pounds crawfish tails
Tony Chachere's Creole
    Seasoning
¾ cup vegetable oil
⅔ cup flour
1½ cups chopped onions
1 large green pepper,
    chopped

1 to 2 stalks celery, chopped
4 to 5 tablespoons minced
    fresh parsley
Several dashes of hot sauce
2 cloves garlic, minced
16 ounces cream cheese
    (use fat free, if desired)
1½ cups water

In a large stock pot, heat vegetable oil and flour over medium low heat. Stir until roux becomes a light peanut color. Add crawfish tails, Creole Seasoning, onions, green pepper, celery, parsley, hot sauce and garlic. Cook, covered for 5 to 10 minutes. Add cream cheese, stirring constantly over medium heat. Stir until cheese melts. Pour in water and cook for 20 minutes over low heat, stirring frequently. Adjust seasonings. Servings: 6 cups.

Jeannie Jones

Seafood and Poultry

Charlie Settoon's Crawfish Etouffee

4 bunches green onions,
  chopped
1 medium white onion,
  chopped
2 medium bell peppers,
  chopped
2 stalks celery, chopped
1 clove garlic, chopped
2 teaspoons chopped
  pimento

3/4 cup vegetable oil
2 pounds crawfish tails
Tabasco, to taste
Worcestershire, to taste
Salt, to taste
2 heaping tablespoons flour
1/4 cup vegetable oil

In a heavy pot, sauté vegetables in oil over medium heat until tender, stirring frequently. Add crawfish and 1½ to 2 cups water to make sauce. Add Tabasco, Worcestershire and salt to taste. In a separate skillet, mix together flour and 1/4 cup oil. Cook over medium heat, stirring until brown. Add to crawfish. Cook covered over medium heat for 20 minutes. Remove from heat and let stand covered for 30 minutes. Serve over rice.

Jan Flagan

Easy Crawfish Etouffee

1 stick butter
1 medium onion, chopped
1 green bell pepper,
  chopped
1 can cream of mushroom
  soup

1 pound package crawfish
  tails with fat
Season to taste with: salt,
  black pepper, cayenne
  pepper, basil, thyme and
  Tabasco

Melt butter in a large cast iron skillet. Add onion and bell pepper and sauté for 3 to 4 minutes. Add soup and stir well to combine. Add crawfish tails and seasonings and cook over medium heat for 20 minutes, stirring occasionally. Serve over hot rice, enjoy! Servings: 6. Cooking Time: 25 minutes.

Julianne Hall

174

Shrimp and Rice Casserole

1 (6 ounce) box Uncle Ben's
   long grain and wild rice
2 tablespoons butter or oil
1 cup diced green pepper
1 cup diced onion
1 cup diced celery
1½ pounds shrimp, cooked

1 teaspoon curry powder
1 teaspoon Worcestershire
   sauce
¾ cup mayonnaise
Salt and pepper, to taste
½ cup white wine
Minced parsley

Cook rice according to package directions and set aside. Sauté green pepper, onion, and celery in butter until tender. In a large bowl, combine vegetables with cooked rice. Add remaining ingredients except parsley and stir until well combined. Pour into a greased 9x13-inch casserole or a round 2 quart casserole. Cover and bake at 350° for 45 minutes or until thoroughly heated. Sprinkle with minced parsley.

Mrs. Roane Waring

M.A.'s Seafood Casserole

Delicious! Always receives rave reviews!

1 cup lump crab meat
1 pound cooked and peeled
   shrimp
1 cup lobster (optional)
1 cup sharp Cheddar
   cheese, grated
1 cup celery, finely chopped
¼ to ½ bell pepper, finely
   chopped

1 cup mayonnaise
1 to 2 dashes Tabasco
Salt and freshly ground
   black pepper, to taste
Corn flake crumbs (corn
   flakes coarsely crumbled
   are best)

Mix all ingredients except crumbs. Place in ungreased casserole dish. Top with ½ inch corn flake crumbs. Bake in preheated 350° oven 30 to 45 minutes or until bubbling. Servings: 6. Pan Size: 1½ quart casserole. Preheat: 350°.

Margaret Ann Eikner

Easy Salmon Loaf

1 can salmon
1/3 cup celery, chopped
1/3 cup onion, chopped
3 eggs
1 cup Cheddar cheese,
   shredded

1 tablespoon lemon juice
1/2 teaspoon salt
1/8 teaspoon pepper
1/2 cup cracker crumbs
1/2 cup mayonnaise

Combine all ingredients and bake in loaf pan for 45 minutes at 350°.
Easy and very good!

Carolyn Gates

Avocado Lemon Butter for Fish

Especially good in the summertime on top of grilled or broiled fish.

1/2 cup unsalted butter,
   softened
1/2 cup mashed ripe
   avocado
2 garlic cloves, minced

21/2 tablespoons Italian
   parsley, minced
51/2 tablespoons fresh
   lemon juice
Pinch salt

Whip the butter with a whisk until very creamy. Beat in the avocado,
garlic, parsley, lemon juice and salt. Chill in refrigerator, then roll into log
shape using wax paper. Cut into rounds and serve on top of fish.
Servings: 6 to 8. Preparation Time: 20 to 30 minutes.

Beth Worley

SPONSORED BY

Jim and Carol Prentiss

Pasta

Cajun Pasta

1 pound crawfish tail meat,
   thawed
1/2 pound Tasso ham
1 quart whipping cream

2 tablespoons Cajun seasonings
2 pounds angel hair pasta
Dash Tabasco sauce, if desired
Fresh grated Parmesan cheese

Rinse crawfish in cold water. Cube tasso ham in 1/4-inch pieces. Pour quart of whipping cream in large skillet; add Cajun seasonings and cook on medium high. Bring cream to boil and simmer to thicken. Stir constantly to keep from scorching. Add more Cajun seasonings to reach the desired flavor. When mixture has been reduced to almost half, add the crawfish and ham. Continue to stir constantly for another 5 to 8 minutes until the crawfish and ham are heated through. Do not over cook. Serve over angel hair pasta that has been cooked and drained. Mix lightly and sprinkle with fresh Parmesan cheese. Servings: 8 to 10. Preparation Time: 45 minutes to 1 hour.

John C. Jones

Penne with Spicy Lemon Sauce

1 cup lemon juice
1 cup heavy cream
1 teaspoon crushed hot
   chilies
2 cups chicken stock
1 teaspoon crushed garlic
4 ounces sweet butter
1/2 box penne pasta
1 bunch green asparagus

2 artichoke bottoms
1 bunch scallions
1 bunch fresh mint
1 avocado
6 raw shrimp
1/2 cup cornstarch
Dash salt
Dash white pepper

Melt butter in saucepan. Add chopped garlic, hot chilies. Simmer for 2 minutes. Add lemon juice, and bring to a boil. Add cream, chicken stock, salt and white pepper. Bring to a boil for 5 minutes. Add cornstarch and water to thicken. Set aside. Dice shrimp and lightly sauté. Add sauce. Add cooked penne. Bring to a boil for 1 minute. Add cooked artichoke, diced scallions and asparagus. Simmer for 1 to 2 minutes. Garnish with chopped mint and a slice of avocado. Serve. Servings: 4.

Folks in the Kitchen wine recommendation: Santa Margherita Pinot Grigio.

Le Dome
Los Angeles, CA

178

Shrimp and Pasta Stir-Fry

1/2 pound medium fresh shrimp
1/4 cup nonfat mayonnaise
1/4 cup canned low sodium chicken broth
1 teaspoon grated lemon rind
1 tablespoon fresh lemon juice
Vegetable cooking spray

2 teaspoons vegetable oil
2 tablespoons peeled and grated fresh ginger
1 clove garlic, minced
1 cup fresh asparagus, sliced diagonally into 1-inch pieces
2 cups hot cooked penne, cooked without salt or fat
1/4 teaspoon lemon & pepper seasoning salt

Peel and devein shrimp. Set aside. Combine mayonnaise and next 3 ingredients in a bowl; stir well with a wire whisk; set aside. Coat a large nonstick skillet or wok with cooking spray; add oil, and place over medium-high heat until hot. Add ginger and garlic, stir-fry 1 minute. Add shrimp and asparagus, stir-fry 3 minutes or until shrimp is done. Add mayonnaise mixture and pasta. Cook until thoroughly heated. Sprinkle with lemon & pepper. Servings: 2. Pan Size: Wok or large skillet. Preparation Time: 5 minutes. Cooking Time: 7 minutes.

Carol Prentiss

Pasta

Fettucine with Shrimp

8 ounces fettucine
1/2 stick butter
2 cloves garlic, minced
4 ounces mushrooms, sliced
1 pound shrimp (2 dozen medium/large), peeled
1/4 red pepper, diced
1 teaspoon dried basil, or 1 tablespoon fresh

1/2 teaspoon oregano, or 1 1/2 teaspoons fresh
1/2 cup cream, warm
1 tablespoon sherry
Salt and pepper
Parsley, for topping
Parmesan cheese

Cook pasta. In large skillet, melt butter, add garlic and mushrooms. Sauté. Add shrimp and red pepper. Cook until shrimp are done. Add basil, oregano, cream and sherry. Add salt and pepper to taste. Drain pasta. Return to pot. Pour in sauce, toss. Add Parmesan cheese to thicken slightly. Top with parsley. Servings: 2 to 3.

Ann Page

Lemon Shrimp with Pasta
A fresh creation!

6 garlic cloves, finely chopped
1 bunch green onions
3 tablespoons olive oil
1/2 pound (31 to 35 count) shrimp

Lemon and herb seasoning
Romano cheese, for topping
Capers, for topping
1 small package angel hair pasta, cooked according to package directions

Sauté garlic and tops of green onions (cut in 1/4-inch slices) in olive oil until garlic is nutty brown. Over medium heat, add peeled shrimp and sprinkle generously with lemon and herb seasoning. Cook until shrimp are pink, about 5 minutes. Spoon over cooked pasta. Grate fresh Romano cheese over dish and sprinkle capers on top. Serve immediately. Servings: 6 medium servings: Pan Size: Large skillet. Preparation Time: 15 minutes. Cooking Time: 15 minutes.

Gay and Mike Williams

180

Mardi Gras Pasta

Thanks to my friend for sharing this recipe.

2 ounces clarified butter
1 tablespoon garlic, chopped
1 tablespoon onion, chopped
1 tablespoon red pepper, diced
1 tablespoon yellow pepper, diced
1 ounce Andouille sausage, julienne
2 ounces jumbo crabmeat

2 ounces crawfish tails
2 ounces peeled shrimp
1 ounce white wine
Juice of 1 lemon
2 cups heavy cream
Salt and cayenne pepper, to taste
Angel hair pasta

Melt butter in saucepan and sauté garlic, onion, peppers and sausage over medium heat. Add crawfish, crabmeat and shrimp. Sauté until shrimp are pink. Add wine and lemon juice and sauté. Add cream, bring to gentle boil. Add salt and pepper. Serve over pasta. Servings: 4.

Annette Poole

Linguine with Shrimp and Red Peppers

1 package tomato basil linguine
1 stick butter or margarine
1 pound shrimp, peeled

1 tablespoon garlic, chopped
1/2 red bell pepper, coarsely chopped

Cook pasta according to directions. Drain and rinse. Sauté garlic in butter. Add shrimp and peppers and cook for several minutes or until shrimp turn pink. Add hot cooked pasta. Mix together and serve immediately. Servings: 4.

Marilyn Newton

181

Pasta

Pasta with Mushrooms, Sherry and Cream

5 tablespoons butter
1 1/2 cups chopped onions
  (Vidalia, if possible)
1 pound fresh mushrooms,
  sliced
1/2 cup heavy cream
2 tablespoons sherry

Thyme, salt and pepper, to
  taste
1 package fresh pasta
Minced parsley
Freshly grated Parmesan
  cheese

In a large skillet, melt butter. Add onions and lightly brown. Add mushrooms and cook a few minutes. Add cream, sherry and spices. Cook about 5 minutes or until thickened. Cook and drain pasta. In a bowl, toss pasta with sauce. Sprinkle with parsley and Parmesan. Servings: 4.

Tim McCarver

Linguine with Turkey Sausage and Pesto
Other pastas may be substituted.

2 tablespoons olive oil
3/4 pound fully cooked
  turkey sausage, cut into
  1/2-inch pieces
1 red bell pepper, diced
6 large mushrooms (about 6
  ounces), sliced
4 green onions, thinly sliced

3/4 pound linguine, freshly
  cooked
1/2 cup purchased pesto
1/2 cup grated Parmesan
  cheese
Additional grated Parmesan
  cheese
Salt and pepper, to taste

Heat olive oil in heavy, large skillet over medium-high heat. Add sausage, bell pepper, mushrooms and green onions. Sauté mixture until vegetables are soft, about 7 minutes. Add pasta, pesto sauce and Parmesan. Toss until mixture is combined. Season to taste with salt and pepper. Pass additional Parmesan. Servings: 4. Pan Size: Large skillet. Preparation Time: 30 minutes. Cooking Time: 10 to 12 minutes.

Elizabeth Woodmansee

Folk's Folly Doggie Bag Pasta

How to feed six people on a single "to go box".

1 (.88 ounce) package dried morel mushrooms
1½ ounces sun-dried tomatoes
1 tablespoon olive oil
1 package Knorr garlic and herb pasta sauce mix
1 cup milk
½ cup water

1 tablespoon butter
6 ounces or more Folk's Folly cooked beef, thinly sliced
¼ cup Parmesan cheese
Salt and pepper, to taste
8 ounces fettucine or other pasta

Follow package directions for soaking mushrooms and tomatoes. Drain mushrooms, reserving liquid. Slice each mushroom into 2 to 3 pieces. Heat olive oil in a deep skillet. Sauté the mushrooms about 3 minutes. Drain and chop the tomatoes. Mix the Knorr sauce with the milk, water and butter according to directions. Add to the skillet with the tomatoes and ¼ cup strained mushroom liquid. Cook, stirring constantly until sauce thickens, about 5 minutes. Add sliced meat and ¼ cup Parmesan cheese and stir until heated through. Cook pasta according to package directions. Toss with sauce in a heated pasta dish. Top with additional Parmesan cheese if desired. Servings: 6. Pan Size: 2 quart. Preparation Time: 10 minutes. Cooking Time: 10 to 15 minutes.

Helen Saino

183

Pasta

Chicken and Peppers Pasta

1 red pepper, coarsely
  chopped
1 yellow pepper, coarsely
  chopped
1 yellow onion, coarsely
  chopped
3 tablespoons olive oil
1 teaspoon Worcestershire

4 large boneless, skinless
  chicken breasts
Hickory smoked salt
3 tomatoes
Small package angel hair
  pasta, prepared
  according to directions
Romano cheese for topping

In medium-size skillet, cook peppers and onion in olive oil over medium heat. Add Worcestershire. Sauté vegetables until tender. Set aside. Grill chicken breasts, sprinkling with hickory smoked salt. Chop tomatoes into one inch cubes and chill. Remove chicken from grill and cut into bite-size pieces. Spoon pepper and onion mixture over prepared pasta. Add warm chicken, grated Romano cheese and top with chilled tomatoes. Servings: 6 medium. Preparation Time: 20 minutes. Cooking Time: 30 minutes.

Gay and Mike Williams

Chicken Spaghetti

*From my mother's kitchen and a family favorite. Makes
3 full quarts for separate casseroles or 1 large dish to serve 15.*

1 onion, chopped
2 stalks celery, sliced
1 small bell pepper, chopped
1/2 stick butter
2 cans cream of chicken
  soup
1 (7 ounce) jar pimentos,
  undrained

1 can Rotel diced tomatoes
1 pound Velveeta, cubed
1 chicken or 6 chicken
  breasts, boiled, deboned,
  cut up
7 ounces spaghetti, cooked
  and drained

Sauté onions, celery and bell pepper in butter. Add soup, pimentos, tomatoes, Velveeta and chicken. Stir to melt cheese. Add pasta and mix thoroughly. Cover and bake at 400° for 15 to 20 minutes. Servings: 15. Pan Size: 3 quart.

Judy S. Hurdle

184

Mary's Chicken Spaghetti

6 chicken breasts	2 pounds Velveeta, cut into
2 large green peppers,	small cubes
chopped	1 can tiny peas, drained
2 large onions, chopped	1 large can mushrooms,
1½ sticks butter	sliced and drained
1 can Rotel tomatoes, chopped	1 (7 ounce) package vermicelli
2 tablespoons Worcestershire	Salt and pepper, to taste

Season and cook chicken in enough water to make 1½ quarts of broth. In a large skillet, sauté peppers and onions in butter. Remove chicken from broth. Save broth to cook vermicelli in. Add Rotel tomatoes and Worcestershire to peppers and onions. Add cubed Velveeta, peas and mushrooms. Cook and add vermicelli. Add chicken that has been pulled from bone and cut in pieces. Salt and pepper to taste. Continue to cook until heated through. Serve immediately or freeze and bake at 350° for 30 minutes or until bubbly. Preheat: 350°. Preparation Time: 2 hours. Cooking Time: 30 to 45 minutes.

Mary Garrett

Spinach Lasagna

For everyone - even people who dislike spinach - like me!

2 small boxes lasagna noodles	1½ teaspoons thyme
2 (10 ounce) packages	1½ teaspoons basil
chopped spinach	1½ teaspoons pepper
4 cups grated mozzarella cheese	2 (16 ounce) jars of your
1 cup Parmesan cheese	favorite spaghetti sauce
4 eggs	with mushrooms

Cook noodles as directed on box. Cook spinach as directed on package, drain and let cool for 15 minutes. Beat together eggs, thyme, basil, and pepper. In a separate bowl, mix spinach, mozzarella cheese and Parmesan cheese. Add to egg mixture. Layer noodles, spinach mixture, sauce and end with noodles. Top with sauce and sprinkle with grated mozzarella cheese. Bake at 350° for 40 minutes covered, then uncover and bake for an additional 15 minutes. Servings: 8 to 10. Pan Size: 10x13-inches. Preheat: 350°. Preparation Time: 25 minutes. Cooking Time: 40 minutes covered then 15 minutes uncovered.

Ann Floyd

Pasta

Dan's Noodles

Based on a recipe by Dan Canale.
This dish makes even better leftovers!

1 large can whole tomatoes	2 tablespoons parsley,
3 large white onions	chopped
1 cup olive oil	4 cups water
1/2 clove garlic, minced	1/2 cup dried mushrooms,
1 stalk celery, chopped	chopped
1/2 teaspoon rosemary	1 package extra wide egg
1/2 teaspoon sweet basil	noodles
Pinch of sage	2 cups sharp Cheddar
1/2 teaspoon thyme	cheese, grated
1 dried red pepper, chopped	1/2 cup Parmesan cheese

In a large pot, break up tomatoes by hand until liquid. Slice onions into half circles and separate. Add to tomatoes. Add olive oil and stir. Add garlic, celery, rosemary, basil, sage, thyme and red pepper. Stir. Sprinkle parsley over mixture. Cook over medium-high heat. In separate saucepan, add water to mushrooms. Boil, cover and set aside for 20 minutes. Add to tomato mixture. Stir. Alternate cooking on low heat and resting on counter for 24 hours. When mixture is ready, cook noodles, grease pan with tomato gravy and layer noodles, gravy and Cheddar cheese. Repeat. Top with Parmesan cheese. Bake at 350° for 30 to 50 minutes. Leftovers can be reheated in a frying pan with butter. Serve with an avocado salad, French bread and a bottle of Chianti. Servings: 10. Pan Size: 9x13-inches (makes 2). Preheat: 350°. Preparation Time: 30 minutes.

Vanessa H. Alley

Mom's Cannelloni

CREPES/CANNELLONI:
1 cup flour
2 eggs
1/4 teaspoon salt

1 cup milk
2 tablespoons melted butter

FILLING:
2 1/2 cups boiled chopped
chicken
1/2 cup well-drained chopped
spinach
2 cups (1/4 pound) chopped
mushrooms sautéed in 2
tablespoons butter

1/3 cup grated Parmesan
cheese
1 egg
1 egg yolk
Salt and pepper, to taste
2/3 cup pine nuts, chopped
(optional)

SAUCE:
1 tablespoon flour
1/4 cup melted butter
1 1/2 cups milk
1 egg yolk

3 tablespoons grated
Parmesan cheese
Salt and pepper, to taste

Mix all cannelloni ingredients. Make cannelloni with crepe maker following instructions or use 7-inch skillet. Place approximately 1/8 to 1/4 cup batter in pan (buttered or sprayed with cooking spray and hot). Swirl batter around to cover pan (quickly), cook until ever so slightly brown. Mix all ingredients in filling together. Spoon 2 rounded tablespoons of filling in center of cannelloni. Spread, roll and place cannelloni in baking dish sprayed with cooking spray. Sauce: Combine flour and melted butter, cook for 1 minute and slowly add milk, salt and pepper. Remove mixture from heat when thickened. Add 1 egg yolk and grated cheese. Pour sauce over top of center of cannelloni and bake at 350° approximately 20 minutes or until heated through. Servings: approximately 6 or 12 to 15 cannelloni. Pan Size: Crepe maker or 7-inch skillet. Preheat: 350°. Preparation Time: 1 1/2 hours. Cooking Time: 20 minutes.

Debbie Drago Wilemon

Manicotti

MEAT SAUCE:

1 pound ground chuck
1 pound ground round
1 large onion, chopped
1/4 to 1/2 cup chopped bell
  pepper

1 (16 ounce) can tomato paste
4 (16 ounce) cans tomato sauce
1/4 teaspoon oregano
1/2 teaspoon pepper
1 clove garlic, crushed

RICOTTA FILLING:

1 package manicotti shells
16 ounces Ricotta cheese
1/3 cup shredded Parmesan
  cheese

2 eggs
2 cups shredded mozzarella
  cheese
Additional Parmesan

Brown beef with onion and pepper, drain, add remaining sauce ingredients and simmer for 1 hour. Cook shells according to package directions. Mix all ingredients for filling. Stuff cooked shells with filling. Put 1/2 meat mixture in large Pyrex baking dish, put stuffed shells on top, add remaining sauce over stuffed shells, sprinkle Parmesan cheese on top. Bake uncovered 375° for about 45 minutes.

NOTE: Can be divided into smaller Pyrex dishes and frozen.

Lina P. Karlson

Pasta Johnnie

*This recipe was given to me by a friend from Verrua, PO,
Pavia (Italy), a small village outside of Milan, Italy.*

2 onions, chopped
2 Knorr chicken bouillon
  cubes
1/2 cup white or red wine
4 tablespoons olive oil
2 cans Progresso tomatoes
  with basil

1 small can tomato paste
Oregano, to taste
Basil, to taste
2 tablespoons parsley
2 pounds fusilli pasta
Fresh grated Parmesan or
  reginato cheese

Combine onions, one bouillon cube, wine and 2 tablespoons olive oil.
Sauté. Add tomatoes and remaining bouillon cube. Cook until tomatoes
are soft. Add tomato paste to thicken to desired consistency. Add
oregano, basil and parsley to taste. Cook pasta in salted water with
remaining olive oil. Add to sauce and mix together gently. Add
Parmesan or reginato cheese to taste. Serve with French bread, Bartard
or Country loaf and extra cheese. Servings: 8. Cooking Time:
Preparation and cooking time, about 1 hour total.

Robert H. Buckman

Spaghetti Carbonara

4 slices bacon
2 tablespoons olive oil
2 tablespoons butter
1 clove garlic, minced
1 cup ham, julienned
  (approximately 4 ounces)
8 ounces spaghetti
1 bunch broccoli flowerets

1/3 cup grated Parmesan cheese
1/4 cup parsley, chopped
1/2 teaspoon salt
1/4 teaspoon pepper
3 eggs, beaten
1/4 cup sliced ripe olives
1 ounce diced pimentos

Cook bacon and set aside. Add oil, butter, garlic and ham to pan. Sauté
slightly. Cook pasta, according to package. When it is almost done, add
broccoli to water. Boil about 2 minutes. Drain. Add spaghetti, broccoli,
crumbled bacon, cheese, parsley, salt and pepper to frying pan. Turn off
heat. Pour eggs over mixture and quickly toss to coat spaghetti evenly.
Add olives and pimentos. Toss. Top with parsley and serve at once.
Servings: 4.

Ann Page

Baked Ziti

1 pound ziti	2 tablespoons chopped fresh
12 ounces ricotta cheese	parsley
2 eggs, beaten	1 (27½ ounce) can
¾ cup grated Parmesan	spaghetti sauce
cheese, divided	8 ounces mozzarella
½ teaspoon salt	cheese, cut into ½-inch
¼ teaspoon pepper	cubes

Cook ziti in a large pot of boiling, salted water until tender but firm, about 10 to 12 minutes. Drain and rinse under cold running water. Drain again. In a medium bowl, combine ricotta, eggs, ½ cup Parmesan cheese, salt, pepper and parsley. Mix to blend well. Toss cooked ziti with 2 cups spaghetti sauce. Place half of pasta in baking dish. Top with ricotta mixture and half of the mozzarella cubes. Top with remaining ziti, spaghetti sauce, mozzarella cubes and Parmesan cheese. Bake at 350° until ziti is heated through and cheese bubbles, 30 to 35 minutes. Servings: 4 to 6. Pan Size: 11x14-inches. Preheat: 350°. Cooking Time: 30 to 35 minutes.

Margaret McNeil

Quick Tomato Sauce for Pasta

¼ cup olive oil	1½ teaspoons salt
1 medium onion, finely	½ teaspoon freshly ground
chopped	black pepper
3 garlic cloves, minced	2 leaves fresh basil or 1
4 cups canned Italian plum	teaspoon dried basil
tomatoes or 2 pounds ripe	3 tablespoons tomato paste
tomatoes	

Heat the oil in a heavy saucepan, add the onion and garlic, and sauté over medium heat for a few minutes until golden. Do not brown. Add the canned tomatoes with their liquid (or the fresh tomatoes, peeled, seeded and coarsely chopped). Cook over medium-high heat for 10 minutes until liquid is reduced by about a third. Add the salt, pepper, basil and tomato paste and let the sauce cook at medium-high heat for 5 minutes more. Servings: Makes about 3 cups. Preparation Time: 10 minutes. Cooking Time: 20 minutes.

Beth Worley

Sicilian Pasta Gravy (Sauce)

Traditional and very old recipe from Sicilian friends.

SAUCE:

1 pound pork neckbones
2 tablespoons olive oil
1 large white onion, chopped
4 cloves garlic, chopped
2 (16 ounce) cans tomatoes
4 (8 ounce) cans tomato paste

1 (8 ounce) can water
2 tablespoons parsley
2 tablespoons basil
2 tablespoons oregano
Salt and pepper, to taste
Crushed red pepper, to taste

4 pounds Italian sausage

MEAT BALLS:

3 pounds ground chuck,
   mixed with 1 pound
   ground pork
1 cup grated Parmesan cheese

1 cup bread crumbs
2 eggs
Salt and pepper, to taste
Chopped fresh parsley
2 tablespoons olive oil

Cook neckbones with olive oil, onion and garlic approximately 45 minutes on low flame. Add tomatoes, tomato paste and water as well as parsley, basil, oregano, crushed red pepper, salt and black pepper. Stir often, reduce to simmer. Cook covered for 5 or 6 hours. You will add tomatoes and water as it thickens. Cut sausage into 4-inch pieces and cook in skillet about medium, pierce with fork to release oil. Drain on paper towels and reserve. Meat Balls: Mix ground meat with eggs until all is moist. Add Parmesan and bread crumbs and mix thoroughly. Add salt, pepper and parsley and mix some more with hands. Shape meat balls, golf ball size or larger. In large skillet, same as used for sausage, cook meat balls in 2 tablespoons olive oil until well browned. You will have to add olive oil as you work your way through the meat. Drain well and reserve with sausage. Add both to sauce for last 1¼ hours of cooking. Simmer and stir often. This is absolutely sensational. Servings: A lot. Pot Size: Very large. Preparation Time: 1 to 1½ hours. Cooking Time: Sauce 5 to 6 hours.

NOTE: You may have to use 2 large pots for sauce or cut recipe in half.

Alan H. Sawyer

Pasta

Angelina Lingua's Meat Sauce

1¹/2 pounds lean ground
   beef
1 cup dry red wine
¹/2 cup side meat (cut in
   cubes)
¹/2 stick butter
4 tablespoons olive oil
1 large onion, finely chopped
2 large cloves garlic,
   minced

¹/2 cup finely chopped
   parsley
1 (28 ounce) can tomatoes,
   coarsely chopped, seeds
   removed
1 (6 ounce) can tomato paste
2 dashes allspice

Marinate ground beef in wine 2 hours while preparing other ingredients. Brown side meat in butter and olive oil. Add onions, garlic and parsley. Cook until soft, approximately 15 minutes. Add ground beef and cook until lightly browned. Add tomatoes, tomato paste, allspice, and simmer on low heat for 2 hours. Remove from heat and take out side meat. Serve over dishes requiring meat sauce. Servings: 4 to 6.

VARIATIONS: To the above add 3 teaspoons oregano, or add ³/4 cup mushrooms, or add rosemary, chicken stock and flour or use ¹/2 cup Italian sausage instead of the side meat and do not remove after cooking.

Louis Lingua

VEGETABLES

SPONSORED BY

Donald H. Farris

Vegetables

Artichoke Bottoms with Spinach

1 (10 ounce) package frozen
   chopped spinach
1 tablespoon chopped onion
1/4 cup sour cream
Salt, to taste

1 (14 ounce) can artichoke
   bottoms
2 tablespoons melted butter
Cracked pepper

Cook spinach and drain well. Place spinach, onion, sour cream and salt in food processor and process until smooth. Mound spinach on each artichoke bottom. Drizzle melted butter over each and sprinkle with cracked pepper. Heat in 350° oven until hot. Servings: 4 to 5 (allowing 2 artichokes per person). Preheat: 350°. Preparation Time: 20 to 30 minutes.

Jane Folk

Asparagus Casserole

This was my grandmother's recipe, a family favorite.

1 1/2 sleeves crushed rich,
   round crackers
4 cans asparagus tips,
   drained
3 to 4 (10 3/4 ounce) cans
   mushroom soup

4 hard-boiled eggs
1 large jar diced pimentos,
   drained
2 cups grated cheese

Crush crackers very fine and spread in bottom of ungreased Pyrex dish. Place asparagus on top of cracker crumbs. Slice eggs; place pimento and eggs on top of asparagus. Next spread entire top of casserole with mushroom soup. Sprinkle grated cheese on top and bake at 350° until cheese bubbles. Enjoy! Pan Size: 3 quart. Preheat: 350°. Preparation Time: 15 minutes. Cooking Time: About 15 to 20 minutes.

Carole C. Moore

194

Baked Asparagus

Great served with manicotti and a green salad.

2 pounds fresh asparagus,
ends trimmed
1 clove garlic, minced
Salt and pepper, to taste
1 teaspoon basil
5 tomatoes, chopped

1/2 cup freshly grated Romano
cheese
1/4 to 1/2 cup seasoned
bread crumbs
2 ounces water

Lay asparagus in baking dish. Sprinkle with garlic, salt, pepper and basil. Top with tomatoes, cheese and bread crumbs. Pour water over all. Cover with aluminum foil. Bake at 325° for 30 minutes. Uncover and bake an additional 15 minutes. Pan Size: 11x7-inches. Preheat: 325°. Cooking Time: 45 minutes.

Loren and Kim Roberts

Broccoli Casserole

1 (10 ounce) package
chopped frozen broccoli,
thawed, and drained well
4 hard-boiled eggs, chopped

2 cups extra sharp Cheddar
cheese, shredded
2 cups white sauce, recipe follows
10 soda crackers
2 tablespoons melted butter or
margarine

In a buttered casserole dish, make two layers in the following order: half of broccoli, half of eggs, half of cheese and half of sauce. Repeat. Top with buttered cracker crumbs made from soda crackers, mixed in melted butter or margarine. Servings: 4 to 6. Pan Size: 2 quart. Preheat: 350°. Cooking Time: 30 to 45 minutes.

WHITE SAUCE:

4 tablespoons butter or
margarine
4 tablespoons flour

1/2 teaspoon salt
2 cups milk
1/8 teaspoon Tabasco

Melt margarine in saucepan or double boiler. Add flour and salt, stirring to a smooth paste. Gradually, add milk and Tabasco stirring constantly. Cook over low heat or double boiler until thick.

Mrs. William M. Frazee

195

Vegetables

Easy Cheesy Broccoli Casserole

1 large onion, chopped
1/2 stick butter or margarine
3 (10 ounce) packages
   chopped broccoli
1 small can mushrooms
2 (10¾ ounce) cans
   mushroom soup

1½ rolls garlic cheese
1 teaspoon Accent
1/2 cup chopped almonds
1/2 cup bread crumbs

Sauté onions in butter. Cook broccoli until tender. Drain. Add mushrooms, soup, cheese, Accent and 1/4 cup almonds. Sprinkle with remaining almonds and bread crumbs. Spoon into casserole dish. Bake at 300° until bubbly. Servings: 8 to 10.

Mrs. Roane Waring

Company Brussel Sprouts
People who do not like brussel sprouts love this dish.
It always receives rave reviews!

4 bacon strips, diced
1 dozen fresh brussel
   spouts, trimmed halved
1 medium onion, chopped
2 tablespoons snipped fresh
   chives or 1 teaspoon
   dried
1 carrot, thinly sliced

10 stuffed green olives,
   sliced
1/2 teaspoon dried basil
1/2 cup chicken broth or dry
   white wine
1 teaspoon olive oil
1/2 teaspoon pepper
Pinch of salt

In skillet, fry bacon just until cooked. Drain, reserving 2 tablespoons of drippings. Add remaining ingredients. Stir over medium-high heat for 15 to 20 minutes until brussel sprouts are crisp tender. Servings: 6 to 8. Preparation Time: 15 to 20 minutes. Cooking Time: 15 to 20 minutes.

Peggy W. Edmiston

Baked Bean Quintet

1 (16 ounce) can large butter beans
1 (16 ounce) can lima beans
1 (15¹/₂ ounce) can red kidney beans
1 (15¹/₂ ounce) can black beans
1 (16 ounce) can pork and beans in tomato sauce
10 slices of bacon
1¹/₄ cups onions, chopped
2 tablespoons chopped garlic (I use garlic in the jar)

1 cup ketchup
¹/₂ cup honey
2¹/₂ tablespoons Worcestershire
1¹/₂ tablespoons dried mustard
2 teaspoons hot sauce
1 teaspoon salt
³/₄ cup barbecue sauce
1 medium onion, sliced and sautéed, set aside

Preheat oven to 375°. Drain all beans, except for the pork and beans. In a skillet, cook bacon until crisp. Remove bacon, reserving 2 tablespoons dripping in skillet. Drain bacon well. Cook chopped onion and garlic in drippings until onion is tender, but not brown. In a large bowl, combine all ingredients (except for sliced onions); stir well. Spray baking dish with vegetable spray. Pour into 9x13-inch baking dish. Place sautéed onion slices on top of beans and bake 30 minutes. Cover and bake another 30 minutes or until heated through. Servings: 12 to 14.

Mrs. Harold E. Crye

197

Rita's Sautéed Green Beans with Garlic and Country Ham

4 cups water	**3 tablespoons butter**
3 tablespoons salt	**3 tablespoons olive oil**
24 cloves garlic	**3 pounds green pole beans**
3/4 pound country ham	**Salt and pepper, to taste**

Cook garlic cloves in large pot of boiling salted water until tender (8 minutes). Lift out garlic and pat dry on paper towel. Cook ham in large skillet in butter and oil until browned. Add garlic and mash with a spoon. Cook green beans in water used for cooking garlic until crisp-tender, drain and refresh under cold water; drain again and pat dry. Add beans to skillet with garlic and ham and heat through. Season to taste with salt and ground black pepper. Servings: 10 to 12. Preparation Time: 30 minutes. Cooking Time: 15 minutes.

Dr. William H. Marsh

Sweet and Sour Green Beans

2 cans green beans, drained and rinsed	**1/2 cup vinegar**
1 onion sliced in thin rings	**1/2 cup sugar**
6 slices crisp bacon, crumbled, reserve drippings	

Place beans and onions in shallow casserole. Mix bacon drippings, vinegar and sugar. Pour over beans. Bake uncovered in 350° oven 1 to 2 hours. Sprinkle crumbled bacon on top.

Lynne E. Fisher

Cabbage Mornay

1 head cabbage	1/2 cup mozzarella cheese
4 tablespoons butter	1/2 cup Parmesan cheese
2 cups milk	1 cup bread crumbs
5 tablespoons flour	

Core and wash cabbage. Cut cabbage and boil or steam for 15 minutes. Set aside. In a saucepan, melt butter, add flour and cook 2 minutes. Add milk and bring to a boil. Add cheeses, whisking constantly. Toss cooked cabbage with sauce, put in casserole and cover with bread crumbs. Bake in oven for 15 minutes at 350°. Servings: 8. Pan Size: 2 quart. Preheat: 350°. Preparation Time: 30 minutes. Cooking Time: 15 minutes.

Emmett D. Bell

Zesty Carrots

1 1/4 pounds carrots, cut into strips	1/4 cup mayonnaise
2 tablespoons grated onion	1/4 teaspoon salt
2 tablespoons prepared horseradish	1/4 teaspoon pepper
	1/2 to 1 cup herb stuffing mix

Cook carrots until tender-crisp. Reserve 1/4 cup liquid to mix with sauce. Grease baking dish. Combine remaining ingredients except stuffing and pour over carrots. Brown herb stuffing in a little butter and sprinkle over top. Bake at 375° for 15 minutes. Garnish with parsley. This sauce tastes good over any combination of vegetables you want to use. Servings: 6. Pan Size: 1 1/2 quarts. Preheat: 375°. Cooking Time: 15 minutes.

Anne Piper

Vegetables

Carrot Soufflé

2 cups carrots (14 to 15
   carrots), salted, cooked
   and mashed
1 stick butter or margarine
2 eggs, well beaten

3 tablespoons flour
1 teaspoon baking powder
1 cup sugar
Pinch of cinnamon

Blend all ingredients and bake in greased casserole dish at 400° for 15 minutes, then 350° for 45 minutes. Serve immediately. (Leftovers warm up very well.) Servings: 4 to 6. Pan Size: 8x8-inches. Preheat: 400°. Preparation Time: 30 minutes. Cooking Time: 1 hour.

Calista Bray

Braised Celery
"Delicate and delicious".

12 ribs celery, cut into
   1-inch pieces
1/2 stick unsalted butter
Salt and pepper, to taste

1 tablespoon fresh lemon
   juice
1/2 cup chicken stock

In heavy skillet, sauté celery in butter, salt and pepper over moderate heat for 5 minutes, then over medium-high heat until glazed and lightly browned. Add the lemon juice and chicken stock, bring to a boil. Reduce heat and simmer until tender, about 5 minutes.

Beth Worley

200

Corn Casserole

2 (16½ ounce) cans yellow
  cream style corn
2 cups grated Cheddar cheese
1 (4 ounce) can chopped
  green chilies
½ cup chopped onions

1 cup milk
2 large eggs, slightly beaten
1 cup yellow cornmeal
1½ teaspoons garlic salt
½ teaspoon baking soda

Combine first six ingredients. Set aside. Combine cornmeal and remaining ingredients. Stir into corn mixture. Pour into greased dish. Bake in preheated 350° oven for 50 minutes. Servings: 8. Pan Size: 11x7x2-inches. Preparation Time: 15 minutes. Cooking Time: 50 minutes.

Judy A. Smith

Baked Corn in Sour Cream

2 tablespoons butter
2 tablespoons chopped
  onion
2 tablespoons flour
½ teaspoon salt
1 cup sour cream
2 (15 ounce) cans whole
  kernel corn

2 tablespoons finely
  chopped celery
1 tablespoon pimento
6 slices bacon, cooked
  crisp, drained, crumbled
  and divided
1 tablespoon minced fresh
  parsley

In large saucepan, melt butter. Stir in onion and sauté until transparent. Blend in flour and salt. Add sour cream and stir until mixture is smooth. Add corn and celery, heating thoroughly. Stir in pimento and half the crumbled bacon. Pour into a greased casserole dish. Top with parsley and remaining bacon. Bake at 325° for 30 to 45 minutes. Servings: 6 to 8. Pan Size: 2 quart casserole. Preheat: 325°. Preparation Time: 10 minutes. Cooking Time: 30 to 45 minutes.

Rep. Joe Kent, District 83

Vegetables

Eggplant Supreme

2 large eggplants
1 pound bulk Italian sausage
1 medium onion, chopped
1 medium bell pepper,
    chopped
1/4 cup oil

2 cloves garlic, chopped
1 large jar Italian sauce
1 pound grated mozzarella
    cheese
1 cup Italian bread crumbs

Cut eggplants in half lengthwise. Scoop out pulp being careful not to split skins. Set skins aside. Cover pulp in water and boil until tender. Drain water and mash pulp. Set aside. Sauté onions and bell pepper in oil. Add bulk Italian sausage and cook until totally brown. Add garlic, eggplant pulp and Italian sauce. Mix well, cover and cook on low heat for 30 minutes. Stuff eggplant skins with sausage mixture. Cover with mozzarella cheese and top with Italian bread crumbs. Bake on a cookie sheet at 350° for 30 minutes. Serve with hot garlic bread and side green salad for a complete meal! Servings: 4. Preheat: 350°. Preparation Time: 1 hour. Cooking Time: 30 minutes.

Norman J. Romagosa

Spinach Stuffed Vidalia Onions

4 to 5 medium Vidalia onions
1 pound fresh spinach
2 tablespoons unsalted
    butter, melted

1/4 cup light cream
Salt and pepper, to taste
Dash of cayenne pepper
Grated Parmesan cheese

Peel onions and core out hole in each center. Place in a steamer rack over simmering water and steam until soft, yet still firm (about five minutes). Remove from heat and cool. Wash spinach well. Remove stems. Cook 1 minute in water. Drain and chop spinach and sauté in melted butter. Add light cream and cook uncovered, until fairly dry. Season with salt and pepper. Fill onions with spinach mixture. Sprinkle with cayenne pepper and cheese. Bake in 350° oven in a greased shallow pan until heated through or wrap in foil and place on charcoal grill to heat while grilling steaks, chops or chicken. Servings: 4 to 5.

Mrs. J. Hal Patton

202

Onion Tart in Fillo with Fresh Thyme

About 12 sheets fillo dough
   14 - 18 inches (cut into
   9x9 inch squares)
Melted butter
1½ pounds Spanish onions
2 to 4 tablespoons olive oil
Fresh thyme, chopped
4 ounces milk

4 ounces heavy cream
2 whole eggs
Salt
Pepper
Ground nutmeg
8 round molds (Teflon) 4-inch
   diameter 1-inch high

Cut the onions in half and slice them not too thin. In a hot skillet, over medium fire sauté the onions in olive oil until very tender and slightly carmelized. If too much moisture, raise the flame. When the onions are cooked, add the chopped thyme, season with salt and pepper to taste. In a bowl, beat the eggs, add the milk and heavy cream, (salt, pepper, ground nutmeg to taste) and mix well. While working with the fillo dough, keep a wet kitchen towel on them. Use three sheets per tart. Start brushing the first sheet with melted butter, then put another fillo sheet on top, brush it again with melted butter, put another sheet, brush it too with butter, then flip over the fillo dough without breaking it and put it into the mold. The last buttered sheet should be in contact with the mold. Fold the dough all around and make the dough over lap the rim by ½ an inch. Fill the dough with the cooked onions (the more onions, the better). Pour the eggs and cream mixture (about 1 ounce per tart). When the 8 tarts are finished, put them on a baking sheet pan, then in a preheated oven at 400° for about 5 minutes. Then slow down the temperature to 325° and finish baking the tarts for 15 to 20 minutes until flaky and golden brown. Remove from the oven, let cool 10 minutes then unmold. When ready to serve, warm up the tarts in a hot oven. Can be served with crisped bits of sautéed sliced bacon around. At René Pujol, I use a bit of Madeira sauce all around the onion tart. Enjoy and BON APPETIT. Servings: 8.

Folks in the Kitchen wine recommendation: Keuntz Bas Pinot Blanc.

Claude Franques
René Pujol Restaurant
New York City, NY

203

Vegetables

Oregano Peas

1 (10 ounce) package frozen
   peas
4 tablespoons butter
1 tablespoon onion

4 ounces sliced mushrooms
1/2 teaspoon oregano
1/2 teaspoon salt
1/4 teaspoon seasoned salt

Sauté all of the above, until peas are tender. Servings: 4.

Ann Page

Scalloped Pineapple
Everyone loves this great side dish, especially men!

1/2 cup sugar
3 tablespoons all-purpose
   flour
1 (20 ounce) can pineapple
   chunks, drained,
   reserving liquid

1 cup grated sharp Cheddar
   cheese
1/2 cup butter or margarine,
   melted
1/2 cup crushed rich, round
   crackers (12 crackers)

Combine sugar and flour, then stir in 3 tablespoons pineapple juice. Add grated cheese and pineapple chunks. Mix well and spoon into a greased casserole. Combine butter and cracker crumbs and sprinkle on top. Bake at 350° for 20 to 30 minutes or until golden. Servings: 4. Pan Size: 1 quart casserole. Preheat: 350°. Preparation Time: 10 minutes. Cooking Time: 20 to 30 minutes or until golden.

Barbara J. Riley

Garlic Mashed Potatoes

Wonderful accompaniment to Snapper Pecan Sandy.

4 Idaho baking potatoes	**3 tablespoons roasted garlic**
Salt	**flavored oil**
Water	**4 tablespoons sour cream**

Peel potatoes. Cut into 1/2-inch thick slices. Place in large pot. Cover with water. Add salt, to taste. Boil over medium heat until tender. Drain off water. Add oil and sour cream. Mash by hand or with mixer until smooth. Season to taste. Servings: 4. Preparation Time: 15 minutes. Cooking Time: 15 to 20 minutes.

John Pfund

Potato Casserole

6 large potatoes	**1 cup milk**
1 stick butter	**2/3 cup green onions,**
2 cups sharp Cheddar	**chopped, tops and all**
cheese, grated	**Salt and pepper**
2 cups sour cream	**Additional cheese for topping**

Boil potatoes in jackets. Chill until cold. Peel and grate. Melt butter in double boiler. Add cheese a small amount at a time. Mix together sour cream and milk. Add to cheese mixture. Add onions, stir together, add to potatoes. Mix well. Pour in greased 3 quart casserole and sprinkle additional cheese on top. Bake at 350° for 45 minutes. Servings: 8 to 10.

Lynne E. Fisher

Vegetables

"Joann's" Hashbrown Casserole

This dish was created right out of our pantry when a friend and I had to take a quick dish to a family in need.

1 (32 ounce) package
  shredded potatoes, fresh
  or frozen, thawed
1 stick butter or margarine,
  melted
1 (10¾ ounce) can cream
  of celery soup
4 dashes Tabasco sauce
8 ounces sour cream, light
  or fat free

1 teaspoon Lawry's seasoned salt
Fresh pepper, to taste
½ small onion, finely chopped
1 can French fried onions
  (optional)
12 ounces finely shredded
  Cheddar cheese
1 stick butter, melted
Paprika (if you don't use the
  onions)

Mix first 8 ingredients together thoroughly. Spray casserole with cooking spray and place ½ potato mix in casserole and top with ½ of the cheese. Repeat. Top the last ½ of the cheese with the French fried onions and drizzle with remaining melted butter. Sprinkle with paprika. Bake at 30 to 45 minutes or until hot and bubbly. (Can also use cream of chicken or cream of mushroom soup and 2½ cups chopped cooked chicken to make a meal.) Freezes well. Servings: 12. Pan Size: 3 quart (9x13-inches). Preheat: 350°. Preparation Time: 15 minutes. Cooking Time: 30 to 45 minutes.

Ann Clark Harris

Potatoes O'Brien

⅓ cup chopped green pepper
2 tablespoons chopped pimento
1 medium onion, chopped
¼ cup butter or margarine

1 (16 ounce) package frozen
  French fried potatoes, diced
1 teaspoon salt
⅛ teaspoon pepper

In large skillet, cook and stir green pepper, pimento and onion in butter until onion is tender. Stir in potatoes, salt and pepper. Cook, stirring occasionally, until potatoes are browned and heated, 15 to 25 minutes. Servings: 4. Cooking Time: 15 to 25 minutes.

Margaret McNeil

Oven Potatoes

2 medium sweet potatoes
2 medium russet potatoes
1/8 teaspoon garlic powder
1/8 teaspoon onion powder

1½ teaspoons paprika
¼ teaspoon salt
¼ teaspoon pepper

Wash potatoes well and peel. Slice potatoes lengthwise into strips (like French fries). Spray pan with cooking spray and place potatoes in pan. Mix all seasonings and sprinkle on potatoes. Bake potatoes at 425° for 45 minutes, stirring often. Servings: 4. Pan Size: 9x13-inches. Preheat: Yes. Preparation Time: 20 minutes. Cooking Time: 45 minutes.

Janet Farris Henderson

Easy Microwave Potatoes

6 medium-size red potatoes
Water to cover potatoes
Butter, to taste

Sour cream, to taste
Salt, to taste
Pepper, to taste

Wash potatoes thoroughly. Slice thin and place in a glass microwave dish. Add enough water to cover bottom layer of potatoes. Place lid on dish and cook in microwave on high 10 minutes. After 10 minutes, stir potatoes, replace lid and cook 5 to 10 minutes longer, until potatoes are tender. Drain water and add butter, sour cream, salt and pepper to taste. Servings: 4. Pan Size: Medium Pyrex bowl with lid. Preparation Time: 5 minutes. Cooking Time: 15 to 20 minutes.

Cathy Cavness

Praline Sweet Potatoes

FOR THE SWEET POTATO MIX:

8 cups baked sweet potato meat (about 6 large sweet potatoes)

3 cups heavy whipping cream

1 cup unsalted butter, softened

1 cup light brown sugar

1/2 teaspoon salt

1/4 teaspoon ground white pepper

1/4 teaspoon ground nutmeg

2 teaspoons ground cinnamon

1/4 teaspoon pure vanilla extract

Preheat oven to 375°. Place cooked sweet potato meat into a mixing bowl. Put the remaining ingredients into a heavy-duty saucepan and cook over low heat just until the butter melts, 3 to 4 minutes. Pour this mixture over the sweet potato meat and blend well with a potato masher or heavy wire whisk. Transfer this mixture to a 9x12x2-inch casserole.

FOR THE PRALINE TOPPING:

2 1/2 cups shelled, unsalted pecans

1/4 cup unsalted butter, melted

1/4 cup heavy whipping cream

1 cup light brown sugar

1/4 teaspoon pure vanilla extract

Combine all ingredients and spread evenly over the top of the sweet potato mixture. Bake in 375° oven until the praline topping begins to brown, 35 to 40 minutes. Serve immediately. Servings: 12 to 15 portions as a side dish.

Folks in the Kitchen wine recommendation: St. Suprey Moscato.

NOTE: To bake sweet potatoes, preheat oven to 250°. Bake until very tender, 1 1/2 to 2 hours. Cut in half and scoop the meat out with a spoon.

Frank Brigtsen
Brigtsen's Restaurant
New Orleans, LA

Sweet Potato Casserole

3 cups sweet potatoes,
   mashed
1 cup sugar, or to taste
1/2 cup butter, melted
2 eggs, beaten

1 tablespoon vanilla extract
1 cup brown sugar, packed
1 cup pecans, chopped fine
1/3 cup flour, all-purpose
1/3 cup butter

Preheat oven to 350°. Mash potatoes together with sugar, butter, eggs and vanilla. Pour into a buttered casserole dish. Mix the brown sugar, chopped nuts, flour and butter until mixture is crumbly. Sprinkle over potato mixture. Bake at 350° for 30 minutes or until topping is lightly browned. Servings: 8.

NOTE: Canned sweet potatoes may be used, but fresh baked are best. Wash and bake about 6 to 8 medium sweet potatoes at 350° for 1 to 1 1/2 hours. Scoop out soft centers and mash with masher or big spoon.

Tricia Seubert

Wild Rice "Risotto" with Winter Squash

I make this every Thanksgiving for my family dinner.

3 tablespoons unsalted
  butter
1/2 pound Chanterelles or
  other mushrooms, diced
2/3 cup wild rice, boiled
  until tender and drained,
  about 2 cups cooked
Salt and freshly ground
  black pepper, to taste
1 tablespoon extra virgin oil
1/2 cup chopped onion
2 large cloves of garlic,
  minced

1 1/4 cups short grain rice (or
  arborio rice)
4 to 5 cups vegetable or
  chicken stock
2/3 cup puréed cooked
  unseasoned pumpkin or
  butternut squash, diced
2 tablespoons aged
  Monterey Jack or
  Parmesan cheese
1 tablespoon chopped
  chives

Heat 1 tablespoon of the butter in a large sauté pan over medium heat until it just begins to brown. Stir in the mushrooms. Cook, stirring until they begin to wilt; then, add the cooked wild rice. Season with salt and pepper, stir and set aside. Heat the olive oil in a heavy saucepan. Add the onion and garlic, and sauté over medium heat for 2 to 3 minutes. Add the short grain rice and stir. In a separate pan, bring the stock to a simmer, and keep hot. Add 2 cups of the hot stock to the short grain rice, and cook, stirring, until the liquid is absorbed by the rice. Add the pumpkin purée or diced squash, sautéed mushrooms and wild rice and another cup of the stock. Stir until the stock is absorbed. Add another 1 to 1 1/2 cups stock, and continue to cook until the short grain rice is just about tender. The risotto can be prepared in advance to this point and set aside for an hour or two. If prepared in advance, add another 1/2 cup stock when reheating the risotto. Before serving, stir in the remaining butter, the cheese and the chives. Season to taste with salt and pepper. Servings: 8. Preparation Time: 1 hour 20 minutes.

Harriet Hussey Radcliffe

210

Wonderful Wild Rice

*Great for a wild game dinner. Fabulous served with
duck, venison, dove, etc.*

1¹/₂ cups wild rice	**Salt**
1 cup diced celery	**Pepper**
1 cup finely chopped onion	**2 tablespoons parsley**
1 cup butter	**¹/₄ teaspoon dried thyme**
¹/₂ pound sliced mushrooms	

Cook wild rice, set aside. Sauté celery and onion in ¹/₂ cup butter until soft. Add rest of butter and mushrooms and cook another 3 minutes. Mix together the rice, vegetables, butter, salt, pepper, parsley and thyme. Servings: 6. Preparation Time: 1 hour.

The Folk Family

Green Rice

*This is always welcome at potluck suppers, as
well as a good side dish at home.*

2 cups cooked white rice	**Scant ¹/₂ cup melted butter**
2 eggs, slightly beaten	**Salt, to taste**
2 cups milk	**1 (10³/₄ ounce) can cream**
1 or 2 small onions, chopped	**of mushroom soup**
1 cup grated mild Cheddar	**Buttered bread crumbs for**
cheese	**topping**
¹/₂ cup chopped parsley	

Mix all ingredients together except mushroom soup and bread crumbs and bake in slow oven 250° to 275° for 1 hour. Take out and spread on mushroom soup and bake 15 minutes. Top with buttered crumbs. Servings: 6 to 8. Pan Size: 2 to 2¹/₂ quart. Preparation Time: 25 minutes. Cooking Time: 1 hour 15 minutes.

Mrs. John B. Marlin

211

Vegetables

Green Rice Casserole

3 cups cooked white rice
1 cup milk
2 eggs, well beaten
1 cup green pepper, finely
   chopped
1/2 cup green onions, finely
   chopped
2 cups parsley, finely chopped

1 cup grated Parmesan cheese
1 cup grated American cheese
1/2 cup celery, finely chopped
2 cloves garlic, pressed
Salt and pepper, to taste
   (white pepper preferred)
1/2 stick butter or margarine

Combine milk and beaten eggs. Add remaining ingredients except butter. Turn into a 2 quart casserole lightly greased with butter, and dot with butter. Bake at 350° about 1 hour.

Lina P. Karlson

Mexican Rice
Delicious!

1 small green pepper, diced
1 small onion, chopped
1 tablespoon oil
1 (10 ounce) package frozen
   corn, thawed

1 cup mild salsa
1 cup chicken broth
1 1/2 cups Minute Rice
1/4 cup shredded cheese

In saucepan cook pepper and onion in hot oil until tender. Add corn, salsa and broth, bring to a boil. Stir in rice and cover. Remove from heat and let sit for 5 minutes. Fluff with a fork and add cheese. Servings: 4. Pan Size: Medium large. Preparation Time: 10 minutes. Cooking Time: 15 minutes.

Carla Johnston

Spinach and Artichoke Casserole

1 can artichoke hearts	1 stick butter, (a must) melted
1 can sliced water chestnuts, drained	8 ounces cream cheese, softened
2 (10 ounce) packages frozen chopped spinach, cooked and drained	3/4 teaspoon red pepper
	3/4 teaspoon salt
	Paprika

Thinly slice artichokes and layer on bottom of round casserole dish. Spread chestnuts over artichokes. Mix melted butter, spinach and cream cheese. Season with red pepper and salt (be careful not to add to much salt or pepper). Spread mixture over artichokes and chestnuts, sprinkle paprika on top. Bake for 30 minutes. Servings: 8 to 10. Pan Size: 2 to 3 quart casserole. Preheat: 350°. Preparation Time: 15 to 20 minutes.

Dee Gibson

Nelson's Spinach Casserole

2 (10 ounce) packages frozen chopped spinach	1/2 teaspoon pepper
2 tablespoons diced pimento	5 eggs, beaten
8 ounces Velveeta cheese, cut up	5 tablespoons flour
1 pound cottage cheese	1 ounce "The Spirit of New Orleans" herbsaint
1/2 stick butter, melted	Parmesan cheese for topping
1/2 teaspoon salt	

Cook spinach according to package directions and empty into colander. Press out excess water. Combine all ingredients in large mixing bowl. Add the herbsaint last, mix well. Spray dish with cooking spray. Spoon spinach into dish. Bake covered for 45 minutes. Uncover, and sprinkle with shredded Parmesan cheese. Cook an additional 15 minutes or until cheese is melted. Servings: 8. Pan Size: 10x10x2-inches. Preheat: 350°. Preparation Time: 15 minutes. Cooking Time: 1 hour.

Nelson McCoy

Vegetables

Quick Spinach

2 (10 ounce) packages
    frozen chopped spinach
1½ cups sharp Cheddar
    cheese, grated
1 egg
Dash of garlic salt

1 (10¾ ounce) can
    condensed mushroom
    soup
Buttered bread crumbs or
    Pepperidge Farm
    dressing

Cook spinach in water for 15 minutes; drain well. Combine with remaining ingredients, except crumbs, in order given; pour in casserole. Bake at 350° until mixture bubbles. Top with crumbs, bake 5 to 10 minutes longer.

Kim and Bishop Norris

Spinach Rockefeller
Great as a festive side dish or dip with corn chips.

2 packages frozen, chopped
    spinach, cooked and
    drained
½ stick butter
1 teaspoon vinegar
1 cup sour cream

1 (6 ounce) roll jalapeño
    cheese, cubed
1 tablespoon instant minced
    onion
Salt and pepper, to taste

Mix all ingredients in baking dish and bake at 350° for 20 minutes or until bubbly, stirring at midway point to mix in cheese. Servings: 6.

Mary Ruth Witt

Pie Pan Spinach

1 deep dish pie shell	1¾ cups cottage cheese
3 slices bacon, chopped	¼ cup grated Parmesan
½ cup chopped onion	3 eggs, slightly beaten
1 (10 ounce) package frozen	½ teaspoon salt
chopped spinach, thawed	¼ teaspoon pepper
and drained well	⅛ teaspoon nutmeg

Bake pie shell 3 minutes at 400°. Reduce to 350°. Remove pie shell. Sauté bacon and onion until onion is transparent, drain. In large bowl, combine remaining ingredients and mix well. Pour into pre-baked pie shell and bake at reduced heat (350°) for 30 to 35 minutes. Let stand 5 minutes and serve. Servings: 8. Pan Size: Deep dish. Preheat: 400°. Preparation Time: 30 minutes. Cooking Time: 30 to 35 minutes.

Barbara A. Smith

Spinach-Stuffed Squash

1 teaspoon crushed garlic	6 to 8 yellow crooked neck
1 stick butter	squash
2 (10 ounce) packages chopped	Salt and pepper, to taste
spinach, thawed and drained	Grated Parmesan cheese
1 egg	for topping
1 cup grated Parmesan cheese	

Sauté garlic in butter for 1 minute, add spinach and sauté 2 minutes until thoroughly combined and heated. Remove from heat, cool to room temperature. Add slightly beaten egg, mix thoroughly, add Parmesan cheese, salt and pepper to taste. Wash squash, remove both ends (most of neck) and split lengthwise down the middle. With a teaspoon, scoop out center seeded section of squash and fill with spinach mixture. Top with Parmesan cheese. Bake at 350° for 20 to 30 minutes or until squash is tender. Servings: 6 to 8 (1 squash each). Pan Size: 9x12-inch glass baking pan. Preparation Time: 15 minutes.

Debora Drago Wilemon

215

Vegetables

Summer Squash Casserole

2 cups yellow squash, cubed
1/2 cup green onions, chopped
1 1/2 tablespoons butter or margarine
1/2 cup grated Cheddar cheese

1/2 cup soft breadcrumbs
1/2 cup milk
1 egg, slightly beaten
1/4 teaspoon salt
1/8 teaspoon pepper

Arrange squash and onion in steaming rack and steam 5 to 10 minutes. Combine squash mixture, butter and cheese; stir until butter and cheese melt. Combine remaining ingredients and stir into squash mixture. Spoon into lightly greased 1 quart casserole dish. Bake at 350° for 30 to 35 minutes. Servings: 6 to 8. Preheat: 350°. Preparation Time: 15 to 20 minutes. Cooking Time: 30 to 35 minutes.

Beth Worley

Squash Casserole

4 or 5 medium size squash, chopped and cooked about 5 minutes or until tender, drain
1 cup Cheddar cheese, grated

2 eggs, beaten
1/2 cup milk
1/2 cup chopped onion
8 to 10 soda crackers, crushed

Combine all ingredients except crackers. Spoon into covered casserole and top with cracker crumbs. Bake at 350° for 40 minutes.

Phyllis Cox

Lizzie's Squash
You don't have to like vegetables to love this recipe!

10 medium yellow squash
2 tablespoons chopped
  onion
1¼ sticks butter, melted
16 ounces sharp Cheddar
  cheese, grated

½ cup brown sugar
1 egg, beaten
Season salt and pepper, to
  taste
1 sleeve crushed rich, round
  crackers

Cut squash into ¼-inch slices and boil with onion. Cook until soft. Drain well. Add butter (reserving ¼ cup), cheese (reserving ½ cup), brown sugar, egg, season salt and pepper. Mix well. Spoon into baking dish. Top with grated cheese, ¼ stick melted butter and cracker crumbs. Bake at 350° for 45 minutes. Freezes well. Servings: 8 to 10.

Elizabeth Gillespie

Green Tomato Casserole

5 to 6 medium green
  tomatoes
Cooking spray
1½ tablespoons sugar
Salt and pepper, to taste
¾ cup bread crumbs
4 tablespoons butter

½ teaspoon oregano
¼ teaspoon basil
Pinch of thyme
Pinch of garlic salt
½ cup Parmesan cheese,
  grated

Cut tomatoes into ½ or ¼-inch slices. Arrange, over-lapping in baking dish sprayed with cooking spray. Sprinkle each layer with ½ teaspoon sugar and salt and pepper to taste. In skillet, lightly brown bread crumbs in butter. Add oregano, basil, thyme and garlic salt. Sprinkle mixture over tomatoes and top with cheese. Bake at 350° for 45 minutes. Servings: 5 to 6.

Lina P. Karlson

217

Vegetables

Zucchini Casserole

4 medium zucchini, cubed
1 medium onion, chopped
1 stick butter or margarine,
    melted

1 package stuffing mix
1 (10¾ ounce) can cream of
    chicken soup
1 cup sour cream

Steam zucchini and onion. Combine butter and dressing. Mix soup and sour cream. Add vegetables. Spray casserole with cooking spray and layer vegetable mixture and dressing mixture. Bake at 350° for 30 minutes. Servings: 6 to 8. Pan Size: 2 quart. Preheat: 350°. Preparation Time: 1 hour.

Barbara and John Moore

Roasted Vegetables Rosemary

Absolutely delicious as a winter side dish with roast pork, lamb or turkey.

3 large carrots, peeled and
    cut into chunks
1 large onion, peeled and
    wedged leaving wedges
    attached to root end
1 large sweet potato, peeled
    and cut into 1-inch cubes
10 to 12 large cloves garlic,
    peeled

3 tablespoons olive oil
1 tablespoon balsamic
    vinegar
1 to 2 teaspoons coarse
    salt, to taste
1 tablespoon fresh
    rosemary, chopped (this
    is necessary, no substitute)
Chopped parsley to garnish

Preheat oven to 425°. Toss all ingredients in a large bowl. Spread vegetables out in a baking pan just large enough to hold them in one layer. Roast in hot oven, stirring carefully once or twice for 45 to 50 minutes. Vegetables are done when fork tender and a toasty, caramelized color. Sprinkle with parsley to serve hot or room temperature. Servings: 4. Pan Size: 10x12-inch roaster. Preheat: 425°. Preparation Time: 15 to 20 minutes. Cooking Time: 45 to 50 minutes.

Nancy Thomas

218

Cranberry-Squash Salsa

Great for a side dish at Thanksgiving!

2 cups butternut squash, finely diced	1/3 cup maple syrup
1 cup fresh cranberries	Zest of 1 orange, grated
2 clementines, peeled (optional, only if not available)	Juice of one lime
	Pinch of cinnamon
	1/2 teaspoon mint, finely minced

Bring a saucepan of water to a boil, add the diced squash. When the water returns to a boil, drain the squash and place in a bowl. In a food processor, chop the cranberries fairly fine by pulsing. Add to the squash. Using kitchen shears, snip the clementine segments in small pieces. Add to squash. Fold in the maple syrup, orange zest, lime juice, cinnamon and mint. Set aside at least 2 hours before serving. May be refrigerated overnight. Servings: 6. Preparation Time: 30 minutes. Per serving: 85 calories, 0 grams fat, 0 milligrams cholesterol, 4 milligrams sodium, 1 gram protein and 20 grams carbohydrate.

Harriet Hussey Radcliffe

Green Tomato Relish

35 green tomatoes	7 cups cider vinegar
16 bell peppers	7 cups sugar
1 head cabbage	2 tablespoons mustard seed
6 large onions	1 1/2 teaspoons turmeric
3/4 cup pickling salt	1 1/2 teaspoons whole cloves

Quarter, then chop tomatoes, bell peppers, cabbage and onions in food processor until medium-coarse in texture. Pour pickling salt over vegetables and set aside for 2 hours. Combine vinegar, sugar and spices in a large saucepan and bring to a boil. Add drained vegetables and bring back to a boil. Remove from stove. Cool slightly. Pour into jars and seal. Servings: 10 pints. Preparation Time: 3 hours.

Nancy Worley

Roberta's Chow-Chow

Roberta was a very special family friend and a second mother to my husband. Since we were married, Roberta in her typically generous manner of keeping her children well-fed, kept us amply supplied with her Chow-Chow, usually giving us a case at a time. Unfortunately, Roberta died a couple of years ago; so in her honor when my mother-in-law and my brother-in-law visit, we make several batches of Chow-Chow over a summer weekend when the produce is at its best. Roberta's legacy continues.

12 medium onions	1/2 cup salt
12 sweet green peppers	1 box pickling spice
12 sweet red peppers	5 to 6 cups sugar
4 quarts cabbage	2 1/2 quarts vinegar
12 quarts green tomatoes	

Chop all vegetables fine in food processor. Combine and mix with salt. Let stand overnight. Drain well the next morning. Tie pickling spice in a cheesecloth bag. Combine spices, sugar and vinegar in a pan. Bring to boiling point and simmer 20 minutes. Add drained vegetables and simmer to desired consistency. Remove spice bag and pack Chow-Chow in hot sterilized jars and seal. Servings: 16 to 18 pints. Pan Size: 12 to 16 quart container. Preparation Time: 1 1/2 hours. Cooking Time: 2 1/2 to 3 hours.

Gwen Parrish

220

DESSERTS

SPONSORED BY

Bob Buckman &
Joyce Mollerup

Desserts

Mimi's Peanut Butter Pie

This is my grandmother's treasured recipe that she has kept secret from all those in her community of Clarksdale, Mississippi, as she has delivered her pies throughout the last 40 years.

8 ounces cream cheese, softened	9 ounces Cool Whip
16 ounces peanut butter	1 teaspoon vanilla
1 (14 ounce) can sweetened condensed milk	1 teaspoon lemon juice
	4 Heath bars, crushed
	Additional Cool Whip

CRUST:

1/3 box chocolate graham crackers   6 tablespoons butter, melted

For crust, crush graham crackers and add butter. Press into greased pie pan. Mix together all remaining ingredients, except additional Cool Whip. Pour into prepared pie crust and chill overnight. Top with remaining Cool Whip. Rich, easy, fabulous! Servings: 8. Pan Size: 9-inch pie. Preparation Time: 20 minutes.

Lou Martin

Grasshopper Pie

25 large marshmallows	2 ounces creme de menthe
2/3 cup milk	1 ounce creme de cocoa
1 cup heavy cream, whipped	1 chocolate crumb crust

Add marshmallows to milk and heat slowly until marshmallows are melted. Cool. Add creme de menthe and cream de cocoa and the whipped cream. Pour into pie shell. Chill at least overnight.

Helen Hardin

222

Rum Cream Pie

1½ cups chocolate wafer
   crumbs
6 tablespoons butter, melted
1½ teaspoons unflavored
   gelatin
¼ cup water

3 egg yolks
½ cup sugar
¼ cup dark or light rum
1 cup heavy cream, whipped
Chocolate for garnish

Combine chocolate crumbs and butter and press into sides and bottom of 9-inch pie plate. Chill 1 hour. Combine gelatin and water in small saucepan. Let stand for 1 minute. Cook over medium heat, stirring constantly until gelatin dissolves. Set aside to cool. Beat egg yolks and sugar until thick and lemon-colored. Gradually stir in gelatin mixture; beat well. Stir in rum. Fold in whipped cream. Pour mixture into chilled crust and top with grated chocolate or chocolate curls. Refrigerate. Servings: 6. Preparation Time: 1½ hours.

Carole Ferrell

Candy Bar Pie

1⅓ cups shredded coconut
2 tablespoons melted butter
2 tablespoons instant coffee
2 tablespoons water

1 (7 ounce) chocolate bar
   with almonds, broken up
4 cups Cool Whip

Combine coconut and butter. Press into pie plate. Bake in 325° oven for 10 minutes or until golden brown, cool. In a small pan, dissolve coffee powder in water, add chocolate bar. Stir over low heat until almost melted. Cool. Fold in Cool Whip and pour into coconut crust. Chill in freezer overnight. Does not freeze solid! Servings: 6 to 8. Pan Size: 8-inch pie plate. Preheat: 325°. Preparation Time: 20 minutes. Cooking Time: 10 to 15 minutes.

Gail Sepich

Desserts

Angel Nut Pie

1/2 cup sugar
1/8 teaspoon cream of tartar
2 egg whites
1/2 cup chopped nuts
3/4 cup semi-sweet
   chocolate pieces

3 tablespoons hot water
1 teaspoon vanilla
1 cup heavy cream, whipped
3 sticks crushed
   peppermint candy

Sift sugar and cream of tartar together. Beat egg whites until stiff. Add sugar. Beat until smooth and glossy. Grease a pie plate and smooth meringue over it to form crust. Sprinkle nuts on top and bake at 275° for one hour. Cool thoroughly. Melt chocolate in double boiler, add hot water and cool slightly. Add vanilla and fold in whipped cream. Fill cooled pie shell and chill for at least 4 hours. Just before serving, top with crushed peppermint. Preheat: 275°.

Buzzy Hussey

Egg Custard Pie

1 cup sugar
4 tablespoons butter or
   margarine, melted
2 tablespoons flour

3 eggs, beaten
1 1/2 cups milk
1 teaspoon vanilla
1 (9-inch) pie shell

Cream sugar and butter together; add flour and eggs, mix well. Add milk and vanilla. Pour into pie shell. Bake at 350° for one hour or until knife inserted in center comes out clean. For coconut custard pie, add 1/3 package shredded coconut after milk and bake. Makes large 9-inch pie. Servings: 8. Pan Size: 9-inch pie pan. Preheat: 350°. Preparation Time: 10 minutes. Cooking Time: 1 hour.

Mrs. D. Wayne Williams

224

Caramel Apple Pie

6 ounces cream cheese,
    softened
1 egg
1½ teaspoons vanilla
3 tablespoons sugar

1 tablespoon flour
1 can condensed milk
12 ounces apples, peeled
    and sliced
½ teaspoon cinnamon
1 (9-inch) pie shell

In a mixing bowl, combine cream cheese, egg, vanilla, sugar and flour. Beat until smooth. Spread over pie shell. Caramelize condensed milk in slow cooker or medium saucepan until thickened. In separate bowl, combine caramel mixture, apples and cinnamon. Gently spoon over cream cheese mixture. Bake at 350° for 40 to 45 minutes.

Edith Jackson Hankins

Mom's Favorite Blueberry Pie

Single crust pie shell
¾ cup granulated sugar
2½ tablespoons cornstarch
¼ teaspoon salt
⅔ cup water
3 cups fresh blueberries,
    cleaned

2 tablespoons butter
1½ tablespoons lemon juice
1½ tablespoons Grand
    Marnier liqueur
Sweetened whipped cream
    for garnish

Bake pie shell according to directions. Combine sugar, cornstarch and salt in a saucepan. Add the water and 1 cup blueberries. Heat to boiling, stirring constantly; boil until very thick, about 15 minutes. Remove from heat; stir in butter, lemon juice and Grand Marnier, cool. Fold in remaining 2 cups blueberries, refrigerate one hour. Spoon into pie shell. Refrigerate at least one hour before serving. Garnish with whipped cream, if desired.

J. Tucker Beck

225

Desperts

Coconut Meringue Pie

1 cup sugar
4 tablespoons flour
2 egg yolks
2 cups milk
2 tablespoons butter

1 teaspoon vanilla
Pinch salt
1/2 cup flake coconut
1 (9-inch) pie shell, baked
Meringue (see recipe below)

In a heavy saucepan, combine sugar and flour. In a small bowl, beat the egg yolks, add the milk and stir before adding to the sugar mixture. Cook over medium heat until thickened. Remove from heat and add butter, vanilla and salt, stirring. Add the coconut and pour into a baked 9-inch pie shell. Top with meringue, sprinkle with additional coconut and bake at 350° until meringue is golden brown.

MERINGUE:
3 egg whites, room
    temperature

3 tablespoons sugar
1/4 teaspoon cream of tartar

While beating egg whites, gradually add sugar and cream of tartar. Beat until peaks form. (Do not allow to become dry.) Spread onto filled pie shell with knife until fluffy.

NOTE: For delicious chocolate pie: use the same recipe but omit the coconut and add 3 rounded tablespoons cocoa (mixed in with sugar and flour).

Nancy Worley

Dorothy's Lemon Pecan Pie

As served at the old Hammett House Restaurant over 30 years ago...
still the best lemon pecan pie around.

3 whole eggs	1 teaspoon lemon extract
1/3 cup butter, melted	Juice of 1/2 lemon
11/2 cups sugar	1 (8 inch) pie shell, unbaked
3/4 cup pecan halves or pieces	

Whisk eggs lightly but do not use a mixer nor beat until foamy. Add remaining ingredients and pour into 8-inch unbaked pie shell. Bake at 300° for 45 minutes, taking care not to brown too quickly.

Mary Ruth Witt

Jimmie Ruth's Lemon Pie

2 cups crushed vanilla wafers	1/2 cup fresh lemon juice (6 to 8 lemons)
1/2 stick butter, melted	4 egg whites
3 egg yolks	3 tablespoons sugar
1 can sweetened condensed milk	

MAKE CRUST FIRST: Combine crushed vanilla wafers with melted butter. Spread in 9-inch pie plate. Bake 10 to 15 minutes or until brown. Let cool 15 minutes.

FILLING: Mix egg yolks with sweetened condensed milk. Slowly mix in lemon juice. Set aside.

MERINGUE: Beat egg whites until peaks form. Slowly beat in sugar. Pour filling into cooled crust, spread meringue on top. Bake at 350° for 10 to 15 minutes or until meringue is nicely browned. Let cool completely then refrigerate before serving.

Jimmie Ruth Pugh

227

Desserts

Harbor Docks Key Lime Pie

1 (14 ounce) can sweetened
   condensed milk
4 egg yolks
3 to 4 ounces key lime juice

1 (9-inch) graham cracker
   pie shell
Whipped cream

In small bowl, combine sweetened condensed milk with egg yolks and beat at slow speed until blended. Slowly add lime juice and beat until well mixed. Pour into pie shell. Bake at 350° for 12 to 15 minutes or do not bake and refrigerate overnight. Serve with whipped cream. Preheat: 350°.

Folks in the Kitchen wine recommendation: Bernkastler Badstube Spatlese.

Harbor Docks Restaurant
Destin, FL

Old Fashioned Pumpkin Pie

1½ cups canned pumpkin
1 cup milk
1 cup sugar
2 eggs

¼ teaspoon cinnamon
¼ teaspoon nutmeg
1 (9-inch) pie shell, unbaked
1 tablespoon butter
Whipped cream

Combine pumpkin, milk, sugar, eggs, cinnamon and nutmeg. Pour into pastry shell. Cut butter in slices and sprinkle across top. Bake at 425° for 25 minutes. Serve with whipped cream.

Mary Ruth Witt

228

Quick Pumpkin Pie

4 eggs	2 teaspoons vanilla
1/2 cup butter or margarine	2 cups cooked mashed
2 cups milk	pumpkin
1/2 cup flour	1/2 teaspoon cinnamon
1 cup sugar	1/4 teaspoon ginger
1 cup coconut	3/4 teaspoon nutmeg

Mix all ingredients thoroughly in a blender or by hand. Pour into 2 (9-inch) pie plates. Bake at 350° for about 50 to 55 minutes or until knife inserted in center comes out clean. The flour will settle to form crust. The coconut forms a topping. The center is an egg custard, pumpkin filling. Delicious.

Laquita Price

Strawberry Snowflake Pie
The best dessert ever.

1 baked (9-inch) deep dish	1/2 teaspoon cream of tartar
pie shell	Pinch of salt
1 quart strawberries	2 egg whites
1 1/2 cups sugar	1/4 teaspoon almond extract
1/2 cup water	

Fill pie shell with whole strawberries that have been washed, hulled and well drained. Put the prettiest berries in the center. Mix sugar, water, and cream of tartar in a saucepan. Cover the pan and bring to a boil. Uncover and continue cooking until syrup "skins" long threads or reaches 250° on a candy thermometer. Pour gradually into stiffly beaten salted egg whites, beating constantly. Place pan in cold water and continue beating until icing piles in peaks. Add almond extract and mix well. Spoon onto pie leaving center uncovered. Cool before serving. Do not put in refrigerator.

Brenda Harris

Desserts

Fudge Pie

1 stick butter or margarine
2 squares chocolate
1 cup sugar
2 eggs, beaten

¼ cup flour
1 tablespoon water
½ teaspoon vanilla
½ to 1 tablespoon nuts

Melt butter and chocolate. Add remaining ingredients and pour into a well-greased and floured pie pan. Bake at 325° for 30 to 40 minutes. Serve with vanilla or peppermint ice cream. Preheat: 325°.

Buzzy Hussey

Easy Chocolate Pie

4 tablespoons flour
1 cup sugar
Dash of salt
2 squares unsweetened
   chocolate

2 cups milk, scalded
2 tablespoons butter
3 egg yolks, beaten
1 teaspoon vanilla
1 prepared pie crust

Combine flour, sugar, salt and broken up chocolate pieces. Add hot scalded milk slowly while stirring. Add butter. Cook slowly until fairly thick and then add beaten eggs. Continue to cook until very thick. Add vanilla. Pour into a prebaked pie crust and chill until cold.

TOPPING:
1 cup whipping cream   Shaved chocolate
Sugar

Whip cream until it begins to thicken. Add sugar and whip until firm. Top each slice of pie with a generous spoonful of topping followed by a sprinkling of shaved chocolate.

Helen Hardin

Chocolate Pie

Family recipe passed on for generations!

1 cup sugar	¹/₈ cup water
¹/₄ teaspoon salt	1 cup hot water
2 tablespoons cocoa	4 tablespoons butter
3 rounded tablespoons flour	¹/₂ teaspoon vanilla
1 small can evaporated milk	2 egg whites
2 egg yolks	1 baked pie crust

In a saucepan, mix together sugar, salt, cocoa and flour. Add evaporated milk and egg yolks. Stir. Add both measurements of water and cook over medium heat until mixture comes to a boil. Take off heat and stir in butter and vanilla. Pour into baked pie crust. Beat egg whites until stiff peaks form. Spread over chocolate filling. Bake at 350° until meringue is golden brown.

Mrs. Fredrick W. Smith

Our Secret Chocolate Meringue Pie

This is a special recipe I have used and shared with only a few people for 45 years...my two daughters' favorite.

CRUST:

3 egg whites	1/2 teaspoon vanilla
Dash of salt	3/4 cup sugar
1/4 teaspoon cream of tartar	1/3 cup chopped pecans

FILLING:

3/4 cup semi-sweet chocolate chips	1 cup of heavy cream or Cool Whip
1/2 cup hot water	Additional whipped cream
1 teaspoon vanilla	
Dash of salt	

Combine egg whites, salt, cream of tartar and vanilla. Beat to a stiff foam. Add sugar gradually; beating until very stiff and sugar is dissolved. Spread into well greased 9-inch pie plate (Pyrex best). Build up sides. Sprinkle bottom and sides with nuts. Bake in a low oven 275° for 1 hour. Cool, then fill with filling.

FILLING: Melt semi-sweet chocolate pieces in top of double boiler over boiling water. Add hot water, vanilla, and salt. Stir until smooth. Cool. Fold in whipped heavy cream or Cool Whip. Fill shell. Chill for 4 hours or overnight. Serve with whipped cream or Cool Whip. Servings: 8. Pan Size: 9-inches. Preheat: 275°. Preparation Time: 30 minutes. Cooking Time: 1 hour, let set at least 4 hours.

Sis Long

232

Kirkland's Old Fashioned Chocolate Pie

My husband is the king of all pie eaters, and this is truly his favorite.

3 heaping tablespoons flour
3 heaping tablespoons
   cocoa powder
1 cup sugar
1 (5 ounce) can evaporated
   milk, then fill can with
   water and add

3 egg yolks
1 teaspoon vanilla
1 stick butter or margarine,
   softened
1 (9 inch) baked pastry shell

In medium saucepan mix all ingredients (will be lumpy). Turn heat on medium-high, stirring constantly about 5 minutes, or until mixture thickens, stirring bottom of pan. Pour into baked pie crust. Top with meringue and bake until golden brown at 375° for 5 to 10 minutes.

FOOLPROOF MERINGUE:
3 egg whites, room
   temperature (10 to 15
   minutes out of
   refrigerator)

1 teaspoon cream of tartar
1/2 teaspoon vanilla
6 to 8 tablespoons sugar

Beat egg whites for 1 minute on high, add cream of tartar and vanilla. Then add sugar, only 1 tablespoon at a time, still beating on high until stiff and egg whites form peaks. Servings: 6. Pan Size: Deep dish crust. Preheat: 375°. Preparation Time: 20 minutes. Cooking Time: 5 to 10 minutes to brown meringue.

Kimberly W. Kirkland

233

Chocolate Meringue Pie

For those who love chocolate, this is a wonderful treat.
Best with homemade pie pastry.

1¼ cups sugar plus ½ cup reserved
⅓ cup all-purpose flour
¼ cup high quality cocoa
2 cups milk
4 eggs, separated
2 tablespoons butter or margarine

1 baked (9-inch) pastry shell
½ teaspoon cream of tartar
1½ teaspoons vanilla in chocolate filling and ½ teaspoon in meringue (optional)

Combine 1¼ cups sugar, flour, and cocoa in a heavy saucepan. In a separate bowl, combine milk, egg yolks, and melted butter; beat, using a wire whisk, until mixture is well blended. Gradually add milk mixture to sugar mixture, stirring until smooth. Cook mixture over medium heat, stirring constantly, until thickened and bubbly, about 10 minutes. Add (optional 1½ teaspoons pure vanilla), and stir. Spoon into pastry shell; set aside. Beat egg whites and cream of tartar at high speed with electric mixer until foamy. Gradually add remaining ½ cup sugar, a tablespoon at a time, (optional ½ teaspoon vanilla), beating until stiff peaks form and sugar dissolves (2 to 4 minutes). Spread meringue mixture over chocolate filling, sealing edge of pastry. Sealing is important to quality of meringue. Bake at 325° for 25 minutes or until golden brown. Cool to room temperature before cutting with knife dipped in cold water. Servings: 6 to 8. Pan Size: 9-inch pie dish. Preheat: 325°. Preparation Time: 20 minutes. Cooking Time: 25 to 30 minutes.

Dorothy D. Thurman

Apple Cake

FOR CRUST:

2¹/₂ cups graham cracker
    crumbs
2 tablespoons sugar

1 teaspoon cinnamon
¹/₂ cup butter, melted

Mix ingredients together saving a small amount for topping. Press into 9¹/₂-inch springform pan covering bottom and sides.

FILLING:

2¹/₂ large Granny Smith
    apples, peel and slice
    thin
2 tablespoons butter
2 tablespoons sugar
1 tablespoon lemon peel
1 tablespoon lemon juice

6 large eggs
2 cups sour cream
2 cups sugar
2 tablespoons vanilla
    extract
Pinch of salt

Melt butter. Add apples, sugar, lemon peel and juice. Cook for 15 minutes, and cool. Heat oven to 350°. Beat eggs in double boiler. Add sour cream, sugar, vanilla, salt, blend well with wire whisk, until thickened. Put apples in pan. Pour egg mixture over apples. Sprinkle with extra graham cracker mixture. Cook in water bath for 1 hour and 15 minutes or until set. Servings: 12.

Billy and Tommie Dunavant

235

Desserts

Applesauce Fruit Cake

This was my grandmother's recipe from the hills of Tennessee. My wife never would eat fruitcake until she tasted this recipe (we even have friends that request this every year).

1 cup butter	1/3 teaspoon cloves
1 cup sugar	1/2 teaspoon nutmeg
2 1/2 cups flour	Pinch salt
1 1/2 cups apple sauce	2 teaspoons soda
1 1/2 cups black or English walnuts	1 cup crystallized cherries
	1 cup crystallized pineapple
1 1/2 cups chopped raisins	1 cup citron
2 teaspoons cinnamon	1 package mincemeat

Line springform pan with greased brown paper. Mix all ingredients together thoroughly by hand. It will be very stiff and difficult to mix. Pour into pan and decorate with additional cherries. Bake at 300° for 2 1/2 hours. Servings: 12. Preheat: 300°. Preparation Time: 20 minutes. Cooking Time: 2 1/2 hours.

Robert Qualls

Apricot Nectar Cake

CAKE:

1 box yellow or lemon cake mix	1 cup vegetable oil
1 (3 ounce) package lemon gelatin	1 cup apricot nectar
	6 eggs

Mix all ingredients together and bake in greased and floured tube cake pan at 350° for 50 minutes. Prepare glaze and pour over cake. Cool completely and remove from pan.

GLAZE:

2 cups confectioner's sugar	1 cup orange juice
1 lemon, juice and grated rind	

Mix together. Servings: 10 to 12. Preparation Time: 50 minutes. Cooking Time: 50 minutes.

Scott Sellers

236

Ida's Carrot Cake

2 cups sugar
4 eggs
1½ cups salad oil
2 cups flour
1 teaspoon salt

2 teaspoons soda
3 teaspoons cinnamon
2 tablespoons vanilla
3 cups raw carrots, grated

ICING:
1 stick butter or margarine
8 ounces cream cheese
1 box powdered sugar

1 cup chopped pecans
2 teaspoons vanilla
Dash salt

Mix and blend sugar, eggs and salad oil. Add flour, salt, soda, cinnamon and vanilla. Add carrots. Bake in 2 or 3 layers at 350° for 40 minutes.

ICING: Mix butter, cream cheese and powdered sugar. Add chopped pecans, vanilla and dash of salt. Spread on cake when cooled. Servings: 16. Preparation Time: 45 minutes. Cooking Time: 40 minutes.

Dawn Mokros

Desserts

Pina Colada Cake

This is a very moist cake. The longer you keep it, the better the flavor. Great!

1 (18½ ounce) package
  yellow cake mix
1 (3¾ ounce) package
  instant vanilla pudding
  and pie filling mix
1 (15 ounce) can cream of
  coconut

½ cup plus 2 tablespoons
  rum
⅓ cup vegetable oil
4 eggs
1 (8 ounce) can crushed
  pineapple, drained well

Preheat oven to 350°. In large mixing bowl, combine cake mix, pudding mix, ½ cup cream of coconut, ½ cup rum, oil and eggs. Beat on medium speed 2 minutes. Stir in pineapple. Pour into greased and floured 10-inch tube pan. Bake 50 to 55 minutes. Cool slightly. Remove from pan. With a table knife or skewer, poke holes about 1-inch apart in cake almost to bottom. Combine remaining cream of coconut and rum. Pour over cake. Chill thoroughly. Garnish; store in refrigerator. Garnish: whipped cream, pineapple slices, maraschino cherries or toasted coconut. Servings: 10 to 12. Preparation Time: 30 to 45 minutes. Cooking Time: 50 to 55 minutes.

Carol Wandling

238

Coconut Pineapple Cake

CAKE:
1 cup butter
2 cups sugar
3 cups sifted flour
1 tablespoon baking powder

1/4 teaspoon salt
4 eggs, separated
1 cup milk
1 teaspoon vanilla

FILLING:
1 cup sugar
1/3 cup water
1 can crushed pineapple,
    drained slightly

1 cup coconut

ICING:
1 cup sugar
1/4 teaspoon salt
2 egg whites
1/2 teaspoon cream of tartar
1 1/2 tablespoons cornstarch

4 tablespoons cold water
1 teaspoon vanilla
6 marshmallows
Grated coconut

FOR CAKE: Cream butter and sugar. Add egg yolks one at a time beating after each addition. Mix together flour and baking powder and beat into butter mixture alternating with milk and vanilla. Beat egg whites and fold in gently. Pour into three greased and floured cake pans and bake at 350° for 30 minutes. Cool in pans. Preheat: 350°.

FOR FILLING: In a small saucepan, combine sugar and water. Bring to a boil and cook until mixture reaches 230° on a candy thermometer. Remove from heat, cool slightly and add pineapple and coconut. Cool. Spread between cake layers.

FOR ICING: Put all ingredients, except marshmallows and grated coconut, in top of double boiler. Cook for 4 minutes beating constantly. Add marshmallows cut into pieces and heat an additional three minutes, stirring constantly. Spread icing over cooled cake. Cover with grated coconut.

Mrs. Thomas R. Price

239

Desserts

Our Favorite Coconut Cake
This cake is better the second day.

1 box yellow cake mix with pudding, milk substituted for water

FROSTING:

2 cups sugar	**1 (12 ounce) package frozen**
1 (8 ounce) container sour	**coconut (reserve 1/4 cup**
cream	**for frosting)**
1 (8 ounce) container frozen	
whipped topping	

Prepare cake according to cake mix instructions substituting milk for water. Bake and sit overnight. Mix all frosting ingredients and let sit overnight. Next day, split each cake layer in half. Frost one layer at a time and stack. Frost sides. Put reserved coconut on top. Refrigerate in airtight container. Servings: 12. Pan Size: 2 round cake pans.

Pat Leary

Key Lime Cake

CAKE:

1¹/₃ cups sugar	5 eggs or egg substitute
2 cups all-purpose flour	1¹/₃ cups oil
²/₃ teaspoon salt	³/₄ cup orange juice
1 teaspoon baking powder	¹/₂ teaspoon vanilla
¹/₂ teaspoon baking soda	1 teaspoon lemon extract
1 (3 ounce) package lime gelatin	

GLAZE:

¹/₃ cup key lime juice	¹/₃ cup powdered sugar

GARNISH:

Whipped topping	Lime slices

Preheat oven to 350°. Place dry ingredients in mixing bowl. Add eggs, oil, orange juice, vanilla and lemon extract. Beat until well blended. Pour batter into 9x13x2-inch pan. Bake 25 to 30 minutes. Remove cake from oven. Let pan cool 15 minutes then prick cake all over and drizzle with glaze. Cover and refrigerate. Serve with garnish. 12 to 15 servings.

Sharon S. Kelso

Mandarin Orange Cake

2 cups sugar	2 (11 ounce) cans mandarin
2 cups flour	oranges
2 eggs	1 pint whipping cream
2 teaspoons vanilla	³/₄ cup brown sugar
2 teaspoons baking soda	¹/₂ teaspoon vanilla

Blend first 5 ingredients. Chop oranges and fold in. Pour mixture into greased and floured pan. Bake in preheated oven at 350° for 45 minutes.

FROSTING: Stir brown sugar into the whipping cream and chill for 12 hours. Add ¹/₂ teaspoon vanilla and beat. Frost cooled cake. Servings: 16. Pan Size: 9¹/₂x13-inches. Preparation Time: 30 minutes. Cooking Time: 45 minutes.

Bonnie Hartzman

Lazy Daisy Oatmeal Cake

1¼ cups boiling water	1 teaspoon vanilla
1 cup uncooked oats	1½ cups flour
½ cup butter, softened	1 teaspoon soda
1 cup sugar	½ teaspoon salt
1 cup brown sugar	¾ teaspoon cinnamon
2 eggs, beaten	¼ teaspoon nutmeg

FROSTING:

½ cup butter, melted	⅔ cup nuts, chopped
1 cup brown sugar	1½ cups shredded coconut
6 tablespoons half-and-half	

Using small bowl, pour water over oats and cover. Allow to stand 20 minutes. In large bowl, beat butter until creamy. Add sugars. Beat until fluffy. Add eggs and vanilla. Stir in oats. In separate bowl, sift flour with soda, salt and spices. Add to creamed mixture. Pour into well greased and floured 9x13-inch baking pan. Bake at 350° for 25 to 30 minutes. While cake is baking, prepare frosting in medium saucepan by melting butter. Add brown sugar, half-and-half, nuts and coconut. Stir while butter is melting. When cake is done, punch holes throughout with fork tines and spread frosting over cake. Place under broiler until bubbly. Serve warm or cold. Servings: 10 large. Preheat: 350°. Preparation Time: 40 minutes. Cooking Time: 30 minutes.

Mary Ruth Witt

242

Southern Hospitality Caramel Cake

A great cake to take for a new neighbor, party or any occasion.

1 yellow cake mix

ICING:

2 cups sugar   **1/2 cup sugar**
1 teaspoon cornstarch   **1 teaspoon vanilla**
1 pint heavy cream   **Pinch of salt**

Bake cake according to package directions. To make icing: Put 2 cups sugar, cornstarch and heavy cream in a deep saucepan and bring to a boil. In a skillet, cook 1/2 cup sugar over medium heat to caramelize. When caramelized, pour into boiling mixture. Reduce heat and stir but do not overstir. Test every few seconds to see if soft ball will form in cold water. Add vanilla and a pinch of salt. Take off heat and stir occasionally until you can put your hand on bottom of pan comfortably, about 5 to 7 minutes. Beat 1 to 2 minutes with a large spoon like you would candy until thick but not hard. Spread over cooled cake. Pan Size: 9x13-inches.

NOTE: Use extra fine granulated sugar.

Marilyn Newton

243

Chocolate Yummy

1 cup all-purpose flour
1 cup finely chopped pecans
1 stick butter or margarine,
   softened
2 (8 ounce) packages cream
   cheese, softened
1 1/2 cups whipped topping

1 1/2 cups powdered sugar
1 large box vanilla instant
   pudding mix
1 large box chocolate
   instant pudding mix
Approximately 6 cups milk
Additional whipped topping

Mix flour, chopped pecans and softened butter. Press into bottom of 9x13-inch pan or glass baking dish. Bake at 350° for 15 to 20 minutes. Remove and cool completely. Mix softened cream cheese, powdered sugar and whipped topping until smooth and creamy. Spread over pecan crust. Mix vanilla instant pudding according to directions on package. (Use about 1/4 cup less milk so that pudding will become very firm.) Spread over cream cheese layer. Mix chocolate instant pudding according to directions on package. (Use less milk.) Spread over vanilla pudding layer. Cover with foil and chill thoroughly. Spread additional whipped topping over chocolate pudding layer. Garnish with chopped pecans or chocolate bits. Eat and enjoy! Rich but not heavy. Preheat: 350°.

NOTE: This recipe can be cut by using small packages of pudding mix and using 1 (8 ounce) package cream cheese with 1 cup sugar and 1 cup whipped topping.

Rip Scherer

244

Hershey Bar Cake

I searched for this "taste" for years and use it constantly.

8 Hershey bars
6 ounces chocolate chips
1 stick butter, softened
1 stick margarine, softened
2 cups sugar
4 eggs

1/2 teaspoon soda
2 teaspoons vanilla
1/2 teaspoon salt
21/2 cups cake flour
1 cup buttermilk
Powdered sugar for topping

Melt Hershey bars and chips in 2 tablespoons water. Beat butter and margarine with sugar, adding eggs and vanilla; mix dry ingredients, adding buttermilk. Mix chocolate with all. Bake at 325° in a greased and floured tube pan about 1 hour 15 minutes. Let stand in oven 5 to 10 minutes. Sprinkle with powdered sugar and serve in a pool of chocolate sauce (recipe follows). Freezes well. Servings: 20. Pan Size: 9 or 10-inch tube pan. Preheat: 325°. Preparation Time: 30 minutes. Cooking Time: 1 hour 15 minutes.

CHOCOLATE SAUCE: (Serve over Fudge Pie or Hershey Bar cake with ice cream or whipped cream.)

4 ounces unsweetened
   chocolate squares
2 ounces semi-sweet
   chocolate chips
1/2 stick real butter, 1/2 stick
   margarine (1 stick total)

1 cup sugar (heaping)
2 (6 ounce) cans evaporated milk
2 teaspoons vanilla

Mix all together and stir until thick (over low heat). Serve hot!

Jane D. Lettes

245

Desserts

Three Musketeer Cake

8 Three Musketeer candy bars
2 sticks butter
2 cups sugar
4 eggs

2 1/2 cups flour
1/2 teaspoon soda
1 1/4 cups buttermilk
1 cup chopped pecans

Melt candy bars and 1 stick butter, set aside. Cream sugar and 1 stick butter. Add eggs. Add alternately flour, soda with buttermilk. Add melted candy and butter mixture. Add pecans. Bake in tube pan at 325° for 1 hour and 10 minutes.

ICING:
2 1/2 cups sugar
1 cup evaporated milk
6 ounces semi-sweet
   chocolate chips

1 cup marshmallow cream
1 stick butter

Cook sugar and milk to soft ball stage. Add chocolate chips, marshmallow cream and butter. Stir until all are melted.

NOTE: This cake is delicious served with or without the icing.

Charlotte Wolfe

Easy Mini-Cheesecakes

3 (8 ounce) packages lite
   cream cheese
1 cup sugar

5 eggs
1/2 teaspoon vanilla

TOPPING:
1 cup sour cream
1/2 teaspoon vanilla

1/4 cup sugar

Mix first four ingredients together. Fill mini-foil muffin tins 3/4 full. Bake 30 minutes, 300° oven. Mix together topping ingredients. Put 1/2 teaspoon mixture on each one plus fruit preserves, if desired. Bake for 5 minutes. Cool. Refrigerate or freeze. Servings: About 48. Pan Size: 2-inch mini-baking cups. Preheat: 300°. Cooking Time: 30 minutes plus 5 minutes.

Inez Franklin

246

Jet's Cheesecake

1 (9 ounce) bag vanilla wafers
1 teaspoon cinnamon
1 stick butter, melted
1/4 cup sugar
4 eggs
1 cup sugar

1/8 teaspoon salt
1 teaspoon lemon juice
2 pounds cream cheese, softened
1 pint sour cream
1 teaspoon vanilla
4 tablespoons sugar

Crush vanilla wafers in plastic bag or process in food processor until fine. Combine crumbs, cinnamon, 1/4 cup sugar and butter. Press into springform cake pan. Use 1 large pan or 2 small. Beat eggs, add 1 cup sugar slowly and continue to beat until thick and lemon colored. Add salt, lemon juice and cream cheese. Beat until well combined. Pour over crust and bake at 375° for 25 minutes or until well set. Remove from oven. Combine sour cream, vanilla and 4 tablespoons sugar. Spread over cheesecake. Return to oven and bake for 10 to 15 minutes longer at 475°. Preheat: 375°/475°.

Mrs. Jessie Thomas Leyman

Italian Cheesecake

1 stick lightly salted butter,
    melted
1/4 cup sugar
2 cups graham cracker
    crumbs
1 pound ricotta cheese
1/2 cup plus 2 tablespoons
    sugar

1 tablespoon flour
4 eggs, separated
1/4 cup sour cream
1/4 cup heavy cream
1 tablespoon vanilla
2/3 cup semi-sweet
    chocolate chips tossed
    with 1 tablespoon flour

In a small bowl, combine butter, sugar and crumbs. Press into pan. Combine ricotta, sugar and flour mixing with a wooden spoon until blended. Add egg yolks, sour cream, heavy cream and vanilla, stirring to blend. Beat egg whites until stiff peaks form and fold into cheese mixture one-third at a time until combined. Do not overblend. Add chocolate chips and stir. Pour over crust. Bake in a preheated 350° oven for 50 to 60 minutes or until center is firm. Cool in pan 30 minutes. Servings: 8 to 10. Pan Size: 10-inch springform. Preheat: 350°. Preparation Time: 1 hour 15 minutes. Cooking Time: 50 to 60 minutes.

Debora Drago Wilemon

247

Desperts

Fondant au Chocolat

Butter 8 aluminum cups (4 ounce size), coat the cups with granulated sugar

ONE:

3 ounces melted butter
1/2 ounce cocoa powder
Pinch of salt

6 ounces melted extra bitter chocolate (Valrhona)

With a hand whip, mix cocoa powder into melted butter. Add salt, and melted chocolate. Mix very well.

TWO:

4 ounces egg whites or 3 egg whites from 3 very large eggs

4 drops lemon juice, fresh strained
1 1/2 ounces powdered sugar

Whip the egg whites with the lemon juice, gradually adding the sugar until stiff. With a rubber spatula fold one into two. Pour or pipe the mixture into the prepared aluminum cups, leaving 1/2-inch from the rim. Bake the chocolate fondant in a preheated oven at 425° for 4 1/2 to 5 minutes. Unmold on the center of a plate and decorate with whipped cream, chocolate sauce and candied oranges. Serve it right away. Servings: 8.

Folks in the Kitchen wine recommendation: Kendall-Jackson Merlot.

René Pujol Restaurant
New York City, NY

248

Munnie's Chocolate Dessert

*My great-grandmother Munnie made this
dessert for special birthday parties.*

12 ounces semi-sweet chocolate chips	4 stiffly beaten egg whites
	1/2 cup powdered sugar
1/4 cup water	1 pint heavy cream, whipped
4 beaten egg yolks	1 large angel food cake

Melt chocolate in double boiler with the water. Add egg yolks. Let cool. Blend with stiffly beaten egg whites and powdered sugar. Fold in whipped cream. Break angel food cake into small pieces and combine this with chocolate mixture. Place in large flat Pyrex or springform pan and refrigerate overnight. Serve with almond flavored whipped cream and top with a cherry. Servings: 12. Preparation Time: 30 minutes.

Jane Folk

Ms. Inell's Perfect Pound Cake

2 sticks butter or margarine	3 cups flour
1/2 cup shortening	1/2 teaspoon baking powder
3 cups sugar	1/2 teaspoon salt
5 eggs	1 cup milk
2 teaspoons vanilla	

Blend butter and shortening and beat until soft. Add sugar a little at a time, blending well. Add one egg at a time beating after each addition. Add vanilla. Mix dry ingredients. Add flour mixture to butter mixture one cup at a time alternating with milk and ending with flour. Pour into well-greased and floured pan. After baking, cool on a rack in the pan for 10 minutes. Remove from pan and continue cooling on rack. Servings: 15 to 20. Pan Size: 10-inch tube pan. Preheat: 325°. Preparation Time: 15 minutes. Cooking Time: 1 hour and 20 minutes.

Inell Chancellor

Chocolate Pound Cake

3 cups all-purpose flour
1½ teaspoons baking
   powder
4 (4 ounce) squares
   unsweetened chocolate
2/3 cup heavy cream
2 tablespoons instant coffee
   crystals
1/4 cup hot water
1½ cups butter, softened

2 cups sugar
5 eggs, room temperature
2 tablespoons brandy or
   cognac
1½ teaspoons vanilla
Sifted powdered sugar
Garnish: edible flower
   petals, lemon leaves,
   candied lemon slices

Grease and flour pan. In a medium bowl, combine flour and baking powder; set aside. Place chocolate squares in top of a double boiler over gently boiling water. Cook, stirring constantly until chocolate melts. Gradually stir in cream. Cool. Dissolve coffee crystals in hot water, stir into chocolate mixture. Preheat oven to 300°. In a large bowl, beat butter and sugar with an electric mixer until well combined. Add eggs, one at a time, beating thoroughly after each addition. Batter should be satiny smooth and fall in ribbons from a spoon. Add flour mixture alternately with cooled chocolate mixture and beat until well combined. Beat in brandy and vanilla. Pour batter into prepared tube pan. Bake for 1¼ to 1½ hours or until a toothpick inserted near center comes out clean. If necessary, cover with foil during last 15 minutes to prevent overbrowning. Cool in pan 20 minutes. Remove from pan; cool thoroughly. Sprinkle with powdered sugar. Garnish as desired. Servings: 16. Pan Size: 10-inch Bundt. Preheat: 300°. Preparation Time: 20 minutes.

Margaret M. Mallory

Granny's Pound Cake

This probably was the first solid food I ate as a baby.
My granny always had one made sitting in her kitchen.

1 cup shortening (Granny
  uses 1/2 butter, 1/2
  shortening)
3 cups sugar
6 eggs
3 cups flour
1/4 teaspoon soda

1/2 pint sour cream
1 teaspoon vanilla
1/2 teaspoon extract,
  whatever strikes your
  fancy that day (coconut,
  almond, maple, etc.)

Cream shortening and sugar. Add one egg at a time. Sift flour several times. Add soda. Add flour, alternating with sour cream. Add flavoring. Pour into pan and bake for 1 1/2 hours at 300°. Servings: 10 to 12. Pan Size: Bundt pan. Preheat: 300°. Preparation Time: 5 minutes. Cooking Time: 1 hour and 20 to 30 minutes.

Kim Manhein

Buttermilk Pound Cake

1 cup shortening
3 cups sugar
1 teaspoon (or more) vanilla
5 large eggs

1 cup buttermilk
1/2 teaspoon baking soda
3 cups flour

Beat together the shortening, sugar and vanilla in mixer at high speed until mixture looks like ice cream; thoroughly beat in eggs, one at a time. Stir together the buttermilk and soda. By hand, stir the flour gradually into the creamed mixture alternating with the buttermilk mixture and mixing only until smooth. Turn into a 10-inch angelcake pan (ungreased) and bake in a pre-heated 325° oven until a cake tester inserted in the center comes out clean, 1 hour and 20 minutes. Do not open oven first hour. Place on wire rack for 10 to 15 minutes.

Joanne Bejach Korges

251

Desserts

Amaretto Mousse

12 ounces cream cheese
1 1/2 pounds powdered sugar
2 to 3 ounces Amaretto
1 ounce almond extract

2 ounces sliced almonds
Sugar cookies for dipping
(Nabisco brown edged
cookies are great)

Let cream cheese come to room temperature. Place soft cheese in large mixing bowl. Pour in 1/3 powdered sugar, 2 ounces Amaretto and the almond extract. Mix with electric hand mixer and add powdered sugar. The consistency should be such that it can be easily spooned or poured. Add more Amaretto if desired and milk if too thick. Serve with cookies for dipping. Sprinkle sliced almonds over top and garnish with a fresh strawberry. This makes a nice sweet for a reception. Servings: 25 to 30. Preparation Time: 30 to 45 minutes.

John C. Jones

Amaretto Delight

Easy to prepare and it brings rave reviews every time, especially from men.

1/2 cup sliced almonds
12 ice cream sandwiches
1/2 cup Amaretto

12 ounces whipped topping
1 package Heath Bar Bits O'
Brickle

Spray dish to prevent sticking. Lightly toast almonds in a 300° oven and set aside to cool. Line bottom of dish with ice cream sandwiches. Punch holes in sandwiches and drizzle Amaretto to taste over them. Mix remaining Amaretto with whipped topping. Sprinkle 1/2 package of Heath Bar chips over ice cream sandwiches. Spread whipped topping that has been mixed with Amaretto over Heath Bar layer. Add another layer of Heath Bar Brickle. Top with toasted almonds. Freeze until ready to serve. Remove from freezer 10 to 15 minutes before serving and cut into squares. Re-freeze. Servings: 12 to 16. Pan Size: 9x13-inch Pyrex. Preheat: 300° to toast almonds. Preparation Time: 10 minutes.

Myra Harding

252

Bananas Foster

In the 1950's, New Orleans was the major port of entry for bananas shipped from Central and South America. Owen Edward Brennan challenged his talented chef, Paul Blange, to include bananas in a new culinary creation - Owen's way of promoting the imported fruit. Today, thirty-five thousand pounds of bananas are flamed each year at Brennan's in the preparation of its world-famous dessert.

1/4 cup (1/2 stick) butter	1 cup brown sugar
1/2 teaspoon cinnamon	1/4 cup banana liqueur
1/4 cup dark rum	4 scoops vanilla ice cream
4 bananas, cut in half lengthwise, then halved	

Combine the butter, sugar, and cinnamon in a flambé pan or skillet. Place the pan over low heat either on an alcohol burner or on top of the stove, and cook, stirring, until the sugar dissolves. Stir in the banana liqueur, then place the bananas in the pan. When the banana sections soften and begin to brown, carefully add the rum. Continue to cook the sauce until the rum is hot, then tip the pan slightly to ignite the rum. When the flames subside, lift the bananas out of the pan and place four pieces over each portion of ice cream. Generously spoon warm sauce over the top of the ice cream and serve immediately.

Folks in the Kitchen wine recommendation: Bonny Doon Vin De Glacier Muscat Canelli.

Brennan's Restaurant
New Orleans, LA

253

Desserts

Banana Pudding

*Two generations of grandmothers used this recipe,
making it affectionately called "Nana" pudding!*

PUDDING:

1²/₃ cups sugar
6 tablespoons flour
4 cups milk
4 eggs, separated, yolks
    beaten

3 to 4 bananas, very ripe
1 teaspoon vanilla
1 bag vanilla wafers

MERINGUE:

4 egg whites
4 tablespoons cold water
¼ teaspoon cream of tartar

6 tablespoons sugar
1 teaspoon vanilla

Measure sugar into saucepan, add flour, gradually stir in milk. Cook over medium to medium high heat, stirring to prevent scorching. When pudding starts to thicken, add small amount to the beaten egg yolks and then return egg mixture to pudding container cooking until thickened. Cool and add the vanilla. Meanwhile, prepare wafers, bananas and make meringue. In 3 quart round dish, layer vanilla wafers on bottom and place a layer around insides of bowl. Peel bananas and slice thinly all over top of wafers. Pour cooled pudding into dish and top with meringue. Brown lightly in 350° oven for 8 to 10 minutes. Servings: 6 to 8. Pan Size: 3 quart saucepan. Preheat: 350° oven. Preparation Time: 20 to 25 minutes. Cooking Time: Total 30 minutes.

MERINGUE: Add cold water and cream of tartar to egg whites and beat on high speed of mixer until stiff peaks form. Gradually add sugar, mixing thoroughly. Add vanilla.

Sharon Miller

254

Bread Pudding

6 slices white bread
Softened butter
4 eggs
1 cup sugar, divided
1 teaspoon vanilla extract
Dash of salt
3 cups milk

1 teaspoon cinnamon
1 (8 ounce) package
    softened cream cheese
Whipped cream for topping
    (optional)
1 ounce Amaretto for topping
    (optional)

Butter one side of bread and cut into one inch squares. Place in a lightly greased baking dish. Slightly beat three eggs. Add to eggs 1/2 cup sugar, vanilla and salt. Mix well. Heat milk; slowly add to egg mixture, mixing well. Pour over bread squares. Sprinkle with cinnamon. Combine cream cheese and remaining 1/2 cup sugar; blend until smooth. Add one egg, beating well. Spread mixture evenly over soaked bread. Bake at 350° for 45 minutes or until firm. If you desire topping, mix Amaretto with whipped cream and top squares of bread pudding. Servings: 8. Pan Size: 113/4x71/2x13/4-inch rectangle baking pan. Preheat: 350°. Preparation Time: 1 hour 15 minutes. Cooking Time: 45 minutes.

Toni Campbell Parker

Christmas Pudding

2 cups sugar
2 sticks butter
4 eggs
1/2 cup bourbon

1/2 box white raisins
2 cups pecan pieces
1 box vanilla wafers,
    crumbled

Melt sugar and butter together and let cool. Separate eggs. Add bourbon to egg yolks and beat until frothy. In a large mixing bowl, combine cooled sugar mixture, egg yolks, raisins, pecans and vanilla wafers. Beat egg whites until stiff and fold into mixture. Pour into soufflé dish and bake at 375° for 20 to 30 minutes. Serve with whipped cream.

Elizabeth Labry

Nana's Lemon Pudding

My grandmother was well-known for her delicious cakes and pies, but this lemon pudding recipe is a family favorite!

4 tablespoons butter	4 tablespoons flour
1½ cups sugar	2 cups whole milk
4 eggs, separated	Whipped cream
2 lemons, juice and grated rind	Lemon slices

Cream butter and sugar. Add beaten egg yolks, grated lemon rind and juice, flour and milk. Beat egg whites and fold into above mixture. Bake in buttered glass dish (9x9 or 9x11-inches) placed in a pan of water. Bake at 350° for 40 to 50 minutes. Serve with whipped cream and lemon slices. Servings: 6. Preparation Time: 15 minutes. Cooking Time: 40 to 50 minutes.

Barbara Williamson

Lime Dainty

1 lime, peeled, grated, juiced and strained (about 2 tablespoons)	¾ cup sugar
	2 tablespoons flour
	2 eggs, separated
3 tablespoons butter	1 cup milk
⅛ teaspoon salt	¼ teaspoon vanilla extract

Beat together butter, salt, sugar, and flour. Add egg yolks, milk, lime juice, lime peel and vanilla. Beat well until smooth. Whip egg whites until stiff and fold into other mixture. Pour batter into buttered 4 cup baking dish and set in a shallow pan partially filled with boiling water. Bake in a preheated 350° oven 45 minutes or until top is lightly browned. There will be cake on top and pudding on the bottom.

Billy and Tommie Dunavant

Dessert Number 7

Joe Thiesman's favorite dessert named after his football jersey number.

1 (3 ounce) box gelatin, any flavor

Whipped topping (optional)

1 (3 ounce) box pudding, any flavor

Prepare gelatin according to package directions. Prepare pudding according to package directions. After pudding is cooked and cooled slightly, spoon gelatin into a custard dish until it is half full. Spoon the pudding on top. It will settle and cool in the refrigerator. If desired, top with whipped topping. Makes a great dessert!

Joe Theisman

Boiled Custard

2 rounded tablespoons flour
1 cup sugar
Dash of salt
7 or 8 egg yolks, depending on size of egg

2 quarts whole milk
1½ teaspoons vanilla

Mix together flour, sugar and salt. Add beaten egg yolks. Put in pan and over medium-high heat add 1 cup milk slowly while stirring. Heat the rest of milk and slowly add to mixture. Cook slowly for 30 minutes stirring constantly until very thick. Add vanilla to custard after it cools.

Scott Sellers

Desserts

Wilhelm Hoppe's Lemon Cream Brulee

LEMON CREAM FILLING:

4 ounces lemon juice

Zest from 3 medium lemons

6 ounces heavy cream

1/4 vanilla bean or 1/2
   teaspoon real vanilla
   extract

3 egg yolks

2 eggs

2 ounces sugar

1/4 pound butter, cut into
   pieces

In a medium saucepan, add the lemon juice, zest, heavy cream, and the vanilla bean. Bring to a boil. In a large stainless steel bowl, whip egg yolks, eggs, and sugar until it forms a ribbon (light and fluffy). Add the lemon mixture into the whipped eggs, stirring constantly. Place the filled stainless steel bowl into a water bath. The water should be 180°. Cook until it becomes thick, stirring occasionally. Approximately 30 minutes. Remove mixture from water bath and stir in pieces of butter until it's melted. Remove vanilla bean and scrape the seeds into the mix. Strain mixture through a fine mesh stainer and pour into the pre-baked pastry shells.

PASTRY SHELL:

1/4 pound pastry flour

1/8 pound cornstarch

1 1/2 ounces sugar

1/4 pound butter, room
   temperature and cut into
   pieces

1 egg

Pinch salt

Combine pastry flour, cornstarch and sugar in a large bowl. Cut butter into dry ingredients until it resembles coarse corn meal. In a small bowl, scramble the egg and salt and then add to the large bowl. Using your fingers, combine mixture until you've reached a homogeneous mass. Cover and refrigerate overnight. Roll out dough on a floured work table to 3/8-inch thickness. Cut to fit individual buttered pie rings.

(continued on next page)

258

Line pie dough with coffee filter and place pie weights or beans and fill to the height of the dough. Bake at 400° until just golden, approximately 20 minutes. Remove from oven and allow to cool. Remove filter and weights. Let's put it together: Leaving the pastry shell in the ring, fill pastry with the lemon cream filling and chill for at least 3 hours. To serve: Sprinkle 1/8-inch thickness of sugar evenly over the entire lemon cream brulee. Broil until sugar is caramelized. Remove pie ring IMMEDIATELY. Enjoy. Servings: 6.

Folks in the Kitchen wine recommendation: Chateau Rayne Vigneau.

Hoppe's at 901
Morro Bay, CA

Strawberry Mousse

This is a recipe Jacqueline Kennedy served for dinners in the White House during the years she was first lady. A light, delicious dessert.

**1 quart strawberries,
washed and hulled
1/2 cup sugar
1/2 cup white wine
2 envelopes gelatin**

**1/2 cup cold water
1/2 cup boiling water
2 cups heavy cream,
whipped**

Reserve several strawberries for garnish. Press remaining strawberries through a fine sieve. Add sugar and wine; stir well. Chill. Soften gelatin in cold water. Add boiling water, stir to dissolve. Cool. Combine gelatin and chilled mixture. Beat in mixer until fluffy and slightly thickened; fold in whipped cream. Turn into greased two-quart mold. Chill three hours or longer. Unmold onto chilled platter. Garnish with remaining berries. Servings: 8 to 10.

Margaret Ann Eikner

Desserts

Tiramisu

1 cup espresso
12 tablespoons sugar
1 cup liquor (your choice,
    brandy, etc.)
3 eggs

2 (8 ounce) packages cream
    cheese, softened
1 pound ladyfingers
1 pint heavy cream
Cocoa powder

Mix espresso, 5 tablespoons of the sugar and liquor. Sprinkle over ladyfingers. Beat eggs until frothy. Add remaining sugar and cream cheese. Blend until smooth. Place half of the ladyfingers in pan and cover with half of the cheese mixture. Place the rest of the ladyfingers in pan and cover with remaining cheese mixture. Whip cream, adding sugar to taste and spread over top. Sprinkle with cocoa. Refrigerate. Servings: 12. Pan Size: 9x13-inches. Preparation Time: 40 minutes.

Sharon Luigs

Strawberry Trifle

Easy and very impressive.

1 (20 ounce) can pineapple
    chunks, drained
1 quart fresh strawberries,
    sliced
3 to 4 whole strawberries for
    topping

1 large container whipped
    topping
1 can condensed milk
1 angel food cake, cut into 3
    layers
1 package slivered almonds

Combine pineapple and sliced strawberries. Set aside. Combine whipped topping and condensed milk. Set aside. In a trifle bowl, layer cake, fruit and milk mixture. Repeat twice. Garnish with whole strawberries and almonds. Servings: 10. Pan Size: Trifle bowl. Preparation Time: 20 to 30 minutes.

Carole C. Moore

Charlotte Rousse
An old family recipe.

3 envelopes plain gelatin
1 cup cold water
2 cups milk
8 egg yolks, beaten
2 cups sugar

1 1/2 teaspoons vanilla (or bourbon)
1 pint heavy cream, whipped
12 stale ladyfingers, split
1 small jar whole maraschino
 cherries, sliced in two

Soak gelatin in cold water. Heat milk in double boiler just to boiling point. Mix eggs and sugar well. Add to milk (note: to keep milk from curdling, work milk and mixture back and forth until each is enough of same temperature not to curdle). Stir and cook 5 minutes. Add gelatin. Stir and cook 3 minutes. Remove from heat, stirring occasionally until mixture cools and thickens. Add vanilla or bourbon and mix well. Fold whipped cream into cooled mixture. Line glass bowl with split ladyfingers (place vertically). When custard is almost set, fill bowl. Decorate custard with cherries placed face down. Servings: 10. Preparation Time: 1 1/2 hours total.

Julia Atkinson

Mama's Lemon Charlotte Rousse
My mother's favorite light lemon dessert. Serve with raspberry sauce.

2 envelopes unflavored gelatin
1 cup lemon juice
8 eggs, separated
2 cups sugar

1 tablespoon lemon zest
1 large container whipped
 topping
24 ladyfingers

Combine gelatin and lemon juice in a small saucepan and cook over medium heat until gelatin is dissolved. Set aside. Combine sugar, egg yolks and lemon zest. Add slightly cooled gelatin mixture and blend well. Beat egg whites until stiff. Fold into egg yolk mixture along with whipped topping. Place ladyfingers around inside of springform pan. Crumble 2 to 3 ladyfingers in bottom. Pour mixture into pan. Chill 2 to 3 hours before serving. Servings: 15 to 20.

Sylvester Thornton

Desserts

Chocolate Charlotte Rousse

1 envelope unflavored gelatin
2 tablespoons cold water
3 (1 ounce) squares unsweetened chocolate
1/2 cup water
4 eggs, separated

1/2 cup sugar
1 teaspoon vanilla
Dash of salt
1/2 teaspoon cream of tartar
1/4 cup sugar
1 cup heavy cream, whipped
18 double ladyfingers, split

Soften gelatin in 2 tablespoons cold water. Melt chocolate in 1/2 cup water over low heat, stirring constantly. Remove from heat, add softened gelatin, stir to dissolve. Beat egg yolks until thick and lemon colored. Gradually beat in 1/2 cup sugar, add vanilla and dash of salt. Blend in chocolate mixture. Cool, stir until smooth. Beat egg whites and cream of tartar to soft peaks. Gradually add 1/4 cup sugar, beating to stiff peaks. Fold into chocolate mixture. Fold in whipped cream. Reserve about 10 ladyfingers for center layer. Line bottom and sides of an 8-inch springform pan with ladyfingers. Fill with half of the mixture. Layer reserved ladyfingers and fill with remaining chocolate mixture. Chill 8 hours or overnight. Servings: 8 to 10. Pan Size: 8-inch springform. Preparation Time: 20 minutes.

Mary Ann Ford

Cream Puffs

1/2 cup butter
1 cup boiling water

1 cup flour
4 eggs

Add butter to boiling water. Bring water back to a boil and add flour all at once, stirring vigorously. Cook until mixture is thick and smooth and does not adhere to the side of the saucepan, stirring constantly. Remove from the heat and cool slightly. Add eggs, one at a time, beating each egg into the mixture until smooth before adding the next egg. Drop the mixture by spoonfuls onto greased baking sheet 1 1/2-inches apart, shaping round with spoon. Bake at 400° for 25 to 30 minutes. When cool, the cream puffs may be filled with pudding or cream and served with fresh berries, chocolate or caramel sauce. Sprinkle with powdered sugar. Preheat: 400°.

Jill Worley

Brownie Fruit Dessert

1 box brownie mix
12 ounces cream cheese
2/3 cup sugar
1 small can crushed
    pineapple
Various fruit (strawberries, kiwi,
    bananas, blueberries)

2 squares semi-sweet
    chocolate
2 tablespoons butter

Prepare brownies according to instructions and cool. Mix cream cheese and sugar; frost brownies. Sprinkle crushed pineapple and various other fruits onto iced brownies. Melt chocolate and butter, drizzle over fruit. Pan Size: According to package directions. Preheat: 350°. Preparation Time: 1 hour with slicing fruit. Cooking Time: 25 to 30 minutes.

Elizabeth Woodmansee

Kathy's Congo Squares
While attending college, I had to make up a recipe and this is it.
I made a 100 on the assignment.

1 box brown sugar
2 3/4 cups plain flour
1/2 teaspoon salt
1 teaspoon vanilla
3 eggs

1 stick butter, room temperature
1 package semi-sweet
    chocolate chips
1 cup chopped pecans or
    other nuts (optional)

Mix all ingredients except chocolate chips and nuts together by hand, batter will be stiff, add chips and nuts. Spread in greased pan. Bake in 350° oven for 20 to 30 minutes. Allow to cool and cut into squares. Servings: 15 to 20 squares. Pan Size: 13x9-inches. Preheat: 350°. Preparation Time: 15 minutes. Cooking Time: 20 to 30 minutes.

Kathy Boyd

Desserts

Vienna Chocolate Bars

Any jelly can be used but a raspberry or red jelly seems to be the best.

2 sticks of butter or
   margarine
1½ cups sugar
2 egg yolks
2½ cups flour
12 to 15 ounces of fruit jelly
   (raspberry, strawberry,
   blackberry)

16 ounce bag chocolate
   chips
¼ teaspoon salt
4 egg whites
2 cups finely chopped nuts

Cream butter with egg yolks and ½ cup of sugar. Add flour and knead with fingers. Pat out mixture on greased jelly roll pan to about 3/8-inch thick. It helps to put some butter or oil on your hands. Bake 15 to 20 minutes at 350° until lightly browned. Remove from oven, spread with jelly and top with chocolate chips. Next beat egg whites with salt until stiff. Fold in remaining cup of sugar and nuts. Gently spread on top of jelly and chocolate mixture. Bake for about 25 minutes at 350°. Let set before cutting into bars. Servings: 36. Pan Size: Jelly roll pan. Preheat: 350°. Cooking Time: 15 to 20 first time, additional 25 minutes.

Sara Cunningham

Peppermint Sticks

These are the "hit" of the Federal Express Legal Department!

BARS:

4 eggs	1 teaspoon peppermint
2 cups sugar	extract or 1/4 teaspoon oil
1 cup cocoa	of peppermint
1 cup flour	2 sticks butter or margarine,
	melted

ICING:

1 box powdered sugar	1/2 teaspoon peppermint extract
1 stick butter or margarine,	Milk
melted	3 drops food coloring

COATING:

2 squares bitter chocolate,	2 tablespoons butter
melted	

BARS: Beat eggs with sugar until thick. Add cocoa and flour. Add peppermint flavoring and butter. Stir. Pour into well greased 11x7-inch jelly roll pan. Bake at 350° for 12 to 15 minutes (start checking at 10 minutes) or until toothpick comes out clean. Makes 96. Do not overbake. Cool, then frost.

ICING: Beat powdered sugar and melted butter until creamy. Add peppermint flavoring and enough milk to make creamy icing. Add food coloring. Color green or pink or any color depending on season (or reason). Spread icing on bars. Put in refrigerator to cool before coating.

COATING: Melt chocolate and butter in small pan. Drizzle or brush over frosted brownies. Place in refrigerator 10 minutes to harden. Cut into fingers, store in refrigerator. Servings: 96. Pan Size: 11x7-inches. Preheat: 350°. Preparation Time: 15 minutes. Cooking Time: 10 to 15 minutes.

Julie Ellis

Desserts

Chocolate Chip Pecan Oatmeal Cookies

2 sticks butter, softened
1¼ cups brown sugar, packed
½ cup sugar
1 package Egg Beaters
2 tablespoons skim milk
1¾ cups flour, all-purpose, unbleached
1 teaspoon baking soda
½ teaspoon salt
2½ cups oats
1 (12 ounce) package chocolate chips
1 cup pecans, chopped
2 teaspoons vanilla extract

Preheat oven to 375°. Beat butter and sugars together until creamy. Add Egg Beaters, milk and vanilla. Beat well. Mix flour, soda and salt. Add to mixture and mix well. Stir in oats, chocolate chips and pecans. Drop by spoonfuls onto cookie sheet. Bake 13 minutes. Cool on wire rack. Servings: Makes about 5 dozen. Preparation time: 1 hour.

Tricia Seubert

Oatmeal Cookies
Everyone loves these.

1 cup light brown sugar
1 cup white sugar
2 sticks butter or margarine
1 teaspoon vanilla
2 eggs
2 cups flour
1 level teaspoon salt
1 level teaspoon soda
¼ teaspoon cinnamon
¼ teaspoon nutmeg
2 cups oats
1¾ cups chopped pecans
2 little boxes raisins

Cream first 3 ingredients, add vanilla, beat in eggs. Add flour sifted with salt, soda, cinnamon and nutmeg. Add oats, pecans, and raisins. Mix well. Drop small teaspoons of dough on greased cookie sheet. Remove to cool when slightly brown. These freeze well and are crunchy. Servings: 6 dozen. Preheat: 350°. Cooking Time: 8 minutes but watch closely.

Sue Adams

Big House Vanilla Ice Cream

7 egg yolks
2 cups sugar
3 pints whole milk
24 ounces whipping cream

2 teaspoons pure vanilla
  extract
Pinch of salt
Pinch of sugar

In a small bowl, mix together the egg yolks and sugar. Put whole milk in a double boiler and add the egg yolk mixture. Cook for about 20 minutes stirring, or until mixture coats the back of a spoon. Remove from heat and let cool to room temperature. Add whipping cream and vanilla. Stir to mix. Add salt and pinch of sugar stirring until well combined. Freeze.

Kyle Patrick

Easy Peach Ice Cream

1 large box vanilla instant
  pudding
1 can evaporated milk
1 can sweetened condensed
  milk

1 cup sugar
1/2 teaspoon vanilla
1 medium can sliced
  peaches
1/2 gallon 2% milk

Mix together pudding and evaporated milk. Add condensed milk, sugar and vanilla. Mix well. Pour peaches and their juice into a blender and process until well chopped. Add peaches to pudding mixture. Pour into ice cream freezer container. Fill to fill line with 2% milk. Freeze according to manufacturer's instructions. Makes approximately 4 quarts.

Louise Callahan

Desserts

Chocolate Ice Cream

A Seessel family recipe. Unbelievably rich, but worth every mouthful!

9 egg yolks
1½ cups sugar
½ teaspoon salt
1 quart plus ¾ quart
   whipping cream

1 pound semi-sweet
   chocolate chips
3 teaspoons vanilla

Beat egg yolks, sugar and salt until light. In a saucepan over medium heat, bring cream to boiling point but do not boil. Pour cream slowly over egg mixture beating constantly with electric mixer. Melt chocolate in a double boiler and add slowly to egg mixture, stirring constantly. Cook mixture over medium heat. As soon as boiling point is reached, remove from heat. Add vanilla and stir. Cool and freeze in electric freezer. Freeze in containers. Makes ½ gallon.

Art and Peggy Seessel

Chocolate Raspberry Drops

1 package Oreo's, crushed
1 package mini chocolate
   chips

½ jar raspberry preserves
Powdered sugar

Mix ingredients. Chill. Form balls and roll in powdered sugar. Preparation Time: 20 minutes.

Pam Gordon

268

Mrs. Sudberry's Peanut Brittle

Quick, easy and foolproof. A favorite to give at Christmas.

8 ounces raw Spanish peanuts	1 teaspoon salt
1 cup sugar	2 teaspoons soda
1 cup light corn syrup	

Grease or spray a jelly roll pan. Using a heavy saucepan, combine the first three ingredients and insert a candy thermometer. Turn heat to high position, stirring constantly until mixture reaches 300°. Remove from heat immediately and quickly stir in salt/soda mixture until foaming occurs. Immediately pour out on greased cookie sheet. Cool and break into pieces.

Dianne M. Papasan

Chocolate Fudge

1 (12 ounce) can evaporated milk	10 ounces marshmallow creme
5 cups sugar	18 ounces semi-sweet chocolate bits
1 stick margarine	1½ cups chopped walnuts
1 teaspoon vanilla extract	

Grease pan and set aside. In large pot, cook milk, sugar and margarine over medium heat (stirring constantly) until boiling. Lower heat and continue to stir for eight minutes. Mixture should be boiling for the full eight minutes. Remove from heat and add vanilla, marshmallow creme and chocolate bits. Beat with mixer on high until completely smooth and creamy. Stir in nuts and pour into greased pan. Let cool for several hours before cutting. I like to make this in the evening and let it sit overnight and it is perfect for cutting in the morning. Servings: 10 pounds. Pan Size: 9x13 inch. Preparation Time: 20 minutes. Cooking Time: 8 minutes.

Kelly Dodson

Desserts

Mama's Pecan Pralines

1 pound brown sugar   **¼ cup butter**
¼ cup water   **2 cups whole pecans**

Stir sugar, water and butter over low fire until sugar is thoroughly dissolved. Add pecans and boil until mixture forms hard ball when tested in cold water. Drop like pancakes on greased platter or cookie sheet.

NOTE: My mother was from New Orleans and as pralines go, these are easy and better than those bought in New Orleans.

Lina P. Karlson

Caramel Fudge

3 cups sugar   **¼ teaspoon cream of tartar**
1 large can evaporated milk   **1 cup nuts, chopped**
½ cup white corn syrup   **1 teaspoon vanilla**
½ cup butter

Mix sugar, milk, corn syrup, butter and cream of tartar in black iron skillet. Cook, stirring with a wooden spoon, until it forms a hard ball in cold water. Remove and add nuts and vanilla. Beat until firm. Pour on buttered plate. Cut when cool.

Shirley Lawrence

KID'S FAVORITES

SPONSORED BY

NewSouth Capital Management, Inc.

Kid's Favorites

Easy Fresh Fruit Dip

8 ounces cream cheese   **13 ounce jar marshmallow creme**

Combine cream cheese and marshmallow creme. Beat with electric mixer until smooth. Serve with fresh fruit.

Marguerite Mooney

Caramel Popcorn

5 quarts popcorn, popped   **1/2 cup light corn syrup**
2 sticks butter or margarine,   **1 teaspoon salt**
** melted**   **1/2 teaspoon baking soda**
2 cups light brown sugar   **1 teaspoon vanilla**

Stir together butter, sugar, corn syrup and salt and bring to a boil, letting mixture boil 5 minutes without stirring. Add baking soda and vanilla, stir and pour over the popcorn. Spread onto baking sheet and bake at 250° for 1 hour. Preheat: 250°. Preparation Time: 30 minutes. Cooking Time: 1 hour.

Jill Worley

White Chocolate Party Mix

1 (10 ounce) package mini
  pretzels
5 cups Cheerios
5 cups Corn Chex
2 cups salted peanuts

1 pound M & M's (plain)
2 (12 ounce) packages
  vanilla chips
3 tablespoons vegetable oil

In large bowl, combine first five ingredients. Heat chips and oil in microwave for 2 minutes, stirring once. Microwave again until melted, creamy and smooth. Pour over cereal mixture and mix well. Place on 3 waxed paper lined baking sheets and let cool. Break apart. Store in airtight container. Servings: 5 quarts. Preparation Time: 15 minutes.

Mrs. Ted Johnson

Popcorn Munch

Kids can help make this and everyone loves it. Makes a great holiday gift.

2 bags microwave popcorn,
  popped
2 generous cups Cheerios
2 generous cups Crispix
6 ounces unsalted dry
  roasted peanuts

1 stick butter
1 cup light brown sugar
1/4 cup light corn syrup
1 teaspoon vanilla
1/2 teaspoon baking soda

Mix dry ingredients together in large bowl. Pour half into another bowl and set aside. In a small saucepan, melt butter. Add sugar and corn syrup. Cook over medium heat until mixture comes to a boil. Lower heat and cook, stirring constantly for five minutes. Remove from heat and carefully stir in vanilla and soda. Quickly drizzle half the mixture over half of the dry ingredients. Add remaining half and drizzle with the rest of the butter mixture, stirring to coat. Spread onto two cookie sheets and bake at 200° for 1 hour, turning and stirring to coat every twenty minutes. Store in a airtight container. Preheat: 200°. Preparation Time: 10 minutes. Cooking Time: 1 hour.

Ann Ball

273

Kid's Favorites

Toasted Pumpkin Seeds

A great treat for fall.

Fresh whole pumpkin   **Salt, to taste**
1/2 cup butter

When you get ready to carve your Jack-O-Lantern, have a bowl ready to put all the seeds in. Rinse all pulp off seeds, then pat dry with paper towels. Spread seeds evenly on cookie sheet and pour melted butter over top. Sprinkle salt over seeds. Bake in oven at 350° for about 45 minutes until crisp and nutty-flavored. Stir, while cooking, every 10 minutes to evenly coat with butter. Cool on paper towels and sprinkle a little more salt on seeds.

"Miss Amy" and "Miss Margaret"
Buntyn Preschool

ABC Applesauce

10 large fresh apples   **1/2 cup sugar**
1/3 cup water   **1/2 teaspoon cinnamon**

Peel, core and slice apples. Place in pot (or electric skillet) with water and bring to low simmer. Add sugar and cinnamon and continue cooking, stirring occasionally, until apples are soft (about 15 minutes). Remove applesauce from pan and put in blender. Purée for about 15 seconds or until desired consistency. Serve warm or refrigerate for several hours and serve chilled. Servings: 8.

"Miss Amy" and "Miss Margaret"
Buntyn Preschool

Reindeer Sandwiches

2 cups peanut butter   1 cup pretzel sticks
10 slices bread   10 red hots
1/4 cup raisins

Using a triangular shaped cookie cutter or a sharp knife, cut a triangle shape from each bread slice. Spread about 1 tablespoon of peanut butter on each triangle. Use two raisins for eyes, pretzel sticks for antlers and a red hot for mouth.

"Miss Amy" and "Miss Margaret"
Buntyn Preschool

Homemade Fries

Potatoes   Seasoned salt
Vegetable oil   Pepper

Slice potatoes into very thin rounds. Do not peel. Soak in cold water for 30 minutes. Drain well and pat dry. Cook in vegetable oil. Sprinkle with seasoned salt and pepper while cooking. Cook until dark brown and crispy.

Charlie Hill

Chi-Cola
Children love this, and so easy to prepare!

8 split chicken breasts   1/4 cup onion, finely chopped
4 tablespoons oil   1 cup ketchup
Flour   1 cup cola

In a large covered skillet, heat oil and lightly brown chicken breasts. Sprinkle with flour. Add remaining ingredients, cover and cook over low heat until tender.

Betty Biedenharn

275

Kid's Favorites

Twinkie Cake

12 Twinkies
1 large can crushed
   pineapple
1 large box instant vanilla
   pudding, prepared

2 to 3 bananas, sliced
8 to 12 ounces whipped topping
Chopped cherries and
   pecans for top

Place Twinkies in pan. Pour pineapple over Twinkies. Spread pudding over this and lay sliced bananas on top. Spread whipped topping over all and sprinkle cherries and pecans on top. Refrigerate until very cold. Servings: 8 to 12. Pan Size: 13x9-inches. Preparation Time: 15 minutes.

Jan Freudenberg

Frothy Heath Bar Cake

This was given to me by a little girl, 8 years old. She prepared this for her mother's birthday. Especially delicious for a light summer time dessert. Very easy and fun for children to do.

Store bought angel food cake
Medium container whipped
   topping

10 Heath bars, crushed and
   divided

Chop Heath bars, and combine with whipped topping, reserving 3 chopped bars. Ice cake with Heath bar mixture. Sprinkle remaining crushed bars on top. Servings: 6 to 8. Preparation Time: 15 minutes.

Jessica Crouch

276

Never Tell A Lie Cherry Pie
Best served February 22nd!

**1 can refrigerator crescent
rolls**

1 can cherry pie filling

Separate individual crescent rolls. Press each one flat on a cookie sheet. Spoon about 3 tablespoons of fruit filling in middle of dough. Fold dough over and pinch together to seal. Bake at 350° for 15 minutes or until golden brown. Servings: 10. Preheat: 350°. Preparation Time: 15 minutes. Cooking Time: 15 minutes.

"Miss Amy" and "Miss Margaret"
Buntyn Preschool

Apple Crisp

**4 to 5 apples, peeled and
sliced**
1 cup oatmeal

1⅓ cups brown sugar
⅔ cup butter
1 teaspoon cinnamon

Place apples in greased pan. Mix remaining ingredients together to make crumbly topping. Place evenly on top of apples. Bake at 375° for 30 to 45 minutes. Servings: 10. Pan Size: 9x13-inches. Preheat: 375°. Preparation Time: 10 minutes. Cooking Time: 30 to 45 minutes.

"Miss Amy" and "Miss Margaret"
Buntyn Preschool

Kid's Favorites

Thumb Print Cookies

1/2 cup butter, softened
1/4 cup brown sugar
1/2 teaspoon vanilla
1/4 teaspoon salt
1 cup sifted flour

1 egg white, beaten
Nuts, finely chopped
Apple jelly, tinted red or
   green

Mix together first three ingredients. Stir in salt and flour. Mix well. Roll into balls and dip lightly in beaten egg white. Roll in finely chopped nuts. Place about 1-inch apart on ungreased cookie sheet. Bake at 325° for 8 minutes. Remove from oven and quickly press thumb into top of each cookie. Return to oven and bake 8 minutes longer. Fill thumb print with jelly.

Kim Ray

Potato Chip Cookies
One of my family's favorites!

2 sticks margarine
2 sticks butter
1 cup sugar
3 1/2 cups all-purpose flour
   (do not sift)

1 teaspoon vanilla
1 cup crushed potato chips
1 cup chopped nuts
   (optional)

Cream together margarine, butter and sugar. Add flour and vanilla, stirring to blend. Add potato chips and nuts; mixing well. Drop by teaspoon on ungreased cookie sheet. Bake at 350° for 13 to 15 minutes or until light brown. Servings: 125 cookies. Pan Size: Large cookie sheet. Preheat: 350°. Preparation Time: 20 minutes. Cooking Time: 13 to 15 minutes.

Mrs. Don P. Smith

278

Peanut Butter Cookies
This was my mom's recipe.

1/2 box corn flakes, crushed
2 cups peanut butter
1 cup honey

2/3 cup dry milk
1 teaspoon vanilla

Mix peanut butter, honey, dry milk and vanilla. Add 1/2 box crushed corn flakes, mixture will be stiff. Roll out on waxed paper to 1/2-inch thickness and cut into desired shapes. Store in refrigerator overnight. Preparation Time: 10 minutes.

L. W. Mitchell

Old Fashioned Taffy

2 1/2 cups sugar
1/2 cup water
1/4 cup vinegar

1/8 teaspoon salt
1 tablespoon butter
1 teaspoon vanilla

Combine first 5 ingredients in a small Dutch oven. Cook without stirring over medium heat just until mixture reaches soft crack stage (270°). Remove from heat. Stir in vanilla. Pour candy onto a well-buttered 15x10x1-inch jelly roll pan. Let cool to touch. Pull candy until light in color and difficult to pull, buttering hands if candy is sticky. Divide candy in half and pull into a rope 1-inch in diameter. Cut taffy into 1-inch pieces. Wrap each piece individually in waxed paper. Servings: about 40 pieces.

Kaye Keeton

Kid's Favorites

Popsicles

1 (3 ounce) box gelatin (any
    fruit flavor)
1 envelope unsweetened
    Kool-Aid (any flavor)

1/2 to 1 cup sugar
2 cups boiling water
2 cups cold water

Dissolve gelatin, Kool-Aid and sugar in boiling water. Add cold water. Pour in molds. Servings: 16 or more depending on size of mold.

Kaye Keeton

Lollipops

2 cups sugar
1 cup water
2/3 cup white corn syrup

Desired flavoring and
    coloring

Combine sugar, water and syrup. Boil to 275° or hard crack stage on candy thermometer. Add flavoring and coloring. Pour immediately onto lollipop sticks laid out on aluminum foil. Servings: 18 3-inch suckers.

Kim Ray

Snow Cream

Snow (fresh, clean and white)
1 egg
1/2 cup sugar

1 teaspoon vanilla
1 cup milk

Mix together egg, sugar, vanilla and milk. Slowly add snow until it reaches the consistency of sherbert.

Kaye Keeton

280

Ornament Dough
Simple and fun to decorate.

4 cups flour
1 cup salt

1½ cups tap water

Mix ingredients with a fork, then knead until dough is smooth.

Jill Worley

Play Dough I (inedible)

2¾ cups flour
½ cup salt
1 tablespoon cream of tartar
2 packages unsweetened
  Kool-Aid

3 tablespoons oil
2 cups boiling water

Mix dry ingredients in large bowl. Add oil and water and mix thoroughly. Knead until smooth. Store in airtight container. This play dough recipe is not cooked. Servings: 4. Preparation Time: 15 minutes.

Susan Burnett
Buntyn Preschool

Edible Playdough

1 cup peanut butter
1 cup honey
1 cup powdered milk

1 cup oatmeal
½ cup mini chocolate chips
  (optional)

Mix all ingredients (chocolate chips are nice for decorating or adding different flavor). Let little hands enjoy kneading and shaping dough then sampling their handiwork. Servings: 4. Preparation Time: 10 minutes.

"Miss Amy" and "Miss Margaret"
Buntyn Preschool

281

NOTES

TRAVEL

SAIL...

SPONSORED BY

Charlie Rodgers

ALABAMA

BRIGHT STAR, Bessemer, AL
V. Lane Rawlins
"Great Seafood."

JOHN'S, Birmingham, AL
George Lapides
"There's no atmosphere, except the food - especially the seafood. Always order the West Indies Salad before the main course, but also get a plateful of their slaw as an appetizer and pour their special homemade Russian dressing over it. This is a cut above shorts and T-shirt style."

ROSHELL'S CAFE AND DELI, Mobile, AL
Humphrey and Gloria Folk
"All the seafood is wonderful. Moderately priced. Try the Oysters Roshell."

DREAMLAND, Tuscaloosa, AL
V. Lane Rawlins
"Great Ribs."

ALASKA

CLUB 26, Anchorage, AK
Pete and Cecil Aviotti
"Converted, yet quaint small house. Owner is the maitre d', etc. Best Alaskan King Crab legs. Expensive; but everything's expensive in Alaska."

ARIZONA

L'AUBERGE DE SEDONA, Sedona, AZ
Jim and Julie Raines
"A great day trip north of Scottsdale. Small and charming restaurant on a stream under huge cottonwoods. Skip dessert and substitute a breath-taking pink jeep tour of the Sedona High Desert."

TROY'S RESTAURANT, West Sedona, AZ
Jabie and Helen Hardin
"The food is delicious. When you step inside you are in another world - Casablanca perhaps. The high ceilings are painted with blue skies and white clouds. A dream of a room done by a Hollywood set designer."

CALIFORNIA

SPENGER'S, Berkley, CA
V. Lane Rawlins
"Seafood is always fresh, cooked to perfection, and served in generous portions."

VENTANA, Big Sur, CA
George Lapides
"High up on a cliff overlooking the Pacific, the restaurant at the resort has the greatest view of any dining spot I've ever seen. Go before sunset for wine on the terrace and watch the fog roll in. Salmon is the thing to get (when they have it). They also have a chocolate dessert that is to die for."

FIVE FOOT TWO, Laguna Niguel, CA
Jim and Julie Raines
"Laid back, Southen California casual, oriental restaurant with a 'smack yo Mama' deep fried/head-on whole catfish with ginger sauce."

CAMPANILE, Los Angeles, CA
Roger and Ann Knox
"Great food. Fabulous bread from La Brea Bakery located next door."

DRAI'S, Los Angeles, CA
Pepper and Livingston Rogers
"Trendy and fun and great food. Great place to see celebs. Late, late dinner times provide the best viewing of the tiniest black cocktail dresses in the world. A great mix of French and California cuisine with good service and pretty people having fun."

LE DOME, Los Angeles, CA
Herbie and Laura O'Mell
"Great Hollywood atmosphere."
Pepper and Livingston Rogers
"A real Continental-European atmosphere with superb food. Many record executives can be found here at lunch or dinner. The most important thing is everyone is treated well and served beautifully."
[See Pasta Chapter for **PENNE WITH SPICY LEMON SAUCE**]

NICKY BLAIR'S, Los Angeles, CA
Pepper and Livingston Rogers
"Italian food at its best, in a suave atmosphere. Nicky oversees everything when he's not playing a part on film shoots all over the world with his best friend, Sly Stallone. Nicky's always been an actor but he really hit it big with this restaurant."

HOPPE'S AT 901, Morro Bay, CA
Loren and Kim Roberts
"Overlooking the Morro Harbor, Hoppe's at 901 is a haven for delicious food, fine wine, and impeccable service."
[See Salad Chapter for **BUTTER LETTUCE SALAD "MOTHER'S STYLE"**]
[See Dessert Chapter for **WILHELM HOPPE'S LEMON CREME BRULEE**]

MILLE FLEURS, San Diego, CA
Tommy and Anne Keesee
"Romantic, elegant bistro featuring French - California cuisine. Best of the best!"

CAFE ROMA, San Luis Obispo, CA
Loren and Kim Roberts
[See Soup Chapter for **ZUPPA DI COZZE**]
[See Meat Chapter for **LOMBATA DI VITELLO AL ROSMARINO**]

ALEUTO'S, San Francisco, CA
Humphrey and Gloria Folk
"Great Dungeness Crab."

BOULEVARD, San Francisco, CA
Jim and Carol Prentiss
"Opened in 1994 on the Bay. Owners of Kuleto's involved in design and concept. We will personally guarantee a delightful evening. Italian and other specialties. Reservations a MUST! Valet parking available."

CHINA MOON, San Francisco, CA
Roger and Ann Knox
"Very creative menu. Appetizers and cookies are a special treat. They have their own award-winning cookbook."

Travel

JULIUS CASTLE, San Francisco, CA
John and Carl Ann Apple
"Excellent food and beautiful view of San Francisco Bay and both bridges."

KULETO'S, San Francisco, CA
Jim and Carol Prentiss
"The best Italian restaurant we have ever been to. Must have reservation, or the wait could be two hours! It is a MUST in San Francisco and only one-half block from Union Square. It is one of our favorites after a long day of fun and shopping. Great for lunch and dinner."

PACIFIC CAFE, San Francisco, CA
Humphrey and Gloria Folk
"Great lunch with six kinds of oysters on the half shell."

POSTRIO, San Francisco, CA
Jackie and Libby Aaron
"Great fish and pasta."
Wine: Williams-Selyem Pinot Noir

SCOTT'S GRILLE, San Francisco, CA
Humphrey and Gloria Folk
"Wonderful bouillabaisse!"

WASHINGTON SQUARE BAR AND GRILL, San Francisco, CA
Jimmy Chancellor
"Great fish entrees. Desserts are fantastic with the chocolate cream sauce."

TERRA, St. Helena, CA
Jackie and Libby Aaron
"Great chicken with pasta."
Wine: Buehler Cabernet Sauvignon

VALENTINO'S, Santa Monica, CA
George Lapides
"You know a restaurant is special when you can make up your own dishes. Once I told them I'd like a fresh artichoke heart, with veal picata on top of it, with fresh crab meat on top of the veal. The waiter said 'no problem.' It was wonderful. Great wine list, too."

ONDINE'S, Sausalito, CA
Humphrey and Gloria Folk
"The poached salmon with champagne sauce is excellent."

FRENCH LAUNDRY, Yountville, CA
Humphrey and Gloria Folk
"Located in the Napa Valley, the food and atmosphere are fabulous. You will feel like you just had dinner in someone's home."

COLORADO

BOGIE'S DINER, Aspen, CO
Humphrey and Gloria Folk
"Great hamburgers and old-style milkshakes to kill for."

PINE CREEK COOKHOUSE, Aspen, CO
Reid and Chris Sanders
"Situated by a babbling brook, the only way to get there in the winter is to cross-country ski or by sleigh. Hot toddies provided upon arrival."

PINION'S, Aspen, CO
Reid and Chris Sanders
"The place to be on the Fourth of July to watch the fabulous fireworks. Wonderful mountain view. Try the Macadamia Ahi and the Pheasant Quesadillas."

SYGYZY, Aspen, CO
Reid and Chris Sanders
"Fabulous food and service. Try the rack of lamb and the brownie and caramel sundae."

WOODY CREEK TAVERN, Outside Aspen, CO
Michael D. Rose
"Woody Creek Tavern is like my favorite Memphis place, Belmont Grill. Off the river, off a horse, or off a pickup truck, there is no dress code and no pretense. Great food and cold beer."

LEGEND'S, Beaver Creek, CO
Humphrey and Gloria Folk
"Try the cockle and mussel appetizer. The catch of the day is always fresh and wonderful."

GROUSE MOUNTAIN GRILLE, Beaver Creek, CO
Trow and Elizabeth Gillespie
"Atmosphere is excellent. Good views and great fireplace. Excellent service. Limousin beef with mushroom sauce is outstanding - wonderful flavor."

LE BOSQUET, Crested Butte, CO
Ralph and Pat Horn
"The cozy, warm atmosphere makes this a great place to unwind after a day on the slopes."
[See Poultry Chapter for **HAZLENUT CHICKEN IN AN ORANGE THYME CREAM SAUCE**]

SOUPCON, Crested Butte, CO
Ralph and Pat Horn
"A warm, country atmosphere in an intimate setting. There are only nine tables."

THE FRESH FISH COMPANY, Denver, CO
Bob Buckman and Joyce Mollerup
"Excellent seafood restaurant."

THE BRISTOL AT ARROWHEAD, Edwards, CO
Humphrey and Gloria Folk
"Great American cuisine and gracious service in a wonderful setting."

THE GASHOUSE, Edwards, CO
Humphrey and Gloria Folk
"Great buffalo wings and baby back ribs. Also great Maryland crabcakes and mountain trout. One of Frank and Kathy Lee Gifford's favorite hangouts."

KEYSTONE RANCH, Keystone, CO
Bob and Martha Hester
"Service is fantastic. We have driven all the way from Denver just to enjoy the wonderful food and fabulous atmosphere. Diners are served in an enormous log cabin with oriental rugs, fine china and silver."
[See Soup Chapter for **QUINCE AND DUCK SOUP**]
[See Seafood Chapter for **GRILLED JUNIPER RUBY TROUT**]

THE SALOON, Minturn, CO
Humphrey and Gloria Folk
"Great Mexican."

Travel

THE STEW POT, Snowmass Village, CO
Willard and Rita Sparks
"Excellent after a hard day on the slopes."

BLU'S CAFE, Vail, CO
Humphrey and Gloria Folk
"A favorite for lunch. Great food at modest prices. American bistro cuisine."

SWEET BASIL, Vail, CO
Jackie and Libby Aaron
"The seafood and ravioli are superb."
Wine: Frog's Leap Merlot

DISTRICT OF COLUMBIA

DYNASTY, Washington, D.C.
V. Lane Rawlins

HOGATES, Washington, D.C.
Humphrey and Gloria Folk
"Wonderful view of the river. Save room for dessert and order the Rum Buns."

NOTTA LUNA, Washington, D.C.
Bob Buckman and Joyce Mollerup

OLD EBBIT GRILL, Washington, D.C.
Bob Buckman and Joyce Mollerup
"Great food, great atmosphere. Close to all the sights."

THE PRIME RIB, Washington, D.C.
George and Jackie Falls
"Like fine restaurants you see in the movies (baby grand with lucite top), good sensible menu presented by skilled, professional servers."

<u>FLORIDA</u>

PETE' S, Boca Raton, FL
Charlie Rodgers
"Excellent seafood and steaks."

CAFE 30A, Destin, FL
Herbie and Laura O'Mell
"Try any seafood dish. Check out the martini menu."

HARBOR DOCKS, Destin, FL
Mike and Nancye Starnes
"Local favorite for great seafood."
[See Dessert Chapter for **HARBOR DOCKS KEY LIME PIE**]

MARINA CAFE, Destin, FL
Humphrey and Gloria Folk
"We are in Destin frequently for business and always love to eat the Sauteed Eggplant and Crawfish at Marina Cafe. Great service in a beautiful setting overlooking the Destin Harbor."

OCEAN CLUB, Destin, FL
Humphrey and Gloria Folk
"Great piano bar and fabulous food."

CRIOLLA'S, Grayton Beach, FL
Humphrey and Gloria Folk
"Only the freshest ingredients available are used in the preparation of their creative entrees. Great decor and great service. For a special treat, try the soft shell crabs."

LAKE PLACE, Grayton Beach, FL
Charlie Hill
"All the seafood is great! Casual atmosphere."

293

Travel

THE GREEN TURTLE INN, Islamorda, FL
Roger and Ann Knox
"May be the best Key Lime Pie anywhere."

CHALET SUZETTE, Lake Wales, FL
Jimmy Chancellor
"A Swiss-American style chalet. Soups are great. A five course, limited menu."

MOORE'S SEAFOOD, Long Boat Key, FL
Humphrey and Gloria Folk
"Try the stone crab claws and Key Lime Pie."

CHINA GRILL, South Beach Miami, FL
Jackie and Libby Aaron
"The veal and pasta entrees are excellent."
Wine: Kendall-Jackson Merlot

JOE'S STONE CRAB, Miami, FL
Joe and Robin Theisman
"Great stone crab claws and potatoes au gratin."

SHULA'S STEAKHOUSE, Miami, FL
Joe and Robin Theisman
"Owned by Don Shula. Terrific filet."

VICTOR'S CAFE, Miami, FL
Pepper and Livingston Rogers
"This is the best Cuban restaurant in Miami. It's pretty and inter-continental, and you never hear English unless it's you. So many different and unique dishes, you'd have to eat here for a month to try all of them. Fish, it seems, can be done 50 different ways, oh, those Cuban-Caribbean flavors. They have a string trio strolling and thank goodness it's not Mariachi music. This restaurant is so good, wished we lived next door."

CHEF'S GARDEN, Naples, FL
Doug and Andrea Edwards
[See Soup Chapter for **CREAM OF TOMATO AND DILL SOUP**]
[See Poultry Chapter for **CHICKEN PICATTA WITH LEMON CAPER BEURRE BLANC**]

CHRISTINI'S, Orlando, FL
Charlie Rodgers
"Great Italian cuisine"

BICE, Palm Beach, FL
Jimmy and Nancy Thomas
"Try the Bread Salad."

DEMPSEY'S, Palm Beach, FL
Jimmy and Nancy Thomas
"The Shrimp and Artichoke Pasta is our favorite."

RENATO'S, Palm Beach, FL
Jimmy and Nancy Thomas
"Great veal chop."

BERN'S STEAKHOUSE, Tampa, FL
Humphrey and Gloria Folk
"They grow all their own vegetables and still dry age their meat. They have a great wine selection and dessert menu. Get a tour of the kitchen and wine cellar for a real treat."

THE OCEAN GRILL, Vero Beach, FL
Jimmy and Berenice Denton

THE RED SNAPPER, Vero Beach, FL
Jimmy and Berenice Denton

GEORGIA

BONES, Atlanta, GA
Pepper and Livingston Rogers
"Pepper's number one pick, because it has such a masculine atmosphere with dark wood paneling, with etched glass panels between tables, and cozy private rooms downstairs. Huge delicious steaks and professional waiters with floor length white aprons ... gives the impression of a French bistro. Do not under any kind of coaching have the onion rings for an appetizer ... have them with your fabulous entree. Frequented by top-drawer business people and many Atlanta celebrities."

BUCKHEAD BAKERY, Atlanta, GA
Humphery and Gloria Folk

BUCKHEAD DINER, Atlanta, GA
Humphrey and Gloria Folk
"A Buckhead landmark serving an American menu. Be prepared for a long wait, but it is worth it. A lot of fun and great food."
Pepper and Livingston Rogers
"The foods that you would like your mother to have made for you. Incredible meatloaf and huge desserts, all served at a slow pace but this place has great food style and cool decor that old-time diners did not. It is noisy, active and fun."

CARBO'S, Atlanta, GA
Pepper and Livingston Rogers
"This is definitely a couples kind of place; romantic and elegant. Great service and Continental food."

CHOP'S, Atlanta, GA
Humphrey and Gloria Folk
"One of the best steakhouses in the country. Huge steaks, great seafood and terrific side dishes. Service is superb."
Logan Young
"Soft shell crabs are the best! Don't forget to try the onion rings with their special sauce. All the seafood is great."

LONGHORN STEAKHOUSE, Atlanta, GA
Rip Scherer
"Try the petite filet steak."

PANO'S AND PAUL'S, Atlanta, GA
Humphrey and Gloria Folk
"There are eight restaurants, all different and all wonderful. Continental cuisine. Impeccable service and excellent wines."

SEAFOOD SHOPPE, Atlanta, GA
Humphrey and Gloria Folk

ELIZABETH'S ON 37TH STREET, Savannah, GA
George and Jackie Falls
"A place where you say, 'can I get that recipe for . . .?' Great cuisine in a fine old home by Elizabeth herself."

HAWAII

MICHEL'S AT THE COLONY/SURF HOTEL, Waikiki
Humphrey and Gloria Folk
"Located in Diamond Head and offering a French Continental menu. Beautiful setting."

297

ILLINOIS

"We buy all of our (Folk's Folly) beef from Chicago. They have the best prime in the world."   **Humphrey and Gloria Folk**

BISTRO 110, Chicago, IL
Roger and Ann Knox
"Casual, consistently good. Right off Michigan Avenue."
Michael and Debbie Folk
"A casual and fun restaurant for lunch or dinner. Old interesting hats are hung on the walls. Reservations are a must!"
[See Soup Chapter for **CURRIED CARROT SOUP**]

BLACKHAWK LODGE, Chicago, IL
Carey and Stacey Folk
"Menu features modern regional American classics. Casual, rustic decor. Don't fill up on the biscuits and cornbread - save room for the smoked chicken pasta or the fabulous barbecued ribs."

CAPE COD ROOM, Drake Hotel, Chicago, IL
Jimmy Chancellor
"Good seafood. They are known for their Book Binder Soup."

CHARLIE TROTTERS, Chicago, IL
Roger and Ann Knox
"Very innovative. Pricey, but delicious. Wonderful vegetarian selections."

GORDON'S, Chicago, IL
Jimmy Chancellor
"A great little Art Nouveau restaurant with Continental cuisine and a jazz combo on weekends."

NICK'S FISH MARKET, Chicago, IL
Humphrey and Gloria Folk
"When we are in Chicago on business, we make it a point to stop at Nick's for escargot in garlic butter."

298

THE PUMP ROOM, Ambassador Hotel, Chicago, IL
George Bryan
"Their double cut pork chops are the best I've ever eaten."

ROSE BUD, Chicago, IL
Charlie Rodgers
"Italian."

SPIAGGIA, Chicago, IL
Humphrey and Gloria Folk
"Italian dining at its best! Wonderful view overlooking Michigan Avenue and Lake Michigan."

TUSCANY, Chicago, IL
V. Lane Rawlins

YOSHI'S, Chicago, IL
Tommy and Anne Keesee
"Jewel box with edible gems! A cafe featuring Japanese-French cuisine. Quiet and charming."

INDIANA

KEYSTONE GRILL, Indianapolis, IN
Joe and Robin Theisman
"Try the stone crab and the swordfish."

KANSAS

GOLDEN OX, Kansas City, KS
Humphrey and Gloria Folk
"An old Kansas City landmark. Great steaks. Be prepared for a long wait, but it is well worth it."

KENTUCKY

BOONE TAVERN, Berea, KY
George Lapides
"About twenty to thirty minutes south of Lexington, but a beautiful drive through bluegrass country. The restaurant is an inn, across the street from Berea College. The inn and the restaurant are owned by the college and run by college employees and students. This is down home food at its best. You can also play skittles in the hotel lobby before or after the meal … if you know what skittles is."

KEENELAND TRACK AT THE CLUBHOUSE, Lexington, KY
Humphrey and Gloria Folk
"They have corned beef and cabbage with horseradish that is the best in the world. They also have a thing called Kentucky Burgoo which is a thick soup with game in it that is different and wonderful."

COACHMAN RESTAURANT, Lexington, KY
Humphrey and Gloria Folk
"Good prime rib."

LOUISIANA

BRIGTSEN'S, New Orleans, LA
Reid and Chris Sanders
"A popular converted cottage serving outstanding, creative, Cajun food. All the seafood dishes are great. Reservations a must."
[See Soup Chapter for **BUTTERNUT SHRIMP BISQUE**]
[See Vegetable Chapter for **PRALINE SWEET POTATOES**]

BRENNAN'S, New Orleans, LA
Humphrey and Gloria Folk
"You haven't been to New Orleans if you haven't had breakfast at Brennan's. Try the Grillaides and Grits with their milk punch."
Mike and Gay Williams
"The desserts are fabulous."
[See Dessert Chapter for **BANANAS FOSTER**]

COMMANDER'S PALACE, New Orleans, LA
Tripp and Jane Folk
"Our favorite place to eat in New Orleans. Try the Turtle Soup Au Sherry and Pan Seared Veal Tenderloin."
Humphrey and Gloria Folk
"New Orleans' most popular restaurant! Outstanding Creole cooking served in an elegant atmosphere. Save room for dessert."

GALATOIRE'S, New Orleans, LA
George Lapides
"Remains the best restaurant in a restaurant city. Crab Meat Ravigotte is an extraordinary main course, along with the stuffed eggplant. The Shrimp Remoulade has the best sauce anywhere. The snails and gumbo are wonderful."

MOSCA'S, Jefferson, LA (across the river on HWY 90 west)
Humphrey and Gloria Folk
"Locals drive out of town to come to this roadhouse. Great Creole-Italian cuisine. The Chicken Cacciatore is our favorite."

PASCAL'S MANALE, New Orleans, LA
Jimmy Chancellor
"A great local restaurant with a nice oyster bar. The Bar-B-Que Shrimp are out of this world."

SAL AND SAM'S, New Orleans, LA
Pete and Cecil Aviotti
"Great for lunch and dinner. Moderately priced. Try the Ossobuco."

MARYLAND

O'BRICKY'S, Baltimore, MD
George Lapides
"The classic newspaper-on-the-table Maryland crab house, but somehow the crabs always seem meatier here. The crab soup is the best, too. It is near downtown and a walk along the harbor is great afterwards. This is a shorts and t-shirt type of place."

JOE THEISMAN RESTAURANT, Dorsey, MD
Joe and Robin Theisman

MASSACHUSETTS

ANTHONY'S PIER 1, Boston, MA
Humphrey and Gloria Folk
"One of the oldest restaurants in Boston. The walls of windows bring the Boston Harbor right into the dining room. Known for their stuffed lobster. Great bar. Elegant atmosphere."

BIBA, Boston, MA
Ralph and Pat Horn
"The food and service are fabulous. International cuisine that's always wonderful is served in an elegant setting overlooking the Public Garden."
[See Seafood Chapter for **GRILLED LOBSTER WITH WHISKEY**]
Jimmy and Berenice Denton
"They serve the greatest mashed potatoes."

LEGAL SEAFOOD, Boston, MA
Humphrey and Gloria Folk
"Known for serving the freshest fish available. Moderately priced."

OLIVES, Boston, MA
Jimmy and Berenice Denton
"Located in Charlestown and specializing in creative Italian fare. Bistro atmosphere. Expensive but well worth it. Reservations a must."

AMERICAN SEASONS, Nantucket Island, MA
George and Jackie Falls
"Menu features seasonal, regional items, some unusual - all well executed. Sit outside!"

CHANTICLEER, Siasconset, Nantucket Island, MA
Mike and Gay Williams
"One of our very favorites."
[See Meat Chapter for **FILET DE PORC AUX ABRICOTS**]

MISSISSIPPI

MARY MAHONEY'S, Biloxi, MS
Humphrey and Gloria Folk
"One of the earliest structures on the Gulf Coast, this home offers a fabulous atmosphere. They are famous for their Buster Crabbe appetizer and soft shell crabs."

LUSCO'S, Greenwood, MS
Humphrey and Gloria Folk
"Private rooms with great steaks and fresh seafood."
Jimmy Chancellor
"An Italian restaurant with good seafood."

DOE'S EAT PLACE, Greenville, MS
Humphrey and Gloria Folk
"Great steaks and tamales! Pick out your own steak and eat in the kitchen. I always had to bring home two dozen hot tamales for Mama."

THE FEEDMILL, Lamar, MS
Willard and Rita Sparks
"A great find in rural North Mississippi."

UNCLE HENRY'S, Moon Lake, MS
Jimmy Chancellor
"New Orleans-style cuisine served in an old roadhouse and gambling joint. There is a juke box for dancing."

CITY GROCERY, Oxford, MS
Jimmy Chancellor
"Their shrimp and grits are something unusual and taste great."

MISSOURI

CAFE DE FRANCE, St. Louis, MO
George Lapides
"Classic French with a modern flair."

DOMINIC'S, St. Louis, MO
George Lapides
"Located on the Hill, Dominic's serves fabulous pastas and veal dishes."

GIOVANNI'S, St. Louis, MO
George and Jackie Falls
"Quite formal, on the hill, anniversary-type place with excellent fare."

GUISEPPI'S, St. Louis, MO
George and Jackie Falls
"Wonderful, old-time, attractive family-operated restaurant, grand pasta and veal - and a great salad."

RIGAZZI'S, St. Louis, MO
George Lapides
"Eat with the people who live in the area. Try the lunch buffet for the fabulous Italian food and have a 'fishbowl' of beer."

MONTANA

THE BEIRSTRUB, Whitefish, MT
Turner and Nan Askew
"The Beirstrub is the home of the 'Backdoor Burger.' Their burger was voted 'Best of the West' by Sunset Magazine, and they also were voted the best 'apres ski bar' by U.S. News and World Report. The Beirstrub, earthy and unique, is where spontaneous fun is created."

CHICO'S, Pray, MT
Pete and Cecil Aviotti
"Chico's seems to appear out of nowhere and is often frequented by celebrities. The Montana trout and flan are excellent. Make reservations one month in advance. It is expensive, but worth the trip."

STAGE COACH INN, West Yellowstone, MT
V. Lane Rawlins
"Great food. Ask for the specialties."

TUPELO'S, Whitefish, MT
Turner and Nan Askew
"This is a new restaurant with Louisiana cuisine brought to Montana by a Memphis girl and her husband."

NEW MEXICO

LA TRAVIATA, Santa Fe, NM
George and Jackie Falls
"Most tender pasta ever, lively, fun cafe, open kitchen with pots a hangin', operatic background music (naturally)."

PASQUAL'S, Santa Fe, NM
George and Jackie Falls
"Lives up to its reputation, popular, upbeat, good food and prices."

SANTA FE CAFE, Santa Fe, NM
Tommy and Anne Keesee
"Asian-influenced southwestern food. Dinner in the garden by candlelight is an absolute must."

<u>NEW YORK</u>

AUREOLE, New York, NY
Mrs. Thomas R. Price
"The soft shell crabs are the best!"

BECCO, New York, NY
Bob Buckman and Joyce Mollerup
"Wonderful Italian food in the theatre district."
Pete and Cecil Aviotti
"Very well-known to locals. Make your reservation a month in advance and when you go, order the Italian Deep Dish Pasta."

BRIGHTON GRILL AND OYSTER BAR, New York, NY
Bob Buckman and Joyce Mollerup
"Very good soups, pasta and fresh fish offered at very reasonable prices. Arrive before 7:30 to get a seat."

CAFE' DES ARTISTES, New York, NY
George and Jackie Falls
"Friendly, skilled service; unusual, but cozy atmosphere; busy, good food."

FELIDIA, New York, NY
Jackie and Libby Aaron
"One of New York's greatest Italian restaurants. My favorites are the veal chop and pasta dishes."
Wine: Antinori Marchese

GRAMERCY TAVERN, New York , NY
Jim and Carol Prentiss
"Great restaurant for after-theater dinner. Unusual format with prix fixe dinners. The place to see and be seen! American cuisine served in a relaxed atmosphere."

Travel

HARRY CIPRIANI, New York, NY
Pepper and Livingston Rogers
"What we love about Harry's is the really cozy atmosphere. If you haven't tried a Bellini, please do. . .champagne and peach juice. . .and then a carpaccio appetizer. This place carries you away to Venice."

IL MONELLO, New York, NY
Bob Buckman and Joyce Mollerup
"Fabulous Italian cuisine and great service."
Pepper and Livingston Rogers
"The consumate Italian restaurant in New York, with fine service."

IL NIDO, New York, NY
Bob Buckman and Joyce Mollerup
"One of NYC's best Northern Italian restaurants."

LA BONNE SOUP, New York, NY
George Lapides
"Not fancy, not well-known, but it's great at lunch or for a quick dinner before the theater or even after a show because it's open late. The specialties are pâté with bread and the fish soup."

LE CIRQUE, New York, NY
William and Tommy Dunavant
"French dishes with Italian flavors."

MONTEBELLO, New York, NY
Bob Buckman and Joyce Mollerup

ONE IF BY LAND, New York, NY
Richard and Buzzy Hussey
"Located in the village in Aaron Burr's former coach house, it is charming for its history and for the fact that it is nestled on a quiet street in the bustling village. In the interior, the walls are mellow old brick. There is a fireplace to welcome the cold visitor and a sofa in front of it to sit and relax. There is live piano music. . .romantic melodies wash over the diners. The menu is Continental. Service is excellent."

PREGO, New York, NY
Bob Buckman and Joyce Mollerup
"Traditional Italian cuisine. Great service. Reasonable prices."

PRIMAVERA, New York, NY
William and Tommy Dunavant
"Superb Italian food."

RENE PUJOL, New York, NY
Doug and Andrea Edwards
"Country French, intimate atmosphere. Located in the theatre district. I
have been going there for twenty years. My father first took me when I
was in college. The same people have been there all these years and
always remember me."
[See Salad Chapter for **WARM SALMON SALAD WITH POTATOES
AND SHIITAKE MUSHROOMS**]
[See Vegetable Chapter for **ONION TART IN FILLO WITH FRESH
THYME**]
[See Dessert Chapter for **FONDANT AU CHOCOLAT**]

SAN PIETRO, New York, NY
Roger and Ann Knox
"Order any of the pastas and lemon ice."

SISTINO, New York, NY
Jim and Carol Prentiss
"Wonderful, friendly neighborhood restaurant serving old world Italian
favorites. Cozy."

THREE GUYS, New York, NY
Bob Buckman and Joyce Mollerup
"Very good and very fast service for breakfast. Reasonable prices."

TRATORRIA DELL' ARTE, New York, NY
Roger and Ann Knox
"Across from Carnegie Hall. Great place to spot famous faces."

UNION SQUARE CAFE, New York, NY
George and Jackie Falls
"A New York favorite, uncommon cordiality, everything is very well
executed - service, food and ambience."

OHIO

MAISONETTE, Cincinnati, OH
V. Lane Rawlins
George Lapides
"Classic French. Maybe one of the top five to ten restaurants in the country. I always go for one of the fish main courses."

JOHNNY'S, Cleveland, OH
George and Jackie Falls
"A suprise find, great atmosphere, cordial, excellent, well-presented veal and beef entrées."

SOUTH CAROLINA

CHARLIE'S, Hilton Head, SC
Jim and Carol Prentiss
"Local coastal specialties with a French twist. The owner is also the head chef. Located on the main highway coming in to Hilton Head. A MUST for elegant food in a relaxed atmosphere in an intimate setting. Reservations required for evening dining! Also open for lunch."
George Lapides
"Locals, not tourists go here. The menu changes every day at both lunch and dinner. The fish soup at lunch is the best this side of Paris and in the evenings, you can never go wrong with the rack of lamb, a dinner order of crab cakes or any of the fresh fish. The desserts are amazing."

SOUTH DAKOTA

THE STOCKYARDS CAFE, Sioux Falls, SD
Rudi Schiffer
"Situated right in the stockyards, this restaurant serves great steak at great, great prices. Our selection ... anything spelled Prime Steak. What else?"

TEA STEAK HOUSE, Sioux Falls, SD
Rudi Schiffer
"This simple restaurant offers steak, steak, steak. The T-Bone is our choice of fare. Inexpensive and simply great food, and a great favorite with the locals."

<u>TENNESSEE</u>

MADISON'S CAFE, Jackson, TN
Humphrey and Gloria Folk
"Simple, delicious food!"

AUBERGINE, Memphis, TN
Sylvester Thornton
"The most memorable meal I have ever had."
John and Carl Ann Apple
"A little touch of New York in the Mid-South."

FOLK'S FOLLY, Memphis, TN
John and Carl Ann Apple
"Best combination of service and fine beef anywhere - our favorite."

PAULETTE'S, Memphis, TN
Loren and Kim Roberts
"Try the Chicken Sicilian. It's wonderful."
[See Bread Chapter for **POPOVERS**]

HERMITAGE GRILL, Nashville, TN
Jimmy and Berenice Denton
"The best French Onion Soup."

JIMMY KELLY'S, Nashville, TN
Humphrey and Gloria Folk
"Don't ruin your appetite with the famous hoe-cakes they serve for appetizers. A local hangout. Great service with an old southern atmosphere."

LOVELESS MOTEL AND CAFE, Nashville, TN
Roger and Ann Knox
"Home cooking. Especially good for breakfast. Biscuits, ham and red eye gravy. Always busy."

MORTON'S OF CHICAGO STEAKHOUSE, Nashville, TN
George Bryan
"The steaks at Morton's are superb."

WILD BOAR, Nashville, TN
Charlie Rodgers
"Continental cuisine."

CAFE ST. CLAIR, Pickwick, TN
Jim and Julie Raines
"Load the cooler with your favorite drinks and load the boat with your favorite friends. Motor over to Aqua Marina at sunset for the prime rib served years ago in Memphis by the late Jack St. Clair and served now by Mark and Madelyn."

TEXAS

CISCO'S BAKERY, Austin, TX
George Lapides
"This is the best breakfast you'll ever have. The biscuits are out of this world and so is the little doughy thing filled with meat that I always order before breakfast. I don't know what it's called. . .I just ask for the little doughy thing and they always get it right."

ANTHONY'S, Dallas, TX
Humphrey and Gloria Folk
"Great lamb tender."

MANSION ON TURTLE CREEK, Dallas, TX
Logan Young
"One of America's top restaurants. Everything on Chef Dean Fearing's Southwestern menu is great."
[See Appetizer Chapter for **WARM LOBSTER TACO WITH YELLOW TOMATO SALSA AND JICAMA SALAD**]

STAR CANYON, Dallas, TX
Roger and Ann Knox
"Tex-Mex, Southwest or wild game-take your choice."
John and Carl Ann Apple
"Wonderful Southwestern food."

GUIDO'S, Galveston, TX
Humphrey and Gloria Folk
"Order the seafood gumbo or oysters on the half shell."

BEEF 'N BIRD ROTISSERIE, Houston, TX
Willard and Rita Sparks
"Many versatile and delicious ways to prepare various fowl. European flare!"

TONY'S, Houston, TX
Humphrey and Gloria Folk
"One of our favorites. Across the street from the Galleria."

VIRGINIA

JOE THEISMAN RESTAURANT, Alexandria, VA
Joe and Robin Theisman

BAILEY'S, Falls Church, VA
Joe and Robin Theisman
"Try the Chicken Spiral Pasta."

WASHINGTON

IVAR'S, Seattle, WA
V. Lane Rawlins
"Best clams in the world. Their motto is 'Keep Clam'."

METROPOLITAN GRILL, Seattle, WA
Tommy and Anne Keesee
"Best steak on the west coast! Fun, action and fabulous food. Be sure and try the fried artichokes."

WILD GINGER, Seattle, WA
Roger and Anne Knox
"Oriental with a different twist. Great place to go with a group and share."

SZECHUAN EAST, Spokane, WA
V. Lane Rawlins

317

WISCONSIN

MATER'S, Milwaukee, WI
George Lapides
"Best German restaurant I've ever been to in this country."

318

INTERNATIONAL

ARGENTINA

LA CABANA, Buenos Aires
Pete and Cecil Aviotti
"Listed as the World's Greatest Steakhouse. Expensive."

AUSTRALIA

IMPERIAL PEKING, Sydney
Bill and Michelle Dunavant
"Ask for a table next to the window for a great view of the harbor and Sydney Opera House. The seafood entrees are great."

BAHAMAS

GRAYCLIFF, Nassau
Charlie Rodgers
"French cuisine"

BERMUDA

FOUR-WAY INN, Paget
Willard and Rita Sparks
"One of the best we have experienced."

CANADA

MILOS, Montreal
Roger and Ann Knox
"Greek seafood. Worth a cab ride."

ENGLAND

LA GAVAROCHE, London
William and Tommie Dunavant
"Excellent French restaurant."

SCALLINI, London
William and Tommie Dunavant
"Great Italian food."

SALE EPEPE, London
Harry and Weetie Phillips

FRANCE

PERE BISE, Village of Talloires near Annecy
Willard and Rita Sparks
"A unique and excellent dining experience."

JULES VERNE, Paris
Danny and Brenda Harris
"We celebrated my birthday here. The city lights are beautiful."

TAILLEVENT, Paris
Willard and Rita Sparks
"Noted as one of the most excellent restaurants in the world."

GRAND CAYMAN

CROW'S NEST
Jim and Julie Raines
"A funky island look and menu at an on-the-beach restaurant. Don't miss 'Nest Mess', a combo of slaw and Caesar salad with jerked chicken."

GRAND OLD HOUSE
Bob Buckman and Joyce Mollerup
"Very good. Expensive. Great seafood and steaks."

PAPAGALLO'S
Bob Buckman and Joyce Mollerup
"At the upper end of the island. Italian cuisine. Very good. Expensive. Worth going back again."

HONG KONG

AMIGO'S
Bill and Michelle Dunavant
"Wonderful atmosphere and great service. There is a Latin string quartet strolling through the dining room."

JIMMY'S KITCHEN
Bill and Michelle Dunavant
"The Shrimp Madris Curry is the finest dry curry dish I've ever had. Great for lunch."

Travel

ITALY

ENOTECA PINCHIORRI, Florence
William and Tommie Dunavant

PASETTO, Rome
Harry and Weetie Phillips

MEXICO

PRIMA TIVA, Puerto Vallarta
Robert and Nancy Williams
"Nestled on a hill overlooking the Pacific, and cooled by the ocean breeze. Order the Snapper."

SAINT-BARTHELEMY

FRANCOIS PLANTATION
Mike and Gay Williams
"Our favorite restaurant in St. Barts. Wonderful food!"

LA MARINE
Christopher and Amy Folk
"Best Dover Sole on the island. Don't miss the mussels served on Thursday nights."

SPAIN

HORCHERS, Madrid
Harry and Weetie Phillips

SWEDEN

THE OPERA HOUSE
Jackie and Libby Aaron
"The seafood and pasta dishes are my favorites."
Wine: Meursault

THAILAND

THE SEAFOOD RESTAURANT, Bangkok
Bill and Michelle Dunavant
"There is a 100-foot-long seafood bar where you walk up and pick your meal to be cooked. All outdoor dining. A very unique experience."

Index

Index

Index

Index

Index

330

Index

Index